Writing to Survive

On Pine Grove's main street, South Tulpehocken. Photograph by Carl Mydans, 1962. Courtesy of *Time-Life*, Inc.

Writing to Survive

The Private Notebooks of Conrad Richter

Harvena Richter

UNIVERSITY OF NEW MEXICO PRESS
Albuquerque

Chapters 7, 9, and 10 were previously published in the *South Dakota Review* (Autumn 1987):130–67.

Library of Congress Cataloging-in-Publication Data

Richter, Harvena, 1919–
Writing to survive.

Bibliography: p.
Includes index.
1. Richter, Conrad, 1890–1968—Notebooks, sketchbooks, etc. 2. Richter, Conrad, 1890–1968—Diaries. 3. Richter, Conrad, 1890–1968—Authorship. 4. Novelists, American—20th century—Biography. I. Richter, Conrad, 1890–1968. II. Title.
PS3535.I429Z86 1988   818′.5203 [B]   87-34237
ISBN 0-8263-1034-6
ISBN 0-8263-1035-4 (pbk.)

Design: Milenda Nan Ok Lee

First edition.

Contents

Chronology

1890,
October 13. Born in Pine Grove, Pennsylvania.
1904–05. Attended Susquehanna Preparatory School, Selins Grove, Pennsylvania.
1906. Graduated from Tremont (Pennsylvania) High School.
1913. Sale of first story, "How Tuck Went Home" to *Cavalier.*
1914. "Brothers of No Kin" picked by Edward J. O'Brien as best short story of 1914.
1915,
March 24. Married to Harvena Maria Achenbach.
1922. Moved from Reading, Pennsylvania, to farm near Harrisburg.
1924. Death of mother, Charlotte Henry Richter.
1928. Moved to Albuquerque, New Mexico.
1934. "Early Marriage" sold to *Saturday Evening Post.*
1937. *The Sea of Grass,* his first novel, published.
1937–40. Intermittent work for Metro-Goldwyn-Mayer.
1940. Death of father, John Absalom Richter.
1942. The Gold Medal for literary achievement from the Society for the Libraries of New York University.
1944. Honorary Doctor of Literature degree from Susquehanna University.
1946. Award of Merit from the Pennsylvania German Society.
1946. Metro-Goldwyn-Mayer filmed *The Sea of Grass.*
1947. The Ohioana Library Medal Award for literature.
1950. Moved from Albuquerque to Pine Grove.
1951. The Pulitzer Prize for Fiction for *The Town.*
1953. Disney purchased film rights to *The Light in the Forest.*

1958. Honorary Doctor of Literature degree from the University of New Mexico.

1960. The National Book Award for *The Waters of Kronos*.

1966. Honorary Doctor of Literature degree from Lafayette College.

Honorary Doctor of Philosophy degree from Temple University.

Honorary Doctor of Humane Letters from Lebanon Valley College.

1968,
October 30. Died in Pine Grove, Pennsylvania.

I have no secrets or formulas for the writer's success, just experiences.

Maroon Notebook I

Introduction

This book was planned originally as briefly annotated excerpts on writing from my father's notebooks and journals, presenting his theories of writing and examples of how he worked. When I began to put it together, the notebooks and his struggle to become a writer seemed inseparable, and I realized that the notebooks would be unintelligible without some account of what he went through.

My father, or C. R. as I shall call him—for he always signed his letters to me "Your father, C. R."—left an enormous amount of working material. There are notebooks filled with single-spaced entries of plot ideas; six volumes of researched "color" of early America, west and east; three personal thesauruses; a series of novel notebooks for his later fiction; but especially what might be called his "writing notebooks" in which he attempted to codify the rules of a salable story or novel—a kind of threshing floor for his ideas. And there are forty-three volumes of journals, one for each year from 1925 to 1968. Except for *The Sea of Grass* and *The Trees*, manuscripts remain of the novels' various stages, most of them now in university special collections.

There is other material, too, and I was first aware of its extent when my parents moved into the Pennsylvania house in the early 1950s. C. R. walled off the northwest end of the attic and fitted it with white pine shelving. Nothing was prettier to him than white pine. It was sanded to a satin finish and lent the room an almost sacrosanct air. In this hidden room, on the shelves and in cartons below them, he kept the manuscripts of his novels and stories, sold and unsold; maps of counties in

Ohio and Pennsylvania, some of prerevolutionary days; endless brown manila folders of letters from agents, editors, publishers, writing friends. Piled in one corner were frayed magazines with his stories, including the early *Forum* with "Brothers of No Kin." The magazine covers of the 1920s and earlier, the different typography, my father's name in a large logo—all mythicized a past that was somehow sealed to me. As a child I had helped him stuff envelopes with direct-mail folders for his publishing business. But now I saw him in an entirely new light. He was no longer "your father, C. R." *and* a writer. He had become a disconcerting blend of both.

It is that blend which I search for now, trying to find what characterized him as a writer and person, and set him apart. Three passions ordered his life: a passion for writing, a passion for America, and a passion for insecurity. The third was perhaps the strongest. Most writers suffer from it to a degree, but my father made insecurity his mentor, his goad. It was fostered in part by the depression years, by the burden of a sick wife and a child, by having no means of supporting himself and family other than by his pen. He used insecurity as a whip to force himself to do better work or at least sustain its quality. Quite possibly, the more he acknowledged the ultimately positive effects of his fear, the more indispensable it became.

C. R.'s writing notebooks were a hedge against what seemed to him to be imminent disaster. The careful analytical outlines of his two most anthologized short stories, "Early Marriage" and "Smoke Over the Prairie," were born out of a desperation that he would not be able to continue selling to the *Saturday Evening Post*. The *Post* and its famous editor, George Horace Lorimer, had brought our family out of debt. (It was Lorimer who encouraged my father to extend a difficult short story into what became his first novel, *The Sea of Grass*.) C. R. was convinced that it was not luck or happenstance but some intrinsic quality, or set of qualities, which made his work salable. If he could analyze these stories, he could repeat the performance and keep the family solvent.

Together with excerpts from his journals, the notebooks present an intimate chronicle of the struggle to be a writer. C. R. began with his mother helping him write his school themes; he ended with the Pulitzer Prize and National Book Award (at that time Faulkner was the only other novelist to have received both honors). The word *intimate* is stressed because the notebooks were written only for himself. They drip blood and sweat. Partly typed, partly jotted in his indecipherable yet confident hand, they pour out a torrent of complaints, fears, promises, plans, and affirmations that he could write. They were a whipping post to which he constantly returned, flaying himself for not writing as he should, setting down rules, uttering cautionary notes. He chafed under the necessity of having to write "salable" stories and novels when more serious work was on his agenda. In his commonplace book a quote from Gide is underlined in both black and red inks: "Art is born of constraint, lives on struggle, dies of freedom." If he sacrificed *The Free Man* by tailoring it to a specific market, other novels, such as *The Light in the Forest*, grew out of the cruel constraint.

The struggle was compounded, as he grew older, by health problems. Commonplace-book entries such as these reflect his concerns. Freud: "I have to be somewhat miserable in order to write well." And Van Gogh: "The more I become decomposed, the more sick and fragile I am, the more I become an artist."

And the older C. R. grew, the more work loomed ahead. In addition to the notebooks mentioned, a number of others remain crammed with jottings and/or outlines for such disparate works as a novel on Shakespeare, whom he particularly loved; a questioning of the problem of suffering to be patterned somewhat on *The Divine Comedy*; a novel on fate called *The Hand*; a long sequence of autobiographical novels of his struggles—

physical, mental, psychic—only two of which were written. Into these notes he poured his quarrel with God, his angers at what America had become, his criticism of modern inertia and appeasement, of ego that refused to be humbled, of intellectual whitewashings of things as they are. Several published articles (see "Individualists Under the Shade Trees") hint at his dismay at the modern order. Some of it leaks out in the Ohio trilogy and *The Light in the Forest*. But the naked angers were never given literary form.

But this is beside the point, and perhaps the material for another book dealing with the way in which his novels were conceived. It is enough here to suggest that C. R.'s main concern in both the written and unwritten novels was the individual's search for the origins of the self, with the personal and national implications that cluster around it. His belief in self-discipline colored not only his philosophical writings but the pioneer novels. It was not a Puritan stance but part of the agonizing relationship he felt existed between himself and the powers-that-be. He had a Greek sense of the ironic, the inherently tragic view of life in which man's adversary is not only himself but darker intelligences whose designs we cannot fathom at this level. The third volume of his personal trilogy was to have been called *Search for Meaning*.

If the self does not administer its own disciplines, life itself does so, and the disciplines and challenges of the frontier became C. R.'s primary subject matter. The villains are the despoilers, those who rape the land, level its forests. The heroes or heroines are those who, rightly or wrongly, fight the despoilers (Frank Gant, Colonel Brewton, Doña Ellen) or those who endure, like the white captives True Son or Stone Girl, Sayward of the Ohio trilogy, or the preacher who is the "simple honorable man." Into these stories come nineteenth-century themes: the power of innocence against the encroaching corruption of civilization, the exploitation of the land. The first is in the tradition of Hawthorne, Melville, and Henry James; the second looks forward to the ecological concerns of today and lends these stories a prophetic quality.

It is far more difficult to analyze C. R. as a person than his writings. His regard for the common people—the cattlemen rather than the kings—and for the rude pioneer individualist suggests paradoxes in his character. He liked to call himself a peasant but, like Turgenev, whose novels he admired, found his loyalties at times divided. To me he once wrote: "You always rebelled when I said I was proud to be a peasant. I did not mean a serf of the soil. I meant that the people from whose loins I sprang, including the blacksmith and justice who was a congressman for three terms under Jefferson, were down to earth, dealing with honest things like strength, religion, sentiment, heart. They were not cynical. . . . They were sincere." When he would quote a family battle cry, "I'm with you in any plot against those aristocrats," he was not siding with the peasant so much as placing himself against those who would despoil or deceive. His ancestors, he sometimes admitted with a touch of amusement, had fought on both sides of the American Revolution, those on the other side being Hessian mercenaries. English, Scotch-Irish, Welsh, Holland Dutch, and French blood was on his mother's side, German and French on his father's. His wife noted that "he was so pleased to know that most of his male ancestors on his father's side were shepherds," which he felt also explained "his love of nature and his liking for solitude."

All of this was combined with a highly tensed nervous system, a volcanic temper which he finally overcame in his seventies. Optimism went hand in hand with his fears. Set against depression and gloom was a special radiance that I can only describe as a fine golden rain of energy that at times poured from him, a kind of incandescence. Sometimes harshly critical, he could also be exceedingly kind. His name symbolized two of his qualities: Conrad, which in German means *keen counsellor*, and Richter, which signifies *judge*. If he judged too keenly, he also nurtured. If he was at times autocratic, he was also possessed of a rare humility.

And he was often shy, painfully self-conscious, retiring. Chosen valedictorian of his high school class, he refused to give his speech. Years later, he had to persuade Alfred Knopf to read his acceptance of the National Book Award for *The Waters of Kronos*. A typical letter declining an invitation pleads that he is "solitary, gloomy, inarticulate, unsociable and generally unfit for autographing party." Yet among a group of close friends he was lively and articulate. He had a marvelous sense of humor, which surfaces in the comic novel *The Grandfathers* but especially in the character of Portius Wheeler of the Ohio trilogy, who reflects facets of C. R. himself.

Looking back at my father working mornings, afternoons, *and* evenings during the depression years, managing to cook and to nurse his ill wife as well, himself often mistaken for the sick one, he assumes a heroic stance. Yet I never considered him then as hero, simply as someone who plied his profession as a carpenter or lawyer might. Only his working place distinguished him from other men: usually the dining-room or kitchen—the center of the house. One walked about very quietly, not wanting to disturb him. Company was rare. Yet what might have been intolerable was lit for me by the excitement that living in a writer's family generates. He read all of his work aloud to my mother and me—first draft to finished story—and thrashed out plots ("thrashed" was C. R.'s word, indicating the energy and punishment involved) as he paced the floor. When a story sold, the joy was enormous. We lived in a state of constant expectation and suspense which gave a heightened color to our lives.

Together with the struggle, the notebooks illuminate the process of writing itself. This is probably the most difficult topic any author can attempt. Writing about writing, to use a simile of William James, is like turning on a light to see how the darkness looks. A few glimpses are afforded in various diaries, letters, and essays of such writers as William Dean Howells, Edith Wharton, Virginia Woolf, Henry James, Willa Cather. But the process is mainly intellectualized; the gritty day-to-day doing of it is missing.

In the late 1940s, C. R. attempted an article about writing. As his journal reveals, he was reluctant to get too close to himself:

> ALL MORNING I TRIED TO WRITE, start piece for THE WRITER I have been asked to do for several years. This is as far as I got:
>
> > "A number of years ago in a careless moment I consented to write something for the editor of this magazine. It was a mistake. I found I did not care to confide my personal experiences in writing. They might be interesting, even helpful to a few but were too personal, intimate. To lay them open would be to give away part of myself. I do not mean that I had any secrets to relinquish but that these experiences, painful, pleasant, tend to form an integral part of me including that part which wants to write, knows how to write, and actually helps to write. And to speak these things to the four winds or throw them out on the printed page is to release my own writing capital and surplus hither and yon."
>
> Naturally, there was nothing to write after that. I tried to think of something else. I tried to write all morning and wasted it. (July 5, 1947)

Not quite ten years later he finished the article, which he titled "My Friend With the Hard Face." It dealt with the benefits of adversity, but it very carefully skirted "those experiences, painful, pleasant" that formed an "integral part" of him. The following January he withdrew the article from *The Writer*. It was never published.

C. R. always said that Selection and Order were the two most important things in writing. My own task has been to select from his notebooks, journals, and letters what seems to be both representative and illuminating, and to arrange it in some sort of sequence that would carry the sense of his growth as a writer and the series of obstacles he would face and be forced to overcome. If it depicts what might be called a success story, it also gives harrowing glimpses into the nightmares and the various private levels of hell through which most people in the creative arts have to travel.

Because readers usually express an interest in a writer's apprentice years, the first chapter covers roughly my father's late teens and twenties, together with an attempt to convey what the writing/publishing world was at that time. The second chapter narrows into the struggle through the depression years to find his own particular type of story and support the family through writing alone. Out of this struggle came his theories of writing and how to plot, which occupy the three chapters following. Glimpses of how several novels were born are given in "The Novel Notebooks," and the vast amount of material he gathered during his life is excerpted in "Characters and Conversations." The final chapters have to do with style and words and writing, voiced for himself or for those who wrote to him.

My purpose in editing the writing notebooks is to present C. R.'s ideas in a way that might be of help or interest to new or established writers. Many of the ideas apply strictly to his own mode of working, but as such can form a helpful critical tool, for they express what he was trying to accomplish as a novelist. Others apply to classic literature of any time and place, and I have found many of the ideas useful in my own courses in fiction writing at the University of New Mexico.

I have not tidied up any grammatical errors or misspellings in the notebooks or journals. The entries are, for the most part, hastily written. C. R. explained: "These are only notes in my journal, mean nothing as writing. They are set down only so I may read back on them and get material or observations, records, and thoughts. They are written for myself alone, never literary" (September 23, 1951). The headings in his notebooks and journals quoted here follow his style of capitalization, including some headings capitalized throughout for emphasis.

The main notebooks referred to in the text, Black Notebook I, Black Notebook II, Maroon Notebook I, and Maroon Notebook II are sometimes abbreviated to BI, BII, MI, and MII. They are catalogued with their contents in the bibliography, where the writing notebooks are listed. Some 25 percent of the material contained in those four notebooks has been transcribed or adapted for this volume. As to material from other notebooks, some seventeen pages, for example, have been used from Notebook 6; from the lengthy collections of eastern and western color and from the three thick thesauruses, only small, sample portions have been excerpted. The attempt has been not to "edit" the notebooks but rather to open the door of the usually locked room in which a creative writer works.

I would like to thank the following for their encouragement or special help: Mrs. Marjorie Sherwood, formerly of Princeton University Press, for her patient enthusiasm for the venture; Professor A. D. Van Nostrand of Georgia Institute of Technology for his perceptive criticism; and Professor David Johnson of Lafayette College and his wife, Jean, for kindly helping to assemble the bibliography.

In quotations from my father's journals and/or letters, the name Harvey refers to my mother, Vene to me.

1

Of Fate and Obstruction

C. R. was a superstitious man—a "thirteener," as he called it[1]—born on the thirteenth of October, 1890. A small notebook on his desk, labeled "New and Unusual Words," listed "tri-skaidekaphobia, fear of No. 13." It wasn't that he feared that number but simply noticed its importance in his life. His name, Conrad Richter, has thirteen letters. His first short story sold in 1913; the first anthology to carry a C. R. story was *The Grim Thirteen*; the title of his first novel, *The Sea of Grass*, runs to thirteen letters as does "Early Marriage," his first story in the *Saturday Evening Post*.[2] Any phobia he might have had was reserved for the number thirty. To a newspaper man, thirty meant the "end" of the story. He died on the thirtieth (October, 1968).

I think that from the start he was painfully aware that fate seemed to play a large part in his life—at least aware that something was operating over which he had little control. He enjoyed early recognition, then a long and seemingly fruitless period of twenty years, culminating in the blackest possible despair. Euphemistically, they could be called apprentice years, a testing time. Actually, they were a long-drawn-out battle in which he very nearly lost his life. Fate, which had awarded him a short story prize before he was twenty-four years old, was named in his journal "fate, the pervert."

That early recognition was Edward O'Brien's choice of "Brothers of No Kin" as the best short story of 1914.[3] C. R. had only started selling fiction the year before. Even though he had to cajole the *Forum* to pay him what they owed, it was the most prestigious thing that could happen to a young writer at that time. Many stories and sporadic sales followed. But some eight years later, in 1922, he wrote to a "story doctor" in Denver that his fiction was not selling, confessing that "There's been a lot of ink spilled about 'my promise,'" citing O'Brien and mentioning that "several others, including Harold Paget, predicted great things of a poor stick like me." If fate had smiled, she had immediately turned her back. Or so he seemed to think.

Several times I heard C. R. wryly tell about a Mrs. Wigton of Pine Grove "who lived in a beautiful home and was a great novel reader." When O'Brien chose his story as the best of 1914, she refused to believe he had written it. "Someone else must have done it in my name. I was too uneducated and had too humble a father."

As *The Waters of Kronos* and *A Simple Honorable Man* show, the family C. R. chose to be born into was a fortunate one for a writer: a country preacher's household with its constantly changing parishes and faces. His mother and aunt were great story tellers; two great-uncles had been editors and writers. Fate, one might say, was on his side. But odd reversals happened. He refused to become a Lutheran minister like his father, turning down a scholarship which would have meant a college education.[4] Instead he became entangled in a series of grossly unsuitable jobs. He felt misunderstood, perhaps even punished. It reinforced his childhood feelings that his parents were not his own.

> Sometimes it seems impossible to me that a boy so indubitably fitted for studies and so unfitted for labor should have been placed successively at stone breaking, culm shoveling, breaker machinery carrying, and work in a dark damp Pittsburg machine shop. My father desired me to become a freight handler at the Reading station, but fortunately there was no opening at the time. It is incredible to me that my parents did not understand my natural bent. . . . (1927 journal)

Yet, as he wrote to me when I was looking for my first job:

> Don't worry about the humble part. It's getting a job, holding it, learning and getting in a little steady wages that count. I carried water, broke stones on the road, labored in the field, sold magazine subscriptions, collected and delivered laundry. Look up the record of most any writer and see the humble things he did. . . . All this discipline, hard effort, concentration, SACRIFICE will breed strength out of lightness and weakness, purpose out of vacillation, a feeling of deep sober enthusiasm. . . . This is the only way I ever did anything. . . .[5]

The obstructions placed in front of C. R., following his graduation from high school at fifteen, were to influence not only his outlook on life and his notions on fate but his theories of fiction. The most important thing in a story would be the strong obstruction, in other words, adversity or trouble, which the main character must overcome (see Chapter 3). "Get your character in a hole," he would counsel me. I suspect that in my father's life the meshing of experience and art was very close. His writing was everything to him; he *was* his writing. It came before all else except my mother's health, although her periods of rest were enforced by his need for absolute quiet while at work.

The next hardships C. R. faced turned out to be more productive. He had fled the "damp machine shop" with a nervous breakdown. Now he had a job with a country bank. Since he earned only fifteen dollars a month and board and room cost sixteen, he started sending news items to the Philadelphia papers. "Some of the news items were printed and paid for at the rate of five dollars a column. . . . I think the biggest monthly check sent me by any of the newspapers was three dollars."[6] But he claimed he learned more about writing as a country correspondent at seventeen than as a reporter or editor.

> Early in my experience I sent in a four or five line item about a woman catching a skunk who killed her chickens. It appeared in the paper as a long two-column spread with a great mass of detail I didn't know & which had apparently come from the state editor's experience and imagination. . . . Two years later when I wrote my first assignment for the Johnstown Journal, the hard boiled & usually drunken city editor called me over bruskly to the city desk. I expected to be fired. He said, "Where'd you work on a paper before?" "No where," I said. "Well, you'll go farther than here," he told me & that was my first encouragement.[7]

This was the first lesson to C. R. of the sweet uses of adversity. He went on to be editor of a country weekly (the Patton *Courier*) and reporter on other Johnstown and Pittsburg dailies.[8] He had attempted writing magazine stories while at the bank, and his success in the newspaper field suggested he might set his sights a little higher. He sent out a sheaf of letters to such prominent authors as Robert Chambers, William Dean Howells, and Upton Sinclair offering his services as a secretary with the hope of learning a little more about writing.

> Nicest answer from Owen Wister although many were kind - Jack London wrote he'd like us to get together but his wife stood in our way which I thought excuse until I read his biography. John Burroughs dampened me and Richard Harding Davis cured me entirely.[9]

The query to Davis was of a different sort, and the answer, handwritten on two small yellow sheets, dated April 4 (circa 1910–11) bears quoting:

> My Dear Richter:
> The only advice I can give you is to go to "headquarters" and wire back. If you have no money, then follow the advice of Checkers and "act like you was broke." What I mean is that

> writing me for advice how to be a war correspondent is not the way to begin. Did you ever read of Macgahan?? and his ride after the Russian army to Kiva? What I mean is that if you really wanted to be a war correspondent you would borrow the money, steal a ride on a freight train, or walk to the Rio Grande. Should you do so, I should be glad to hear from you again. I am yours, ...

Where C. R. landed was not in the middle of the Mexican war but as private secretary and business manager to a wealthy society woman in Cleveland. The circumstances were anything but "humble." A photograph of C. R., one foot on the running board of his employer's chauffeur-driven car, shows a prosperous and handsome young fellow with a bit of bravado—what they called in those days a "swell." His next venture was investigating a silver mine in the Coeur d'Alenes in Idaho, and he returned by way of California and Mexico in order to say he had traveled "widely" on the next job application. By 1916, a year after he had married, he had founded a small publishing company in Reading; tried to introduce the pretzel, then merely a local Pennsylvania-Dutch delicacy, to the sophisticated New York audience and failed; published a children's magazine for which he wrote everything with a dizzying array of pseudonyms; sold a number of short stories to Vitagraph and Biograph for one-reelers; and acquired a literary agent.[10]

The failure of the pretzel promotion seems, in retrospect, a kindly quirk of fate. But even if the role of pretzel tycoon had not put an end to his writing, it might have set it on quite different and more esoteric paths, for he would have been able to write what he wanted to, not what would sell. Certainly the failure must have *greitzeled* him, to use a Pennsylvania-Dutch expression, for he sent his agent, Harold Paget, a box of pretzels as if to prove their worth. They were pronounced delicious.

Harold Paget, with his sister Cora, ran an agency that handled not only fiction and nonfiction but dramatic and screen material. The several manila folders of correspondence—the Paget sheets small with a large brown heading—have an air of friendly excitement. The letters were encouraging. By the end of 1917 C. R. wondered whether he shouldn't quit his small publishing business to write full time.

My mother prodded him to do so. In 1916 Paget had estimated that within three years C. R. "should be making anywhere between $5,000 and $10,000 from your magazine market alone."[11] Now Paget answered him by saying, "You have made such very decided strides in your work since we have handled it. . . . I should most certainly say that your work and the chances warrant your staying at writing." However, Paget wondered about "the sacrifice it would mean under the circumstances."

The question of whether to strike out on his own is reflected in a 1925 story to the *American* called "Derickson's Gagoo" in which the main character finally realizes he is neurotically holding onto his job just as his small daughter does to her gagoo (security blanket). Derickson cuts the strings, and his former employer, admiring his courage, promises Derickson his account.

But in 1917 C. R.'s own small daughter had arrived and there were too many paying projects to chuck it all. My father wasn't a gambler; he liked what he could call "The Sure Thing." In addition, his need to be original was met by highly successful sales writing. Company executives called his letters "ingenious," "radical," "original without being offensive."[12] When his Handy Book Company in 1925 published a pamphlet *Seven Sales-Writing Principles*, the advertising and sales techniques would be some twenty years ahead of their time. So were his attempts to market his children's magazine. In 1917 his *Junior Magazine Book* offered young subscribers their own name printed on the cover, such as *Betty Baker's Magazine*, instead of *Junior Book*.

Strangely, World War I scarcely affected C. R.'s life. His married status exempted him from service. The war was an ocean away, and editors kept reminding writers and agents that they didn't want stories about the war—nothing but the light and frivolous. C. R.'s next best story of the early years, "The Laughter of Leen," about a young German fraulein who had lost her family, had a hard time finding a market, although it would be widely read on the lecture platform.

Yet in spite of the taboos (no racial mixtures, for example), the war and postwar years were a wonderful time for a young writer. Newsstands displayed a multitude of short story markets. A camaraderie seemed to exist between agent, editor, and writer that is unheard of today. In the innumerable letter files from 1912 on is an array of well-known names and witty correspondence from editors such as Isobel M. Patterson, whose column on books signed I.M.P. had put her into the contemporary literary spotlight; or letters begging for more work (though declining the particular story) from such as Edward Bok or Sinclair Lewis.[13] The almost fierce formality that my father was later to adopt with agents and editors was absent. Criticism was gentle, generous; editors seemed to regret turning down a story and invited submissions endlessly. Although agents charged for postage, it was little enough ($1.65 for nineteen submissions, for example), and they offered abject apologies when they felt a story should be returned to the author.

Borrowing from his sales techniques C. R. sent out jaunty letters like the following:

June 23, 1922

The Editor,
Harper's Magazine
New York
Dear Sir:

It merits little shame to hold in regard the offspring of one's flesh.

> This is the offspring of my mind. Handle it without care as much as pleases you, but know that I thought a fond mite of it or I would not have paid you the compliment of giving you privilege of refusing it board and room.
>
> Yours sincerely,

And circa 1922, a first draft of a letter probably not sent:

> Dear Mr. Lorrimer [*sic*]:
>
> Should these twenty or thirty pages of sweat and tungsten hit THE SATURDAY EVENING POST, please communicate to a lucky devil by the name of,
>
> Yours very truly,

The sense of adventure in the publishing market stemmed in part from the large number of magazines who put out a plethora of short fiction. Wide-circulation weeklies such as the *Saturday Evening Post* and *Colliers* used up to five short stories an issue, yielding a yearly market of over five hundred stories; lesser semislicks such as the weekly *Liberty* did likewise. The women's monthlies, unlike the beauty-food-home-decorating periodicals of today, crammed their pages with fiction (*Good Housekeeping, Woman's Home Companion, Ladies' Home Journal, Cosmopolitan, Red Book*) and a host of others such as *Delineator, College Humour*, the *Country Gentleman*, and the *American* (to which C. R. sold nine stories) were still in full swing. Lesser markets—like *Elks*, the *Munsey Magazine, Outlook, People's Magazine, Everybody's, Every Week*, and various syndicates and illustrated Sunday newspaper editions—swelled the potential.[14]

And the typical short story of the twenties tended to be light, somewhat frothy, often moral. C. R. churned out stories with attention-getting titles such as "The Man Who Had His Block Knocked Off," "Sitting on Sally," "Over the Hill to the Rich House," or "Bad Luck is Good Luck." Short-shorts were in vogue then, and in 1921 he formulated a plan (later pasted in his November 1927 journal with the comment, "I was astonished to find these thoughts written by me. . . . What astonishment and shame as I read this brazen proclamation of only seven years ago"):

I FIND MYSELF???
October 2nd, 1921 Sunday a.m.
I will write stories a thousand or
less words each.
These will be offered four or more at a time
to be printed, as, for example
"TONY THE UNDRAMATIC"
And Other Stories
I will be neither Bruce Barton
nor David Grayson but
Conrad Richter, Pioneer
It will be successful because
short things attract.
It will do good because I can
present in SHORT FICTION
ONE THOUSAND HELPFUL IDEAS
where otherwise I could but
write a hundred.

There is a snapshot of my father in his teens sitting on the front steps facing himself—an image splice. In several of the children's stories he wrote for his *Junior Book* the main characters meet their exact duplicates. In retrospect there seem to have been two Conrad Richters during his twenties and early thirties—one an adventurous young fellow with endless ideas and enterprise, the other a suppressed artist, loving solitude, nature, biding his time. It was fate that forced him into the latter role.

In an article written in 1957 for *The Writer* but withdrawn, C. R. referred to adversity as "my friend with the hard face." Whether he considered adversity and fate as one and the same is unclear, but he told me more than once that if I did not do certain things, the powers-that-be would force me into the proper actions, presumably with some suffering on my part. This followed his theory of self-evolution, a disciplining of the self to avoid the harsher disciplines of fate. By the time this fatherly advice was administered, C. R. had learned just what fate can do.

Yet in another sense, the pattern was set far earlier. When he became engaged to my mother, C. R.'s future father-in-law warned him that several of the family, including her mother, had died from tuberculosis. My mother, he predicted, would contract it too. "Why then she needs someone to take care of her," was C. R.'s answer. In a seemingly idealistic but actually very wise gesture, C. R. shouldered the responsibility. In the beginning the cost would seem very high.

In 1922 C. R. moved from Reading to a country farm near Harrisburg for my mother's health, moving his business to the state capital where it became the Good Books Corporation. But although the five and a half years at Pine Tree Farm were idyllic, my mother's health grew more precarious. In 1928 C. R. sold his business and the farm, and we headed west. The early American valley in Pennsylvania would furnish C. R. with material for his 1964 novel *The Grandfathers* and backwoods characters for his Ohio trilogy. But the move to New Mexico would change the entire course of his life and writing. Ultimately, it worked out for the best. But in 1928 trouble was right around the corner; the "friend with the hard face" would move in with the family for six long years.

2

Finding His Own Type of Story

The years between 1928 and 1934 might be called "the panic years." They included the stock market crash, in which C. R. lost all the money he had invested, and the year the banks closed. If fate had planned a way to force him into writing full time, it couldn't have done the job more effectively. Not only did C. R. lose all his money, but to cover his margins he went deeply into debt.

The irony was that the income from stock dividends—substantial at the time he invested in July of 1928—was to have freed him to write what he wanted.[1] Now that freedom was snatched away. In order to pay for food and rent, he was compelled to write pulps, which paid as low as half a cent a word and demanded the kind of mass-tailored plot he was trying to get away from. In the summer of 1929 he wrote in his journal, "I am like a ship that is slowly but steadily being sunk. . . . I seem drunk with the sense of tragedy and defeat." A year later, in an entry titled The Darkest Road, he laments:

> This is the bitterest lane I have as yet had to travel. Stocks decline almost daily - Stories have come back from the wood pulps. I pick them up - the magazines - and am made sick by their terrible characters - continuous, unreal action like puppets kept ceaselessly dancing by strings - Yet I must slave over these stories while outside at night are a sky & moon I dare not look at and in the mountains are flowers & pines. . . . I must be coarse and toil over action fictions for invisible readers.

C. R. had written sporadically during the Pine Tree Farm period.[2] In the two years since he came west, two stories had sold to the *Farm Journal*, one to *Munsey Magazine*, one to *Triple-X*, and three mining stories about "Broady, the Hard Rock Man" to *Blue Book*. The total gross for 1930 would be $1,256.60, less the agent's 10 percent. Two local pulp writers, Paul Everman of Albuquerque (who died of tuberculosis in 1934) and T. T. Flynn of Santa Fe, were making a good living in the wood pulps and encouraged C. R. to try his luck with them. My mother's illness precluded his trying to find a job.

I don't remember reading any of the pulp magazines my father professed to loathe. But from the typewriter, which now went all morning, afternoon, and evening, came characters like Lazy Dee, Bull Pup Brown, Windy Cox, Jawbone Kelly, Two-Word Talley, Singin' Jim, and the Singing Sheriff. For the latter two, C. R. wrote the western songs himself.[3] The writing was spare; the characters were unusual; the plots were stripped for action with a surprise denouement. C. R. had read his stories to my mother and me since the days at Pine Tree Farm. He did now more than ever, and today I can still sense the magic that radiated from his goose-neck lamp as he read these tales aloud to us. The first paragraph laid down character, situation, suspense. The plot *had* to work. If his stories during the 1920s had been criticized as light, or the action as unbelievable, the pulps cured him of this. The character's life, reputation, or living was at stake. The odds (or obstructions) against the characters were formidable. The overcoming of the obstructions wasn't through chance but by the character's own hard work, endurance, special knowledge, and cleverness.

What his "friend with the hard face" had done for C. R. was to make him aware of the value of the strong plot obstruction and the closely knit structure of the plot itself. He was learning how to assemble the tough skeleton of the stories he would later flesh out for the *Saturday Evening Post*. Without the pulps as teacher, he often said, he would have been unable to write the later stories.

C. R. was also led, in quite another way, into concentrating on portraying character. It was the one thing he could do to make the stories interesting for himself. The pulp editors, who claimed to like characterization, sometimes criticized C. R.'s stories for having character primary and plot secondary. In his later short stories, as well as his novels, the characters always predominate. In "The Simple Life," for example, it is the cowboy Doane Williams, with his complex mixture of recklessness and good humor, whom the reader remembers more strongly than the unusual plot.

If there was a struggle to submit to the grade-B pulp market, another kind of struggle was taking place whose outcome would deeply affect C. R.'s work. That was the search for his own kind of story. His commonplace book has a quotation from Willa Cather at the time she was writing *One of Ours*, saying how she had been drawn back to the Nebraska prairie in her work, how her "deepest feelings were rooted in this country" (Omaha *World Herald*). She had been "trying to work in a sophisticated medium and write about highly developed people whom I knew only superficially." Below that clipping is appended in longhand:

> Find Myself:
>
> Reading modern stories in Good Housekeeping today (June 17, 1933) after avoiding reading for 2½ weeks . . . I see *clearly* what Vene has told me - that I do not know modern life, color, character & talk nearly well enough to write modern stories. I can see also what she did not tell me - that I do not like modern life, color, characters & talk, so how can I enthuse enough about it that the editor or reader classes me as a modern?
>
> What authentic life with lift do I know & like? That I can do.
> Western - old days - ranch, Santa Fe
> Colonial Penna & Ohio, Virginia
> Mexican romances with Mexicans

Foreign with non-modern characters
Mountain { with non-modern characters
with mountain people
Older Days (a generation ago) & Older Days to Present

The modern-life stories that C. R. was unable to sell during the 1930–1933 period had the frothy titles of the 1920s: "Romance is Dead," "Son of a Gunness," "Don't Believe Anything," "Debtors Be Gay," "You Don't Understand," "Pat As She Pleases," "Let 'Em Drown," "Dancing on Water," "Gloria's Violent Ray." The last brought enthusiastic response, although no sale, and was considered quite original. But none were C. R.'s type of story.[4] On the other hand, a yarn bought by *Woman's Home Companion*, "The King Was in the Kitchen" (C. R.'s title: "He Walks in Spinach"), was tied to hearth and reality, with a touch of "lift."

Lift as a concept was important in C. R.'s growing apprehension of his own kind of fiction. Before or in 1933 he began to compile Notebook 6, the most personal of his writing notebooks, filled with admonitions to himself, passages from his journal, quotations about writing, and excerpts from writing of others which especially moved him. From the opening section's eight pages captioned Build Success With Your Own Type of Story:

> Every successful writer has a talent for only one, or at the most, two types of stories. His name, success is built on this type among editors & magazine readers. His name stands for it. It is doubtful if he could have grown successful with half a dozen different types even if he had talent for all & time to acquire the authenticities & radiance for each field. . . .
>
> My talent seems to be for a type of story that lifts you . . . - something warm, tender, noble, beautiful, intense - a background, life etc. transfused into something rich, golden, shining. For short I will call this "lift." People like to be lifted so long as their reason is not insulted. My successful stories to

> better magazines the last 3 years, as well as before, had it - [The] High Places, Heart of [a] Horseman, White Flower. . . .
> But a successful lift story must also today be New, seemingly Real-Life, Uniform, Not too Sweet or Perfect and the other requisites of my stories. My stories that had lift & didn't sell the past 3 years were defeated by their faults. . . .
> Not any subject can be transfused to a golden splendor by me. I can only take those things that so move me.

Willa Cather, whose prairie stories influenced C. R. probably more than those of any other writer, had pointed out this necessity for being moved/motivated. "Almost never," she wrote (this contained in the afore-quoted clipping but also copied out in longhand and underlined by C. R.), "did I find a manuscript that was written because a writer loved his subject so much he had to write about it."[5]

The compulsions that drove him to keep Notebook 6 are reflected in such admonitions as this one, pasted on heavy blue-grey paper and doubtless meant to make himself "buck up" (a phrase he was particularly addicted to) when he became too discouraged:

> The terror & shuddering I have had taught me that, although it is good to go to H & V (1) to see if an idea part is all right (2) to read story part to them
> It is Weak and Injurious
> to go when I have only complaint
> That only drops me down in the mire
> I Must Do Most Myself
> Affirm! "I can write stories that sell"
> Discipline! Make yourself write 1,000 words.
> Repeat "The fault is mine. It is up to me to
> plot & write salable stories"
> Overcome
> H & V deserve a few releases from worry and
> some luxuries

This is followed by a section entitled Quotations on My Work & Working copied out of his journals. On the first page:

October 24
1933

Writing Cheer

I have a trade. I have written & sold over $17,000 worth of stories. $7250 in the last four panic years.

From January 1931 to October 1933 I have written 30 pulps & sold 20. 66 2/3 sales. If all else fails, we can make a living in pulps.

I am understanding more technique every day - every month - both in pulps and smooth papers.

Today on ride among poor little farms off main roads below town, I said, "These poor people have nothing new until spring - but I have ships out, some of which must come in this winter & I can plough my land & raise crops all winter & the rest of the year, too."

I repeat "I can write stories that sell." I think, "I can write stories that sell." I believe "I can write stories that sell."

The years from 1929 to early 1934 appeared to alternate between promise and gloom. In 1931, in which he sold three stories to *Liberty*, he grossed nearly $4,000. 1932 brought in only $1,465. A sampling of journal entries—an excerpt or perhaps only the underlined heading—taken from these years offers a window to the black outlook of his fears. If he did not allow himself to complain to his wife and daughter, here in the privacy of his journals he could attempt to distance, or at least confront the terrors by putting them down in black ink.

1930.

(Feb. 14) Harvey has been home from the sanitarium for ten days. We are too poor to afford a maid. I am doing the cooking and Vene finely helping when she is home from school.

(April 22) [stockman who lived across the street asked C. R. his business.] When I apologetically told him it was writing for magazines & occasional books, he said, as if not to make me feel small by comparison with his superior profession, "We all must have some sort of business to make a living."

(April 29) My word machinery does not function.

(June 23) . . . cashed at the market a check for $1. on the Harrisburg bank in which my checkbook showed a balance of $1.42. I brought home a loaf of bread & a dozen eggs, laid them on Harvey's bed & we all gloated over them.

(June 26) We have not had meat for days.

(July 18) I am too tired & discouraged at times to believe that a story of mine shall ever sell - or that I can ever write another.

(Sept. 17) <u>A Long Way to Go</u> No story has sold for months. There are 13 mss. out right now. The market hesitates. Business hesitates. Pessimistic rumors & opinions again appear in the newspapers. It seems that something must break our way very soon. The law of averages demands it. And yet I have the feeling that I may yet have a long way to go.

(Oct. 1) <u>Blackest for Days</u>. For the first time in days I sat down at the piano tonight. But I did not enjoy it so much as I should if I had not thought I were tempting the fates. I could hear them say, "He's happy again. By morning he'll be recovered enough to apply some more screws."

(Oct. 31) <u>The Long Night</u> Everything seems darker than ever. No story has sold for months. No money for coal, light, heat, milk. I marvel at my calmness.

(Nov. 8) <u>Two Stout Weapons</u>
(1) Strength Before All! (Strength first - & always beneath!)

(2) I have a trade!
We counted up yesterday that I had sold $10,000 worth of stories. I have given 15 or 20 years to the work. Plots come & work out more easily than ever - even though they are not currently selling.

1931
(Jan. 16) Brighter & Busier
A few stories have sold. My health is better. . . . My stories are longer!

(March 14) Purple Moods
Week before last & again today I had hours of dark discouragement. It seems incredible that I shall ever sell enough stories to make my living by it.

(April 3) Black, Black, Black
Stocks go down slowly but surely every day like last year. I have had to borrow on the two stocks held outright. . . .
Some days I am black with discouragement, hopelessness, desperation. Some days I have hope enough stories will sell to carry us through to better times.

1932
(Jan. 22) Dark, Dark!
Not a sale since early in November, except the smallest I have made for many years - $65 gross!

(March 26) Easter Eve
We priced flowers tonight for Harvey & found nothing decent to give her for a dollar. When we came home I told H. She replied indignantly, "I never dreamed you would look for any in our condition, or I'd have warned you that I'd much sooner have a beefsteak!"

(April 5) Black, Black, Black [C. R. thinks his agent not sending out stories—says she's written him when he's received no mail.] I owe the bank $100 interest unpaid and the milkman for 2 months. Two insurance policies would have lapsed but a short while before the last day, a mysterious extra dividend appeared from the company which paid all but $6 of the premiums due. Then a check from my father for $50 paid a little rent & household bills. Today $6 in dividends will allow me to buy paper, ms. cover & a new typewriter ribbon. . . .

(June 8) Lately it has not seemed to matter much if I lived or died - slaving at magazine fictions.

(June 27) Dark, Dark, Bitter! [C. R. had heard nothing from his agent for a month—a story Colliers was considering fell through.] And in all this distress, Paul Reynolds, said to be one of the best literary agents in the country, writes to handle my work! What irony!
I find myself saying "Thank God I only have a lifetime & 42 years of that are gone!"

(Aug. 2) An Author Again.
Today I received in one mail a letter from Reynolds that he was taking "Little Lower Than the Angels" over "personally" to McCalls - and a letter from someone in Brookline asking permission to reprint "King in the Kitchen" for Braille for the blind. For the first day in a long time I felt I was an author again.

(Aug. 20) Black, Blacker Yet
No story has sold for 4 months except one in June for $54. . . .
I never seem to sell a story until I give up all hope.

(Sept. 24) Black, Black
No stories had sold despite our almost certain expectations. . . . I walk outside & am surprised to see sun shining & to find the ground holding me up. "I can walk - that is something I can do anyhow" I tell myself.

(Dec. 5) Dark, Dark

1933
(no date) The Zero Hour
The Strain for Relief
So often the last several years of trouble, I feel that an earthquake is about to happen - shake down the house. And I am not worried at all but rather exhilirate in the relief that it cannot add to my debt - & the excitement will be a change at least. Of course my reason knows it will not happen, but my unconscious straining for relief fosters it.[6]

In March 1933 the banks closed. We were in Tucson, Arizona (having stayed in a mountain cabin near Albuquerque until Christmas because the off-season rent was only fifteen dollars per month) and grocers would not accept C. R.'s checks on the Albuquerque bank. The March 11 entry is titled Black Again:

> The last few days have reminded me of such days at 720 West New York[7] - the same desperate feelings. But then I had hope of working back into the magazines. Now I have worked back & fallen out again. Short Stories picked out "Mason Climbs Mtn" as the best story in the magazine in 1932 & I felt that although smooth papers had rejected me, I was at least good for counting on a living from pulps. Now tonight after reading my last few perhaps I doubt even that.

There is little in the 1933 journal until December. Then the entry captions follow the down pattern: Low Discouraged. Had Been Fine - Blue Today. Blue Again. Blackest Yet. *Short Stories* had cut his rate. It had now been four years since the stock market crash, and although he was amazed how much his writing had improved over the preceding two years, the sense of desperation was growing ("Shudder inside" from an entry on December 14). The following day, and indeed for the remainder of the month, a new awareness of plot seemed to be growing:

> We plan now to all gang on plot for 1 or 2 days all day etc till we have it - then I write day & night to get it out. . . .

On that day he wrote 3,000 words (1,000 was par). Then the next day (captioned Plot Trouble) he wrote 1,000 words in the morning.

> After lunch stuck on plot found the part before the end was not right. We tried to plot it out before supper & sat until 10 PM at supper table. A dozen times I said this was the most tricky & involved plot I ever tried to do. But finally by sticking to essentials—what was necessary like "he must do it himself on end" etc., I worked it out going back to knock out the last 1000 words & change the part. . . .
>
> Resolved to spend more time going [over] & recounting essentials of plot in first place - until it is fool & trouble proof. Tomorrow we go over this again. The thing or trick is to go over the story synopsis again & again attacking it from every angle, weighing, questioning each part for flaws - seeing that it gets hero in trouble at start & gets him deeper to climax & never lets him out or promises to let him out.
>
> (Dec. 16) Plot Huddles Improving
> H & V, especially latter, are getting better on plotting - listening better - staying with ship - not wishing to run away at first indication that I have some idea how to fix it. H. stuck firm & V. asked questions & made good criticisms.

When things went bad—whether regarding health, money, or writing—C. R. would figure out a new plan of action. It might be retiring early for proper rest, or planning the day on a minute-by-minute schedule such as the following (January 11, 1934):

> We will get up - H & I - as soon as she (Vene) leaves, at 20 minutes to 8. That means nearly 10 hours sleep. Desk at 8.30. Nearly 4 hrs work in A.M. I do dishes (breakfast & dinner) & get to work at 1.30 to 5.30. Again at 6.30 to 9.30, making 11 hours for my day.
>
> 11 hrs work
> 10 hrs sleep
> 3 hrs misc.

Several weeks earlier, in late December, C. R. had evolved two other plans. One was to put $500 in postal savings "when we had a windfall & never touching it except for life & death." The other was a schedule my mother made out for him (this not included in the journal) so that "my work comes first & all things arranged so I can produce so much." That day he wrote 3,600 words.

Christmas was lean. On December 28 his energy rises again:

> Enthusiasm for Pulps
>
> . . . P M called on Everman - had dandy visit. Enthusiastic on pulps. He gave me name of markets for my Western duds. . . .
>
> I Have a Business
>
> I realize tonight I have a business - pulp stories - mail them myself - write lots of them.

Two days later "The Singin' Texan" sold to *Blue Book* for $175. "It changed my outlook & I decided to hold over Grama Grass - cheap pulp for quick money - & do a smooth paper as scheduled." This one was "Valhalla," which would sell that summer to the pulp *Blue Book* although the *Post* had been interested in it. The next story he began plotting was "Early Marriage."

Curiously, the darkest entries of the journal are in the nine days between the time he mailed the story (Sad Mailing Early Marriage) and the day it sold, February 16, 1934:

> (Feb. 9) Fate, the Ruthless Herder
> This A M more blue than weeks & weeks. I can see fate driving me closer and closer to ending it. . . . I feel like a sheep or calf who is herded toward one direction. He tries to break away in that direction or to escape in this, but fate, the herder, turns him back. And at last he finds himself between the wide wings of the corral that leads to the slaughter house. If I wait too long, H & V will have barely enough to pay my debts when I go [insurance policies about to expire]. . . .
> Fate, the Pervert
> I am afraid to entertain a hope, lest fate make it ghastly having a terrible opposite come true - . . .

That same day C. R.'s journal recounts how he started out "this noon to prepare an article for *Atlantic* in excerpts of a man's journal, a man who commits suicide." By the time he finished "reading my own journals of these four hard, terrible years" he felt "how terrible it would be to die by your own hand." The deep gloom persisted for another week. Looking back, it appears as if fate weren't quite the "pervert" C. R. envisioned it as being, for on December 18 he took a poem I had written to the printers for use as our Christmas card, read proof on it, and did not see until later that "they had been printed with the word *wealth* instead of *wreath*" (emphasis mine). Within two months the mysterious forecast began to be fulfilled in a modest way.

The day that "Early Marriage" sold, C. R.'s journal heading read Blackest! The Post Buys:

> This A M came a thick letter from Reynolds. I felt a clip inside, which usually means a check attached. But when I opened it eagerly, it contained (1) a letter from Reynolds not thinking much of Early Marriage (2) rejection from Short Stories saying Mountain Man was trite (3) rejection from Argosy saying Stuff

> of a Ranger didn't measure up (4) letter from Argosy (in answer to mine) saying it didn't want any more Singing Jim stories but might be interested in another western with "a number" of my original western songs. I had counted on Mountain Man with Short Stories because it had almost gone to Liberty & Country Home while Mason Climbs the Mtn which was almost the same subject, wind on Mtn top, & which didn't draw a letter from a magazine, was selected as S.S.'s best story of the year. I do not think I was ever so blue. I couldn't borrow from K———now because I couldn't tell him I expected any sales. I didn't. I was completely sunk. I told H. I was a failure & asked if she would mind much if I ended it all which would give her $21,000 & enable her to pay my debts. . . .

A little later the doorbell rang. It was the telegraph boy, with "the utterly incredible news that the Post had taken Early Marriage." But C. R. was less than overjoyed. Tears kept rolling down his cheeks.

> Never before had any acceptance affected me like this. Now, I think, I realize the terrible thing we are up against. Before, when a story sold, I felt our troubles were over - everything would sell now. But now I knew another sale will be just as much of a miracle & it sobers me, saddens me.

My mother said that the sale "was timed perfectly as if by fate," for we were down to ten dollars. But the rescue was incomplete; the pain of the experience remained. With that pain was a heightened flow of energy, a kind of creative adrenalin which would give C. R. a psychological dependence on disaster—or at least on the fear of it. I suspect, too, that the repetition of a sequence of deep trouble and last-moment deliverance made him see his life in terms of fiction. It was a continuing pattern of obstruction and (partial) release/fulfillment. His adversary was Fate or God; his journal in the 1930s bears such captions as Fate Still Against Story or God's Hand Against Me. When, later, he would think on those days, he would feel nostalgia (although unwilling to go back because of their pain). "We had the best time," he wrote March 23, 1961: "Our coming out of the not-have to the have. . . . We were bred in the richness of lack for the poverty of surfeit."

Surfeit. Lack was painful, but C. R. was suspicious of surfeit. Although he would work several times for Metro Goldwyn Mayer, Fortune was as great an adversary as Fate. A quotation from the Chorus of *Agamemnon*, heavily marked in an anthology on his desk, confirms his feeling about it:

> Great fortune is a hungry thing
> And filleth no heart anywhere,
> Though men with fingers menacing
> Point at the great house, none will dare,
> When Fortune knocks, to bar the door,
> Proclaiming: "Come thou here no more!"[8]

3

Plots and Outlines

C. R. always claimed he wasn't a natural writer. "It is not a native talent but has been slowly built, grafted on the rest of me, bought in sweat, blood, and despair."[1] This sense of inadequacy was still another fiction that he employed to fuel himself to work even harder. Although the sale of "Early Marriage" confirmed his ability on one level, on another it was frightening: he would have to repeat the performance and, if possible, improve upon it. Four days after the sale he noted in his journal:

> Still Pessimistic
>
> I feel today and tonight as if the story sale of Early Marriage was only a fluke - that I have a hard year ahead, that I am no more than before. Plotting all day on Long Drouth and I am a bit dazed & stolid - a little of the band across my head. . . .

But in "Early Marriage" C. R. had found his own kind of story, and it became a touchstone for him. On a notebook page marked "Read Often," he summarized the story's unity of time, place, and action:

> Most Important
> One Straightaway
>
> Plot story with one important obstruction & one straightaway time scene as in Early Marriage.
>
> If previous stuff must be cited, go back & bring out whatever is necessary in Recalling, Conversation, etc.

> But start with the one big thing & make it action, detail, suspense from beginning to end, with added trouble & complication as in Early Marriage but nothing new to introduce, just all added obstructions of one thing.
>
> You save time on writing & have more enthusiasm & interest for action suspense.

"Early Marriage" had taken only two weeks from the initial plotting to the final typing—eleven actual days of writing. Nearly two weeks after its sale he again commented on the problems with the new story:

> I Must Have Active Story
>
> The trouble is that Long Drouth has a passive plot. 1st they wait while drought happens to them. 2nd it does not happen quick like flood, enemics, shipwreck, etc.
>
> It lasts over months & years. 3rd, they are not in particular danger - their cattle are merely dying off. . . .
>
> Early Marriage in comparison had a plot that started with danger about to engulf them any time & once the journey was begun it was action to finish.
>
> Oh for more such plots!

Most of the agony in plotting, which fills pages of C. R.'s journals, seemed to be in trying to locate the problem itself. In "Long Drouth," once he realized what was wrong, he made the obstruction an active rather than a passive one by having the drouth postpone the engagement and marriage of the girl.[2] Through this and other exasperating problems in working out the first *Post* stories he developed his major theories of plot.[3] These are set forth in the two outlines of "Early Marriage" and "Smoke Over the Prairie" given in the appendix. Four main points from them are encapsulated in what C. R. termed "primary considerations" in starting to plot a story:

I Universal theme of authentic duty and fresh idea
II Theme fulfillment definite (usually has to do with marriage or none)
III Chief powerful obstruction is to theme fulfillment out of which come other obstructions
IV Strong opening obstruction of chief obstruction that leaves a strong situation

These four points can be said to constitute a universal blueprint for the short story and novel. The term *obstruction* denotes the obstacle or impediment to the action the character must take, and is the most important concept in any plot. Upon the obstruction or obstructions hang the suspense and forward movement of the story. Implicit in the blueprint is what C. R. terms Theme Action, by which he meant "the things done by the character in going ahead & doing authentic duty," in other words, the action of the plot itself. If examined closely, Theme Action can be seen as a way of unifying the story. What the character desires or requires, the obstruction to the fulfillment of that desire, the action taken to circumvent the obstruction, and the fulfillment itself are all cut from one piece of cloth.

The term *authentic duty* is an important one and refers to what a character must do in the particular circumstances in order to fulfill an obligation, to the character himself or to someone else. The word *authentic* refers not only to its rightness within the plot but in the confines of custom, time, and place. For example, in the short story "Early Marriage" it is Nancy Belle's duty to arrive at Gunstock by her wedding day. The "authentic" aspect is the difficulty in rough pioneer times of fulfilling what seems today a simple obligation. The term *authentic* is important in understanding C. R.'s particular quality. It means being truthful to the people and their times, portraying characters and events as they were rather than what fiction might dictate. My father felt scorn for many Western writers who sacrificed truth for drama; not a note of his own fiction rings false, and the reason for this can be glimpsed in the abundance of notes he gathered from old-timers and historical records (see Chapter 8). This transcription of thousands of small details of character and action, place and object, comprised what he termed authenticities. They made the scene and people spring alive. A note in a folder gives his aim as a writer:

> To present life not only so it may be authentic, interesting and provide for interpretation, if possible on several levels, but so the reader may find and lose himself in the true mood and feeling of the life in question as actual experience.

The dual outlines for "Early Marriage" and "Smoke Over the Prairie" occupy some nine single-spaced pages in Black Notebook II and remained a criterion that he consulted for all of his subsequent work. The outlines are given in tandem; each major point is worked out in both stories. This was doubtless comforting for him, for the outlines confirmed the rightness of his ideas. They were road tested. If the story didn't run, there was something wrong with the plot to which the outlines would alert him.

In addition to analyzing just how the two short stories are worked out in detail, the outlines touch closely on just how C. R. attempted to portray the American frontier. "Man in authentic duty" is "pitted against frontier, desert, mountain, or against civilization etc." The universal themes bear on birth, death, youth, love, marriage; the seasons, the land, and the forest. Of primary importance are the courage and integrity of pioneer characters, what he termed the "power" of these people, whether a young girl calmly going across dangerous territory to be married, or a freighter baron with vast business holdings whose domain spanned a thousand miles. These "power" characters are delineated not only through plot action and personal characteristics, but through contrast with other characters, with scenes, and with events. Moreover, they must not be trite characters but authentic, different, enhanced by the aforementioned authenticities of color and atmosphere.

C. R. lists them as the Strong Individual American Character you Like or Admire and Who Goes His Way despite All. Even the most ruthless of C. R.'s major characters (excepting Snell Beasley in *The Lady*) have qualities one can admire. It would have been very difficult for him to deal with characters he did not like; they fired him with enthusiasm to write the story, as did certain qualities, listed in the outline as Richness, Power, Atmosphere, Family, Nobility, Sweep, and Beauty, which contributed to the Lift described in the next chapter.

Many of the headings in the outlines suggest that everything must be tested. Are the root causes that make situations natural? Do Theme Fulfillment and Obstruction fit naturally together? Does Something Good come out of it? Does it contribute to Country, to America? Is it New, Fresh, Subtly Done? Is the Solution one which is Real Life, that Lifts, is not Trite, Sweet, or Perfect? And is there a Gripping, Strong, if Possible Ringing and Exciting Climax that Tops off Story and its Emotion—Unexpected if Possible?

And if cause and effect, obstruction and theme fulfillment are tested, action must be compressed, the obstruction or situation be "squeezed," by which term C. R. meant the increasing of a feeling of suspense or danger. It is difficult to study the outlines without sensing something of the power that C. R. attempted to incorporate into them, a power particularly related not only to the American past but to America itself.

The two story outlines were probably done sometime in 1935 or 1936. "Smoke Over the Prairie" was begun in January of 1935, and although the *Post* was buying everything he wrote, either for themselves or the *Ladies Home Journal*, the stories were getting more difficult for him. ("Smoke" ran 9,000 words and took some three months to write.) In February he complained, Stuck Again, Plot Wrong; and some ten days later ran into the trouble of differing obstructions and theme fulfillments for Frank Gant and his daughter Juliana. Two days later he resolved the problem (the theme fulfillment for Juliana is positive, that for her father, negative; but in the finished plot they mesh perfectly).

But the journal headings over the next several years show that he had metaphorically exchanged one set of problems for another. Crawling with Difficulty. Terribly Discouraged. I Am Getting Frantic. Can't See How We Can Ever Make It. I Must Keep Jaws Clenched. Wrong Again. This Damnable, Damnable Story. I'm Terrified Tonight. Still a Terrible Impossible Job (the last three while writing *The Sea of Grass*).

The opening page of Black Notebook II (dated "Jan '35, O.K.'d Jan '36"), probably written as he was starting to plot "Smoke," restates his plot problems and gives a keen insight into the nature of his short stories:

> WITH IT, YOU CAN WRITE BIG STORIES
> WITHOUT IT, YOU CAN ONLY WASTE TIME AND FAIL
> IT IS THE FIRST THING TO GET AND STEP UP
> POWERFUL, EVEN VIOLENT, EMOTIONAL SYMPATHY-OBSTRUCTION, NATURAL, NOT FICTIONAL

> After working nearly three months on States Woman ["As It Was in The Beginning"], I found after reading it . . . that the latter two thirds of the story were a wretched failure because I did not see to it that I had a POWERFUL EMOTIONAL OBSTRUCTION to Theme Fulfillment.

> My stories are compressed novels and if I do not fill them with strong, violent obstruction, I will never write them. Make sure of this before wasting time writing that can never be replaced. They can be the familiar old Western situations, if they have suspense, power and emotion, for they always

> can be adapted in a new way, from a new viewpoint and character and made more rich with real color and background.
>
> Also, these big obstructions and situations are necessary on which to hang your rich color. The powerful situations arouse the energy flow so you can weave in things in which you are interested, color, atmosphere which Reynolds says is my strongest quality. . . . You must feel the strength, the story and enthusiasm which is the only way you know if you have enough to illuminate a story, to hang a story on - that strong pull inside of you.

> This and the supplementing requirements of a powerful plot situation seem to be:
>
> 1. HERO'S THEME FULFILLMENT - has to do with Marriage & Home if possible.
> 2. CHIEF OBSTRUCTION TO HERO'S THEME FULFILLMENT - MUST BE POWERFUL TO STIR UP VIOLENT ENERGY FLOWS
> 3. OPENING OBSTRUCTION Laying Issues of Chief Obstruction and leaving a Greater Obstruction than opening of [story]
> 4. SQUEEZED. STEPPED UP.
> 5. CHARACTER DECISION & OBSTRUCTION ACTION TOWARD THEME FULFILLMENT [4]

C. R.'s recognition that his short stories were compressed novels was astute. An entire family's lifetime, situations symbolic of the period, or the sweep of an historical era are contained in a single story. C. R.'s insistence on a powerful obstruction had its positive effect in that it made the story easier to write. The negative aspect was that a strong obstruction tended to imply a longer, more complicated story. Early in Black Notebook II C. R. advises himself:

> Important
>
> Write only an incident for story - build it up - start it in 1,000 to 1500 words as in Early Americana - Leave book-length plots

such as Smoke Over Prairie & His Cattle on a Thousand Hills to novels.

Do this in plotting & save months of . . . labor each year.

Not the whole picture - just one character's view or slant of it and the few things he saw of it. . . .

"His Cattle on a Thousand Hills" became *The Sea of Grass.* One installment lengthened to two, and finally to three. Even as a short novel it is tremendously compressed.[5] The lifetime of the Colonel and Lutie, the birth and death of a renegade son, the cattleman-nester feud which had far-reaching ecological as well as sociological implications, all are contained within the slim 33,000-word volume.

The novel sold to MGM (Katherine Hepburn and Spencer Tracy played the leads), and the family was out of debt. But for some years after, C. R. was extremely critical of the book. An undated entry in the Black Notebook II (sometime after 1936) refers to a New Plan he had started in 1934.

At least two or three simple Early Marriage–Valhalla stories between every bigger one. The simpler ones to sell, to bring money, to give you confidence & satisfaction - the occasional bigger one to hold or build your reputation.

Even in the bigger story, purge yourself of following faults of The Sea of Grass.

1. I have been writing longer & longer sentences - saying "and" at the start of nearly every sentence. I must go back to Early Americana & Smoke Over Prairie.
2. I must have conversation on every page.
3. I must have strong situation like Early Marriage & Early Americana.
4. I must compress into one or two big continuous dramatic scenes.

The early reviews of *The Sea of Grass*, now considered an American classic, were not kind. Critics complained about the melodramatic plot or the lack of poetic unity. In later years C. R. would not look at reviews; only if there was an extremely favorable one would he allow my mother to read aloud several choice phrases. A journal entry (February 9, 1937) captioned Said So Before But Never True Till Now - All Is Lost reflects his dismay at early reviews and fears of the novel not selling. That these tended to be universal terrors which writers experience probably never occurred to him, and it would have made little difference if it had. The stage fright simply meant that the problems of writing did not end with the completion of the story or novel. They extended—in an almost malicious manner—through every phase of publication and reprinting. Included in the above journal entry is a cry of anguish which points up the always dubious relationship between a writer and his public: "One thing I know - that neither H. V. or even I know literature or good books - we know only what we like or think is good."

By 1949 (journal entry of January 30) his view toward *The Sea of Grass* had long since changed:

> WRITING A POWERFUL STORY FOR NOVEL. Then one can spend time on the beautiful. I was directed to this today by reading an excerpt from Emily Bronte's Wuthering Heights. "I lingered around them, under that benign sky; watched moths fluttering among the heather and harebells; listened to the soft wind breathing through the grass; and wondered how anyone could ever imagine unquiet slumber for sleepers in that quiet earth." I saw that this was my success in The Sea of Grass, the combination of powerful story and delicate beauty, but I felt I could carry the idea to greater success. It seems made for me and my short novels.

Following are excerpts from pages of Model Plots and Obstructions. Unless otherwise indicated, they are from the Black

Notebook II and are original. They fall mainly under the headings of different varieties of opening obstructions. A number of pages show ways of increasing the suspense/interest of the obstruction. Not included are pages of climaxes and solutions taken mainly from other writers' stories and novels that C. R. used as models. Also not included (see Appendix B) is a nine-point outline with many subheadings on Plotting the Story. Most of the ideas in this outline occur elsewhere in the notebooks, and the points appear to be a checklist meant not only to assure a well-designed plot but to stimulate the mind as the actual plotting was taking place.

Prefacing the section:

Plots to Consult

Richard Matthews Hallet said he would sell his soul any day for a plot. He meant, as I have found out, a story that has

(1) Natural consecutive action as a trip somewhere against odds
(2) Something like this at one time
(3) Trouble that can engulf terribly at once

Following this is a list of Model Plots to Consult, each with at least half a dozen examples:

<u>Dangerous Journey</u>, <u>Mission</u>
<u>Going to Kill Someone - Revenge or Failure</u>
Righteous reason to kill another or self but fate intervenes
<u>Alden - Standish - Priscilla</u>
<u>Dramatic Crisis</u>
What will certain people do under dramatic crisis!
<u>Fault Keeps Character from Succeeding</u>
<u>Accuse Other of What You Do Yourself</u>
<u>Hates or Scared of Something - Does it in End</u>
<u>Mistaken Identity</u>
<u>Atavism - Reversion to Type</u>
<u>Injustice, Discrimination</u>

Criminal (or Like one) Just Once for Good Reason
Taking the Easiest Way (against reader's wishes)
Mother, Father etc. Forbidden From Their Children
Beloved Human, Animal or Other Friend or Possession To
Be Killed or Destroyed
Struggle with Animal for Life or Death
Struggle with Inanimate for Life or Death
Friendship With Man, Animal etc. [example of C. R.'s "Brothers of No Kin" - friend gives up hope of eternal life for friend]
The Closed Market
Villain Succeeds Well Until Disaster
Capture or in Danger from Enemy & Escape
Character Study True of Many
Accomplishment of Authentic Duty Against Odds
Seek for Something Everywhere & Find It At Home
Character Used to Luxury Gets Pleasure out of Being Common
(opposite of Cinderella
plot of famous film It Happened One Night)

"I Am Thankful for My Outline Book," C. R. says time and time again. He might spend days "ransacking my brain" for a plot and finding nothing. But upon "rearranging Model Obstructions," he would feel "ideas & confidence" returning.[6] Some of the Model Obstructions are lists of generalized predicaments, such as drouth, blizzard, a death sentence, injustice, discrimination—Those That Arouse Suspense for Entire Story. Others, more interesting and specific in nature, are listed under Fresh Significant Ideas for Chapters, Stories, Characters. They might be a "strong plot obstruction" such as (M II):

> One who begins to realize he is a Cain. Not Cain the murderer with his mark which is the thing generally thought of with Cain, but the one who found he hadn't favor with God like his brother or wife. Things went wrong. No matter how

he tried people did not like him. This has possibilities, universality.

Or Strong Original Real-life Obstructions (story) for chapter or more (M II):

Peddlar who murdered his family

Discover baby skeleton when tear down house

Gentleman has 5 children by negro slave or poor white servant (he is bachelor). He sees them daily without feeling any pity at their destitute, dirty lot.

Boys pull down house of ill fame. Boys praised & given whiskey reward. Start of such a woman in town.

Girl charges child to leading citizen. No one will arrest him.

Father going with other woman while mother ill & after she dies. Oldest boy follows him.

Accused murderer denies it. Rope breaks on gallows. Does it mean a sign? Go ahead & he confesses.

Man dying. Asks for a little life from each of children. Wife says "Look on baby before you die." "Blessings of God of Abraham, of Isaac, and of Jacob rest upon you."

Strange face looks in window. Girl 5 yrs old golden hair. The next baby came couldn't keep, etc. Suspense of keeping that child alive.[7]

The ———'s and his witch-life wife & how her first child was the leading citizen's and he made her marry——— & the contrast of this girl with her half sisters in the big house.[8]

Or on a page by itself (BII):

Obstruction Minor Original

Navajo has beautiful horse. White boy wants to buy it. He (Navajo) is going to end life & kill horse to have him to ride in next land. Can't seem to save that intelligent, beautiful horse. How it would affect a girl.

Or excerpted from pages on Love Obstruction or Separation (BII):

Fathers are bitter enemies.
He drinks or has serious failing - gambler like in Showboat
She has an unfortunate past
His father or brother has done something to family
She sends him away, is later sorry & can't find him
He goes to war or some dangerous role, abroad, to South America for 5 years
One loves the sea, the other hates it - one the tropics, the other not
Father, grandfather, mother or grandmother forbids him coming to house
Only a soldier or Indian fighter or scout in love with baronial cattleman's daughter
Comes back & finds wife married in absence. Thinks he is dead. Loves her new husband more than he. How will they get along. He sees how better new husband does things than he[9]

Beginning a story with a strong obstruction was not quite enough for C. R. The obstruction confronting the character should not immediately be spelled out; rather it should be surrounded by mystery which would raise suspense and interest in the reader. C. R. termed it Obstruction Mystery. Four beginnings illustrate the manner in which this could be handled; in each case, information is withheld from the reader.

Reader knows something wrong. Hero knows what is wrong but reader does not.

Reader knows something wrong but hero does not seem to know or feel it.

Reader knows something wrong. Hero also, but both he [reader] & hero do not know what.

Another tells hero something is wrong & leaves without telling what.

Following this C. R. lists a series of model beginnings "with obstruction mystery" taken from his own and others' work. Excerpts:

> Reader does not know what is seriously wrong, but he knows something is. Hero and other characters know what but do not talk about it. Go ahead with their plans despite it.
>
> Early Marriage

> Unknown unfriendly armed men call on Sabina's husband. She is not told why - as husbands were then.
>
> New Home

> Rigidity settles over frontier feud town - something has happened but the details kept from young girl.
>
> Square Piano

> Negro leers at playing boy, repeats mysterious words boy does not understand.
>
> Ambuscade [William Faulkner]

> You do not know who stranger (leading character) is & he or she is interesting & different & unusual enough to want to know. An old bleary pioneer in <u>Valhalla</u>, a mocking tattered

Mexican on a wonderful horse in Hoofbeat, Heartbeat. A girl stranger who insists on doing unusual thing of taking out marriage license to wed man never seen as in Rose Wilder Lane's Object Matrimony.

Original ideas for openings with Good Suspense Strong Obstruction:

Two men with gold & a girl crossing country in old days, desert or mountains, and one knows that if he sleeps other will kill him & have gold & girl. Not a word said or if said, done so, in double meaning so girl should not know. The other hates him. Memories. The earlier part of story comes in. Or just a journey to someplace - after robbing wagon train - in old days of plains perhaps - in time of Foard Hudspeth [in "As It Was in the Beginning"]. Needs an epic American theme.

One small camp of settlers after another cut down by Indians. Find one or two scalped & horribly mutilated. Yet never see an Indian. Steadily this terror grows. Much more than if a great mass of Indians had been seen. Something dark, might appear anywhere any moment.

Dying of thirst in desert - thinks of his boyhood & love in well-watered valley.

A letter unopened or verdict in a murder case not given - waiting in jury box - & reviews past life etc. & story of murder - after enough terror & grim suspense has been raised in reader by look of spectators, & grim authority of court - death cell picture in paper etc.

Gypsy predicts string of things ending with terrible catastrophe - that person will be killed - or hero will kill someone. String up to last comes true. (Latter can come true in different way than expected.)

Luck runs high but man does not quit - rides on - reader feels he is going to lose everything soon - can't last.

Stranger asks man if he will act as if he is her husband for an emergency (she is beautiful) or dying man gives custody of money to hero to take somewhere without explanations about where he got money.

He can't remember where he saw other before. Then suddenly he does & pales.

Two men appear on one horse & stay all night, their story not quite ringing right or not explained at all why one horse.

Julia N———thinks of her father - he did everything for them, for her, but died in mid-ocean & buried at sea & had no word from him or knew what he was doing there etc.

They are staying in home on overland trip through pioneer country when someone comes to take her brother aside. He says they will go at once without any reason. Or man in party who is told something dies or leaves before he can tell it & they face night in this place alone not knowing what will happen but knowing something will.

C. R.'s last word on the obstruction echoes his previous warnings to himself, but brings the discussion up to the date of November 27, 1947 (Maroon Notebook I):

I resolve to write only novels and stories with
STRONGEST MOST POWERFUL OBSTRUCTIONS
on which to support spiritual or other theme,
To give breadth and depth and strength and sales to short novels

ONE STARK, VIOLENT, COMPLETE, OVERWHELMING OBSTRUCTION

I began it with my short stories, EARLY MARRIAGE, LONG DROUTH, EARLY AMERICANA, NEW HOME, etc.

I continued it to some degree with THE SEA OF GRASS, much more in THE TREES.

Since then, except for chapters "FACE AT THE WINDER" and "WOLF BITE" in THE FIELDS and the voyage across in THE FREE MAN, I have neglected it to the decline and fall of my reputation and standing and success.

For instance, the voyage should have been all of THE FREE MAN, or the tragedy continued in as stark and violent an obstruction. And the taking of the children in TACEY CROMWELL should have been followed by a worse effect of this obstruction until it was overwhelming and complete.

4

Primary Writing Principles

With the sale of *The Sea of Grass* to MGM, the most difficult personal obstruction (outside of my mother's health, which had considerably improved) was overcome. So was much of the difficulty of story plotting. In the years that followed, C. R.'s focus would shift away from plot theory to principles that concerned themselves with more subtle aspects of writing.

These principles, "revised May 13, 1946," when he had just finished the second volume of the trilogy, *The Fields*, occur toward the start of the Maroon Notebook II.

NOVEL & SERIAL PRINCIPLES

1. Theme, Subject, with significance, importance, power
   - 1A. Check breadth, depth, height
   - 1B. Thoughts on the subject by characters or writer

2. Freshness, Originality.
   - 2A. Fresh idea or ideas for novel, chapters, character
   - 2B. Original thoughts by character or writer

3. Lift, Beauty, Feel
   - 3A. Characters with lift, radiance, life
   - 3B. Chapter novel ideas with lift
   - 3C. The beauty and feel of the background, place

4. Strong story, plot, with violent obstructions and suspense and powerful climax . . . (all necessary under your delicacy and restraint)
   - 4A. Strong, powerful, unforgettable, perhaps hard

obstruction characters as Brock, Seely, Tacey, Jake Tench.[1]

4B. Obstructions for novel and chapters.

4C. Contrast of characters.

4D. Contrast of scenes.

5. Rough Reality
   - 5A. Unsweetened common things of life, people, so reader is left with indelible impression of reality.
   - 5B. Unsweetened talk.
   - 5C. Action of people - tell it in action.

6. Form
   - 6A. The viewpoint
   - 6B. The length

7. The Writing
   - 7A. A pure style

Each of these seven principles was expanded in the notebook pages that followed. The two most important are those of Freshness and Lift. Significant in another way is Principle 5, Rough Reality, which signals a move away from artifice toward life, a move that involved a struggle between two aspects of C. R.'s character. If the roughness never quite gained the upper hand, tempered always by the "delicacy and restraint" alluded to in the outline, the tension between roughness and restraint became one of the strongest characteristics of his writing. Like most of the jottings in his writing notebooks, the principles constitute varied attempts to understand his own method and refine it. At times they assume the guise of strong counsel, so that Notebook 6 and the Maroon and Black Notebooks were a kind of Bible for him, filled with admonitions and dire prediction, and fear of hell fire if the commands issued to himself were not obeyed.

Principle 2 Freshness

Principles I had Forgotten until Now (Sept. 19, 1939)

If I want to do western stories for the Post, I must be writing on the West a long time and thinking on it so the common ordinary ways of writing these Western things are an old well worn story to me, and I cast around for new ways to tell it.

My success with Post Western stories was wholly because of the new vein I opened. That vein was telling it from a woman's point of view, the effect on women. The same stories told from men's viewpoint with all the feel and feeling of men had been done to death. They were no longer real. But the same stories told from their women's viewpoint and with the interest in and effect on their family and family life were new and seemed real and stronger.

Early Marriage, Long Engagement, New Home, Frontier Woman, Square Piano, and Buckskin Vacation were all done from this angle and Smoke Over the Prairie had the boy angle and family life, principally effect on and sympathy for his mother and sister. The only ones from men's point of view were Early Americana and As It Was in the Beginning, and these were very original and different, especially the latter in scene and plot.

The inescapable conclusion is that my oldtime Western Post stories MUST be either in a new vein as the angle of the effect on family or women which makes it very human and real, or must be a fresh, unhackneyed setting and plot if from man's point of view. . . .

This freshness done in several ways. . . . Br John [black servant of Southern woman going west] is killed not in wagon train attack which would be stereotyped but going for water in river bed, and conflict is over getting his body. Early Americana had lonely buffalo hide settlement for locale and original idea of having to kill a woman [if Indians attacked] and then falling in love with her. As It Was in the Beginning had having to get . . . a wife to take care of him in land where women were scarce and how he trades with Indians for her. The Square Piano had shooting feud but coupled with first piano [in territory], musical entertainment in town and from boy's family angle [viewpoint of small younger sister] that gave it a freshness.

IT IS IMPORTANT THAT IT BE DIFFERENT, ORIGINAL IF POSSIBLE, FRESH, OUT OF THE ORDINARY. LIFE AND EARTH ARE ENDLESS, PROLIFIC WITH IDEAS, NEED NOT BE REPEATED.

Principle 3 LIFT

Driving past St. Vincent's Academy in Albuquerque gave me the same feeling that it did the other night . . . of the character of those nuns in this early wild town as in Denver in the old days - a plain almost ugly four story building run quietly by nuns in ugly plain garb, faithful to their belief here in wild places. In other words, <u>what looked like a building or institution causing an emotion in me was only the lengthened shadow of human beings.</u>[2]

CHARACTERS WITH A LIFT [excerpted] Principle 3A

Kit Carson who sits in Palace of Governors and loves his half-breed children

The man who never asked for anything

The boy who broke his arm to read[3]

Rose Berger who could have been a great singer but stayed in P.G. [Pine Grove] and sang to her farmer children

The Reber girl, rejected by her father, who became so beautiful

King Charley, the tavern keeper who kicked King Louis of France out of his hotel

Jack Best, the outlaw, whose eyes danced

Sam Locke the gambler, plus the saloon man who was the only one could keep peace in Tascosa

Madame Blennerhasset, mistress of the island, the most gracious lady the pioneers ever knew, a picture riding through woods in scarlet riding habit

CHAPTER IDEAS WITH LIFT [excerpted] Principle 3B

A small boy who walks to the top of the Blue Mountain to see the world

The light in the wheat field. And when it is cut, the light is gone.

To a boy or child . . . the feel of getting awake in the Estancia Valley in a great blue cloud of sky. That blue vault over you. Start with it. There it hung in the world, blue, blue, clear. Under it was only a valley, etc.

THE FAR MAN. Seen on the top of a distant hill. So far away in the misty air he seemed like a thread against the sky. Who is he? Is he a man, was he a man or what his life. (Significance here). What was his dress, his age, his face and his ideas in life?

Talk of the sea or some other far place by those kept from it, perhaps in the forest, some of whom knew it intimately &

some who never saw it & ask & hear about it, as thirsting children. The feeling for it done by this contrast.

MONTAGU STEVENS, the Englishman, who fought for his country, then spent all his and his wife's fortunes in New Mexico, an alien country, and in his old age and poverty walked up and down the streets of a town in that alien country thinking of his England now at war, that he would be buried here in this country far from home, thinking of that land Shakespeare describes so well, "this England." AND THIS MOST OF ALL, that small island of the world that sends its sons and daughters all over the globe and yet remains the center of his and the world's being, the heart pumping out the blood. His feel for it, for even I feel it very strong.

IDEAS WITH LIFT AND SPIRIT [excerpted]

The Flowers Open When Their Time Comes, despite snow, cold. So in a war with things terrible & girl thin & half developed her love affair happens.

My Other Self. On Penny Hill 35 years later I could see in the twilight the boy, my other self, come along. He was so different than I am now, lacking in money, knowledge but what I wouldn't give to be him there now.[4]

The Light Under the Door. In the photo. It is the kitchen that lies beyond. Mother is there & Joe & Fred as boys & Dad. If I could only open that door and go through![5]

The Star Below. On the mountain so high that stars are below.

The Vision On the Sea. The cords that hold up the earth & fastened to the stars, dragging the sea & earth with them.[6]

Strong man takes care of his weak, not too-strong-minded son. They die following each other. Man in grief, worrying about his boy. Who will take care of him there? And when he dies, it is man who is weak and boy strong.

The Shadow of Peter in a sermon. That the shadow, the name & reputation of man does more than the man can do. People were laid in Peter's shadow to be healed.

THE TOWN HAS TWO TOWNS: one down here, one up in the cemetery. Frank Christ coming back to P. G. said he knew various people had died yet not till he got back and walked the streets did he realize how dead the town was of people he knew - that they had all gone up there. And Claude Mengel said, coming down from the cemetery, "Those up there should be down here and most of those down here should be up there." A story or chapter built on this idea, the people who are up there, the rich and lively and lovable and beautiful.

NOVEL OF BOY'S INTIMATIONS OF IMMORTALITY. He is born into an humble Pa. Dutch family but remembers beauties and asks questions that are treated queerly. Angels have no wings. [his parents are] Not his mother and father. Perhaps his father is preacher but boy not interested in church. It doesn't seem right. He asks in his mind when he comes to German or Lutheran Choir in town when he leaves home, "So you too are bound up and must cope with these German bodies." Those words of Wordsworth, "And hear the children playing on the shore" haunt him.[7]

A SPOT LIKE UNITYVILLE in the juncture of two mountains, remote, or in the crook of Roundtop and the mountain, protected from the winds, with the mountains overhead, back in the last place, at the source of the waters, where everything is dewy and virginal.

PRINCIPLE 5 ROUGH REALITY

THE HARD IMPACT OF THE ROUGH, UNEVEN REALITY OF LIFE

This may affront at times as in Wuthering Heights or Grapes of Wrath, seems unreal. Yet it will leave a strong, real, indelible impression.

"The plots, the story part of THE SEA OF GRASS seem all right. What I need is more solid, STARKER, REALER WRITING. I need Frost and Steinbeck to sober me down and offset my delicacy." [excerpted from journal for Maroon Notebook II]

5A UNSWEETENED, OFTEN INDELICATE BUT EARTHY AND REAL TREATMENT OF INCIDENTS OF COMMON LIFE - NOT WRITTEN DELICATELY AS YOU USUALLY DO. OTHER HARD THINGS THE WAY PEOPLE ARE.

Frank Gant naked in his bath in front of Indian and boy

Lawrence's account of Daufa and his boy friend

Prominent men of Atlanta had to say they spent night in sporting house

Ruth getting a husband [Boaz] by lying with him on threshing floor

Teddy Blue Abbott, the young cowboy, steals pillow out of poor homesteader's, his partner the other. Probably only ones for miles.

Reading THE TREES over August 17, 1939, there were not nearly enough strong things told with a hard natural impact like Genny going crazy and what she said. I looked forward to seeing her crazy as a bedbug through all the rest of the chapters, the crazy things she would do, common things like Aunt Esther would. And Achsa's going away with Louie would have been far stronger and more natural defying them, saying she was going, no she would never see them again, she wouldn't stay and Sayward couldn't make her and off she goes after a violent session without looking back, instead of the delicate way you handled it.

Also wanted more common impact things like "the spittle she blobbed on the stone," cutting themselves in last chapter.

5B UNSWEETENED DIALOGUE   PAGES OF IT   NOT A DIALOGUE SENTENCE SUMMING UP WHAT WAS SAID BUT GIVING EFFECT OF LIFE, PEOPLE & SUM OF ROUGH TALK

Talk is half the business of active life. It should be half of a book.

The talk, the answers should be different yet natural and authentic, not what expected. Speaker goes off on something else. Combats, lashes, ridicules, unexpectedly agreeable, as all life with motives.

V. said where Sulie crawls in piles of leaves and says she won't come out till she comes with a litter hanging to her dugs, should be only one of many things to say, to give the effect of reality and action.

The dialogue in [chapter of] Sulie lost, "Whar's Sulie?" "She never came home with the cows." "When was this?" Sayward told him. "She ain't out yit?" should have been vastly more of this through book.

More real talk like "If it should happen Achsa ain't thar, you kin fetch it home to me and tell me," which carried with it suspense, her reasoning, the possibilities which is the way people's talk carry their thoughts shrewdly. They do not think to great lengths.

5C THE ACTION OF LIFE, PEOPLE. NOT THEIR THOUGHTS BUT DOINGS. LET READER FIGURE OUT WHAT IT MEANS. ALWAYS DOING SOMETHING, CROWDED WITH DOINGS. BOOK SHOULD BE LIVED

> Things should be lived, not told. If one is to enjoy the good feeling of a warm kitchen, he must first live in the cold outside. Then the reader will experience the warmth of the kitchen when the character enters it, as in life.

Under Principle 4, discussed in the last chapter and so omitted here, another important principle or technique emerges: that of *contrast*. An excerpt from Notebook 6, dated November 3, 1945:

> Beauty & Contrast. I have woefully neglected these high friends of mine. Return, Connie. Pursued faithfully, they will lead from Sea of Grass into still richer pastures I have been blind to. Gather yourself on the high lights of beauty, contrast, advancing story as you go. Look for beauty, woo it. The goal - to create drama in beauty and contrast.

I suspect that the combination of the two (which appear unrelated on the surface) has to do with the contrast of a grim situation with the beauty of landscape or character. One of C. R.'s favorite ways of starting a short story (the first two paragraphs of *The Sea of Grass* also use the technique) was to contrast the present with the more golden past, creating a frame that sets off the emotion of earlier times. "Early Americana" begins: "It has slipped almost out of reality now, into the golden haze that covers Adobe Walls and the Alamo, so that today, behind speeding headlights or in the carpeted Pullman, it seems as if it might never have really been." Then follows a description of the Staked Plains and "that rude, vanished, half-mystical buffalo settlement, Carnuel." Again, he uses contrast but in a different way. The usually roaring settlement, filled with freighters, hunters, and hide buyers, is ominously silent. No one has come by for days.

The best of the *Post* stories have a carefully engineered superstructure of contrasts which clothes the plot so that, deceptively, it appears to be not an arbitrary arrangement but rather a casual development of circumstance, as in life. Characters, scenes, landscapes, emotions, actions, and situations are contrasted with each other so that a tension is created between them, a kind of slant rhyme heard in the reader's mind. In Black Notebook II, C. R. lists several pages of different types of contrast, accompanied by brief illustrations from his own and other's writings:

Character to Character
Character to Scene
Character to Event[8]
Character to Same Character at Other Time
Color Contrasted to Color[9]
Color Contrasted to Events
Present with Past[10]
What Character Thinks to What [he] Says
What Character Thinks or Says to What [he] Does[11]

Possibly the most important observation regarding contrast is "*that before one thing happens to a character, the other must be expected*" (italics mine). C. R. illustrates the rule with a story he was working on at the time for MGM, "Paths of Glory": "if character is to have glory of son's military funeral. . . . she must be humble person and son should be person to whom in life there was the opposite of glory." A gloss on this occurs on another page of Black Notebook II: "What contrasting circumstances will make this climax most effective on reader? Her son is no good, looked down on by everyone."[12]

Principles 2, 3, and 5 (very little of 6) form the main body of the Maroon Notebook II.[13] Notes on Theme, the first of the principles, occur in Black Notebook II, probably the one C. R. refers to so often and which he returned to again and again (see Chapter 3).[14] He would pore over the various themes—some sixteen pages—stopping to jot down notes on an idea which particularly appealed to him. This would be entered in another notebook (such as Yellow Notebook 2), much as if bacteria were placed in a solution favorable to their growth.

The overall caption of the sixteen pages is in itself cautionary, designating the area he dare never stray from:

> Universal Epic Theme - Idea of Real People
> In Their Native Environment, Life & Work

Under the subheadings are included titles of his own and "model" works of others as well as general topics. Since these repeat themselves (one entry for model, another for original ideas) they have been excerpted and grouped together under the single category.

The Background The Theme

State Fair — Desert Song — Main Street
The Rock — Grand Hotel — Street Scene
[original] The Nearer East (mysterious, aloof, home life of Mexico aristocrats)

History The Theme - Perhaps Historical Character

Silver Dollar — The Big Parade — First Piano [The Square Piano]
Mutiny on the Bounty — House of Rothschild — Cleopatra

Well Known Something in Life The Theme

Bread — Success Story — Brown's Hat
Calm leisure & joy of living in older days
The Strong peace of men & women of ideals

Well Known Legend The Theme

The Second Lillith — Agamemnon

Americana

[these range from John Brown's Body to Cimarron to stories of

The Erie Canal & Days to Ruggles of Red Gap.] The heading here is:

Americana, if possible (1) With Gusto (2) the American idea

[a page follows of C. R.'s original ideas, titled as above]:

History & ancestors of an American family as known by old aunty who is always telling them

The Star Spangled Banner. The emotion of the older generation who sang it, felt it, the sensation of its muttering parts & the climax "Through the night our flag was still there." As boys, youth, men, age.

Rio Grande - West of the Pecos

Man on Horseback - The Plains

Smoke Over the Prairie
(The Coming of the Railroad)

The First———

The Buffalo

State Road

The First Fence - Before & After Fencing

The Chisum [Chisholm] Trail - The Santa Fe Trail

Cap & Ball Rifle

The Grant[15]

Race of Trail Herds

Captured by Indians & not knowing parents[16]

> Inanimate & Nature against Man fighting in Authentic Duty [these include "The Sea against man, The Mountain against a railroad, The North against a man, A New Wild land against homesteaders," etc.]

The second group of themes is related to Life Events, with headings such as Birth, Death, Marriage, Youth (boy at 15 says he is a man etc.), Friendships, The Service He Belonged To, Home. The third and last group comprises Personal Character: Courage; Manhood; Integrity, Loyalty; Womanhood, Motherhood: Sacrifice, Generosity, Nobility. It is consistent with his objectives that the second and third groups especially suggest ideas "with lift." So does the entire group of "Americana" themes, most notably "Man on Horseback." Had it been written, this might have been one of C. R.'s greatest novels. It not only has a powerful visual title (C. R. felt the best titles have the quality of *motion*) but is symbolic of many facets of the pioneer experience. Notes on the novel crop up here and there, some seventeen pages in the Maroon Notebook I alone. To follow these is to glimpse the way a theme begets a story, gathering ideas and material to itself like the proverbial snowball.

"Man on Horseback" began as an idea for "an artistic Western - symbolic" for the *Saturday Evening Post*, and appears on his work agenda for 1950. It concerned "a definite series of events ending with his establishment as an important business man in the West. . . . And it is then that he sees who the figure in the vision is on horseback - himself." The real character my father wanted—and possibly this kept him from writing the novel for the *Post*—was someone like Kit Carson, a man who loved his Indian wife and half-breed children.[17] A series of short stories was sketched out, with several pages of possibilities which included a strong wife who made a trader out of him. But what C. R. really hoped for was "a novel giving the feel of a place—the plains," and the hero "a real Western character as you know them as contrasted with other fiction Western characters - mild, gentle, strong, powerful, pioneer flame in his eye when aroused, & yet easily swindled, trusting etc."

Preliminary notes for the short story series:

A symbolic conquest of the West

The stage of the plains & its romance

A slight man, a mere man, who becomes more than a man on a horse - idea why.

Perhaps Kit Carson - quiet spoken.

He may have been apprenticed to a saddler - & is a quiet man like Albert Decker who had made saddles but never ridden them - he might have been the one hold-back of a mighty family. . . . When he found himself on horseback he felt himself above man - could think better - do more - as Hudson found himself exhilirated on the back of a good horse. Gave him a sense of power. "It lifts a man above himself. . . ."

He refused . . . certain project, say to leave St Jo or other place for West but when he is on horseback, he goes or agrees. Also to ask girl to marry him. When she says she will when he owns saddlery shop or is a partner, he decides to go West instead.

Men overjoyed he is to go along. Quiet, cautious, always could depend on him. Keen grey eyes. Always un-exaggerated. Heard alarming things while keeping on working, then made a simple remark, mildly, that generally fit. But when pushed, absolutely resolute.

When he returns from conquest there is a power in him he didn't know he had. He could feel his employer sense it & yield to him when he comes in. Offers him partnership. But he refuses it. He is going west.

From the following page:

> Should be in town on edge of prairie on which events take place in story on horseback.
>
> Beginning should be vision of a man on horseback riding into plains - a mist - kid may always have that picture - dream it - never can quite see his face - end is this man is hero in story - sees his face plainly now in same vision or dream.
>
> The exaltation of a common man. He is this man on horseback. This is the idea. Gives it a symbolism, a meaning, & yet a mystery, an obscurity.
>
> He could never see who this figure on horseback was - then on the end he sees - and it's himself. Has always dreamed it - wanted to find him.

The theme of freedom entered into the story at one point:

> Goes for freedom and finds that Indian woman and children bind him and then as governor.
>
> MAN ON HORSEBACK
>
> On horseback signified freedom, escape, adventure. (Don't bring in that a man felt bigger on horseback at all). There was grass and game to be had on horseback and endless trails and country to see.
>
> Part 1. Boy longing, sees men on horses, mother makes money on share in expedition. He goes, comes back and puts it into bank, saves it and daughter married. Shocked. Goes. She agreed to wait for him.
>
> Part 2. He is trader in this Indian camp and marries an Indian girl and lives with her and life in Indian camp and Indian feelings and psychology - goes to fort as partner -

> Part 3. In Palace of Governors and his pain and affection for his Indian halfbloods. Decision. The result of his search for freedom. It doesn't exist anywhere. Age, nature, always waiting to entwine you, etc.

The search or quest motif (at one point in the notes the trader-hero is characterized as a kind of Ulysses, stopping at the various prairie ports) was a forerunner of other psychological themes, such as a search for meaning or for one's place in life which occupied his later novels. Of no other unwritten book, save perhaps *The Angry Saint*, did he leave so many notes.

From his journal of January 7, 1949:

> DESPERATION ABOUT OUR FINANCES STIRS UP GOOD. The thought of having to do Westerns again depressed me. But when I went over the most likely Western, MAN ON HORSEBACK, in my mind, I saw it had what SEA OF GRASS & THE TREES had and none of my others save the first part of THE FREE MAN. That was A Fresh Significant American Historical Theme-Idea, if it can be so called. . . . TACEY did not have such a universal theme of American historical fact. . . . Now MAN ON HORSEBACK has it, the giant power and vision it gave men on horseback to conquer the wild savage West. It is very difficult to put what I mean into words, but I feel it, and it occurred to me how ironical if this later book, which I put aside because it was a Post serial for money, had more American significance in it than anything I did in its stead.

C.R. with his mother, father, and brothers Joe and Fred, 1894.

Above left, C. R. looking at himself, Reading, Pennsylvania, circa 1906.

Below left, C. R. with his dog Montie, White Deer Valley, Pennsylvania, 1908.

Above right, C. R. at Cleveland, Ohio, 1912 or 1913.

Above left, C. R. with pince-nez, Reading, 1914.

Below left, C. R. wanted a natural pose for a magazine, 1920s.

Above right, Working for MGM, Los Angeles, 1940.

Above left, C. R. and Blanche Knopf on the Millersburg ferry, Susquehanna river. Photograph by Alfred A. Knopf, 1940.

Below left, C. R. at Hillside, Dauphin, Pennsylvania. Photograph by Alfred A. Knopf, 1940.

Above right, Harvena A. Richter at Hillside, Dauphin. Photograph by Alfred A. Knopf, 1940.

C. R. in the early 1940s (place unknown).

5

Tensing the Mind

For all the agonies C. R. went through in writing, quite possibly the worst were the days or weeks spent beginning a story or a novel. He adored research. Spinning out a plot, seeing new ideas come out in the weave, induced a creative exhilaration that he would have found difficult to live without. But all the time the tension was building. Metaphorically, he was walking on level ground, but ahead was the mountain. The image could be enlarged with crevasses or obstacles in the path, but mostly it was the sheer drudgery of the climb that dismayed him. He was always terrified he couldn't make it, and if he did, what would be waiting for him at the top?

He was a slow writer, or so he said. As early as 1937 he wrote to Bernard de Voto: "I am painfully slow in getting things down on paper as I see and feel them, creeping while others dance and run." Twenty-two years later he wrote A. B. Guthrie: "I write slowly and started late. My first novel was at the age of 46 and I have to work to catch up to you fellows who got up earlier in the morning and still have much of the day ahead of you."

C. R.'s professed slowness was, I think, like his feeling of not being a born writer, another invented myth. Except for *The Town*, which took three years, a new novel appeared every twenty-four months. Often one or more short stories were turned out during this same two-year period. Most of his novels were fairly short, but their very compression, as mentioned earlier, was time consuming. In 1943 he lamented that

> . . . I used to be a very fast writer and would turn out a story in a day or two, working night and day. Then I didn't have

> much to say. Now when I have more to say than I can in several life times at my present rate, I have become a snail-like writer, beating it out as best I can and replanning and rewriting until something in me is more nearly satisfied.[1]

There is a long tradition of the writer as a kind of wordsmith, hammering out ideas in white heat on a mental forge. C. R. had his own phrases for this: *tensing the mind, building the fire*. From Notebook 6:

> WILL TO WRITE
>
> Set down and prepare consciously for work by TENSING THE MIND TO THE TASK OF WRITING - so many minutes or hours of mental tension on the subject in question.
>
> Worry over non-accomplishment for days finally puts what I call steam under the proper cells and I get to work. Try to do this by conscious tensing. I must work. I dare not waste an hour.

From his journal, summer of 1937:

> I think I must stay at home and tense on my story, get steam up under it, make the fire hotter under it by telling myself I must do it today. Then I can work. I cannot spend my time all over the world or it will turn no engines for me. I have barely enough steam for my own tea kettle and I must blow and blow till it is hot. Nothing after all matters to me but work accomplished. Pleasure is nothing, except it be pleasure by accomplishment.

From his journal, summer of 1950:

> I am indebted to chance or Providence perhaps that I am physically lowered and tensed. In my early twenties I had great power for writing, would do a story almost in a day and

> night. I had facility but little content or critical ability. Now my sense of enjoyment and enthusiasm is so low that I must find or work for something unusually good and important and moving to move me. It leaves me less of a writer and more of an editor. The editor in me coaxes and drives the writer in me and sits over him constantly with a red pencil saying this isn't good enough and that isn't important or interesting. Both parts of me know that if I brood over it long and desperately enough, something better will come, usually a combination of several ideas of methods discarded. I call it building a fire under me. My writing seems to run by steam rather than electricity. The latter can be turned off and goes to work, but one must build a fire for some time under the boiler before steam is made in enough pressure to start turning the wheels.

There was an alternative to mind-tensing, and that was building up steam through reading another writer—a running on borrowed energies. From Notebook 6:

> SUGGESTIONS FOR MAKING YOURSELF WRITE
>
> Read Don Byrne and note his enthusiasm for - his Irish people, his uncle and aunt, the stable man, their strength, beauty and individuality - for his country, county, land, its bees, birds and all the things peasants say about them - for all the eerie and paradoxical and strange things in his country which made him glow in them all the more - for the contrast of characters, rough violent language and the observation of grave beauty and understanding.
>
> Read Byrne for the Irish lilt like "the immense loneliness of the sea and the plumcolored whales" but say it of the scene you are writing about, and the words will write themselves down as they do tonight.
>
> Make yourself write on and on without stopping and weighing. That habit has nearly broken you. Write it down. Let it sing along. There is no tune, no swing, once you stop.

> Write a synopsis of what you want to say in the chapter, the effect you want to give. Reflect on it. Get it down.
>
> I notice that when I make myself rest between chapters, feeling that I deserve a day or two to rest or catch up on errands, etc., it is terrifically hard to start again and I must lose several more days before steam can be worked up and the style in my words. I should be where there is no occasion to rest between chapters but to finish one and start another same day and go on while the strain and temper are on.

With the ever-goading necessity of earning a living, C. R. had little trouble with writer's block. Most of the time "blocking" had to do with not having the right plot. But occasionally he became so tense that nothing would start the fire. At those times my mother provided the relief. A 1934 journal entry tells of not being able to write and asking my mother to come into the room with him until he could finally begin. "She left the room and I went on and wrote 1000 words on the typewriter in two hours." From the March 1951 journal:

> I MISS HARVEY'S CLOSENESS. This morning I was low and upset - by my health, by my nerves, by worry over house . . . when I asked H. to come in living room and sit near me. Gradually I relaxed and as I did, strength returned and hope and promise. She reminded me that at times in past she used to just come and sit in room when I had a difficult place to write and then I was able to do it. . . .

When they fled Pine Grove for the cooler altitudes of Hazleton or Williamsport in the summer, my mother would rest or read in the hotel room while my father wrote. It was a curious accommodation that the fates had arranged: my father needed quiet for his writing, and my mother required a great deal of rest. Had my mother possessed the normal energy of a well person, both the marriage and writing career would have gone up in smoke. I expect that unconscious foreknowledge played its part. C. R. took almost painfully solicitous care of my mother; she in turn provided the Sayward-like calm and strength indispensable to him. *The Trees* bears the dedication "for Harvey."

The warmth and closeness of the family, most particularly my mother, dictated where he would write. The place had to have the "fluid of life," what might today be called the "right vibes." C. R. could sense immediately upon entering a particular house or room—and we lived in a long series of rented houses—whether he could work there. It dare not be too large or imposing. He wrote for a questionnaire:

> What Makes the Ideal Study. For me, a moderately small room in a house in which we live and where there is consequently the fluid of life which, although unseen, is very evident to me and which I can assimilate and feed on. I don't know how. A hotel room in which my wife lives with me does as a substitute. But a very large house or work room where this fluid is thinned or dissipated by space, or an office or hotel room alone where there is no fluid at all, I cannot work in.

In the Pennsylvania farmhouse where we lived from 1922 to 1928, his desk was at the end of the downstairs hall, a kind of cubbyhole nonetheless close to the heart of the house where he always liked to write. But the summer kitchen, only a few feet away from the back porch, didn't work out at all. In 1926 C. R. had it turned into an elegant studio with hardwood floor, two oriental rugs, fieldstone fireplace large enough for an applebutter kettle; but he could never really write there, in spite of an early notation: "I like my summer kitchen study & especially the fire in its Franklin stove. There is nothing more calmly pleasant than to see a fire, to hear the lap, lap of the blue & red tongues like waves on a small shore."

By the time he worked for MGM in the late thirties, he had tried several times to work in a hotel room and "couldn't do a tap." In Hollywood he refused a private bungalow and secretary and wrote at home. In our last house at 11 Maple Street, Pine Grove, he put his large walnut desk in the diningroom. It was a light sunny room with a graceful wallpaper, which he chose himself, of blue and yellow butterflies on white. A swinging door led to the kitchen. It proved a perfect working place for the eighteen years that remained.

But the thought of owning a house was an anathema to C. R. 11 Maple Street was purchased only because, in 1950, World War III seemed imminent, and food and gas would be more readily available in Pine Grove where we had family and friends. Gas was an all-important commodity. It made possible his only means of relaxation (he had no hobbies other than research and reading): that of taking small drives in late afternoon or traveling from place to place in search of stimulation. Constant change fueled him. His journals are full of speculation as to where the best place would be to live: the Southwest, California, Pennsylvania, North Carolina. In the fifties and sixties he and my mother went to Florida each winter. As soon as the frost came, some chemical change also seemed to occur in my father; he became inordinately restless. Mid-November or mid-December (to escape holidays which took too much time away from writing) became deadlines for leaving, which my mother, who liked to stay put, was rarely able to stave off. He constantly daydreamed of having five or six houses scattered throughout the U.S., each taken care of by someone so that when he and my mother arrived, all would be fresh and ready for them. In that way, packing would be held to a minimum. In reality, the car was always loaded to the roof; the days of packing exerted a heavy strain.

For C. R., "tensing the mind" might be said to be accompanied by a number of rituals. One was a no-talking breakfast;

his thoughts were already gathering. Even in later years he was at his desk by 8:00 or 8:30. He would first go over the work of the day before, correcting or rewriting. It was, in a sense, clearing away the clutter. Then he could start afresh. His desk never needed tidying—it was scrupulously neat; and his pencils never needed sharpening—they were automatics with slip-on erasers. Or he might use a lifetime pen with blunt point and black ink. He didn't smoke or drink coffee as he worked; he was too finely tuned for stimulants—they simply made him ill. His only fetish was a small balsam pillow, about three by four inches, which he kept in a desk drawer. It brought the smell of the north woods, which he loved keenly.[2]

Sunday mornings were reserved for answering letters. It was the only day he didn't feel a compulsion to write, which is not to say he wouldn't work on his notebooks or research in the afternoon. No letter from a reader went ignored. It was at times a prodigious task. But the only time he hired a secretary was to try to dictate a story. It didn't work out; another's presence made him self-conscious.

Tensing the mind meant, to some extent, tensing the body as well (viz., My Jaws are Clenched, from his journal). And it meant finding the least inhibited way of getting his thoughts on paper. Was the flow more direct to pen or typewriter? His journal carries a running argument for a number of years on their respective virtues. He seemed to feel most natural writing with his pen, and the journals up to the middle nineteen thirties are in his nearly unreadable scrawl, which at first glance has the quizzical glide of Arabic.

For the pulp stories he used his typewriter. Writing by hand would have been too slow. A September 1932 journal entry tells of rewriting the day before "entire 6,000 words of a second draft, revising as I went & today typed it off. . . . The previous day I had typed most of Henry's Noble Blood. Typed therefore 16,500 words in 3 days."

Pen was reserved for the slicks. First drafts of the early *Post* stories were done entirely in pen. By November 1, 1934, he was ready for A Trial Experiment in Writing:

> 1. Writing 1st draft on typewriter as I have not done in any of Post or L H J stories but which I am trying in hope that I can turn out more work. Last story took me 2½ months by hand, and I am already 1 1/3 months on this by hand with little done.
>
> 2. I am not trying to write literarily at first, but am just forcing myself to put it down & will then either revise & retype again or again, or completely rewrite by hand, believing I will have more confidence & make more speed, avoiding the endless faltering, because the first draft is already done! I need only rewrite & rewrite & that I have always been able to do quickly and well (knock on wood).

By 1937 he was carrying on a lively debate:

> Of what use is writing it by typewriter if it is drivel? On the typewriter I run on and on. When I have something genuine & pressing to say, something I feel very much, I want to do it by hand.

The following day:

> Pen and Typewriter Again. Discounting that it will probably change as soon as I say it, I can write so much easier and better with a pen than a typewriter these last days. Easier to pick up the book and pen. Easier to set down thoughts. In front of the typewriter I freeze every few lines. . . .

The second to last entry closes on a cautionary note, which he underlined: "But I should always write plainly." He did not necessarily follow this admonition. He had a curious and very individualistic hand which, as mentioned, appeared illegible.

Word endings like "ing" tended to be merely a slurred line. Notes taken at their source, jotted down while someone was talking, were in an even thornier shorthand, and C. R. would often ask my mother to decipher a passage for him, which she usually could do. She was an amateur handwriting expert, and it is a pity that she left no analysis of his script. He rather prided himself on his signature. The capitals are large and free flowing; the hand in general has a certain confidence and artistic quality about it. His impatience comes out in the speed and line-slurring, often forgetting to cross *t*s. It is very much at odds with the picture of himself that continuously emerges from his journals, distraught, unconfident, without the smallest touch of self-esteem.

Most of his novel and story outlines and synopses were first done in pencil or pen, to be transferred later to the typewriter. So were chapter beginnings. But the early typewritten pages are hand corrected until they are nearly indecipherable, crammed with the tension of getting the story in motion. A manuscript could go through countless drafts; a page could expand into 10A, 10B, 10C, and so forth. When an attempt was made to sort out the many manuscript versions of *The Waters of Kronos*, only approximate drafts could be discerned; they ran into each other like water. My mother had learned early the value of writers' manuscripts; carefully she fished everything out of my father's wastebasket, smoothed the sometimes crumpled pages, and stored them away thriftily, so that every step remains of C. R.'s later novels. The pages are mostly white, although the beginnings might be done in pencil on yellow paper, a relaxed gesture C. R. adopted so that the flow might come more easily.

His own typewriter was always a portable—first a Royal, on which he wrote *The Sea of Grass*—later several Remington noiseless machines. They were easy to carry around in his car and set on his knees to write. If he needed a change, he would drive off with the typewriter in search of a quiet country lane where he could work undisturbed, stimulated by the freshness of the scene.[3] His typewriter always went with him on a vacation trip. The word vacation is used with reservations; whenever my parents settled at one spot for a day or so, C. R. spent the mornings working. One year it was decided that he needed a real vacation—no typewriter allowed. As soon as they reached their destination he disappeared, coming back somewhat sheepishly with a rented machine.

C. R. was always nervous away from his writing, in a figurative and literal sense. Afraid of losing his manuscript, he took it in the car with him whenever he left the house, even carrying it in a brief case into the theatre in case the car was stolen. This fear was not irrational. Not only is there a long historical list of manuscripts burned by accident, but *The Trees* almost suffered that fate. C. R. and my mother were traveling about Ohio in a trailer, living among the great trees to get the feeling of them. One morning when they stopped for gas the attendant mentioned that smoke was coming out of the trailer's chimney. Because there had been a breakfast fire in the cookstove, they assumed the smoke came from that and almost drove off. My mother, however, insisted on checking. A pillow protecting a reading lamp, which the jolting had accidentally turned on, was on fire. It was just inches away from the manuscript of *The Trees*.[4]

Tensing the mind was C. R.'s way of getting in the right mood for work. It was elusive, as he noted in his journal: "THAT HIGH, LAVISH WRITING MOOD. I must cultivate it, stir it up" (November 11, 1934). When retyping the last pages of the first draft of a story for MGM, he wrote jubilantly:

> THE GRAND FEEL OF THE WRITING FLUID
>
> . . . I was so nearly done and there was so little to correct and it seemed so fair that I felt the old writing fervor. . . . the feeling was especially noticeable in the fingers. It is as if the brain

> pours a magic power into the fingers and they pound the keys with a sustained rush and the jolts of the keys become almost velvet. (December 29, 1937)

But usually a chapter would be "still a stone wall" to climb over (March 24, 1939) and he would comment on the frequent waste of "vital forces and effort" as he "struggled through, forced through, crucified myself through" a revision which, the next day, had to be thrown away (November 19, 1938). In later years he would feel "a renaissance of writing spirit" less frequently (June 15, 1946). He had learned that "the most painful slow work is usually my best" (August 19, 1952). It was at such a time that he was the most critical. This resulted in feeling himself not so much a writer as "a struggler of expression, a digger of words, an arranger of sentences, an editor of deletions and substitutions, then all this over again until it is more nearly right" (September 23, 1954). Thinking back on the days when he "was young and energy flowed" to his brain and "the words leaped to clothe the thought," he realized that those thoughts "were simpler, easier to express." His "critical faculty" had grown meanwhile; the "thoughts were more difficult and the energy less."

Another debate he carried on with himself was whether to write a first draft straight through and revise later, or make each section or chapter perfect as he went along. He usually opted for the latter. His first draft "must be completely beaten, changed around, till it is done" (June 17, 1944). Only then could he go on. Yet revising went on through the proof stage, bringing "to a head the unresolved problems of the original writing, phrases or sentences that didn't quite satisfy" (October 24, 1949). The rewriting itself was exhausting.

> I REALIZE AT LAST the terrible expense of energy, concentrating, pouring ones self out that I do when finishing up a book. It seems so easy, so nearly done, that I feel I can do this in a

> short time and make every effort to do so. . . . It's the rush and pressure after the long pull. Rewriting seems so easy and yet to bring it out in my mind the way it should be I give my all.
>
> THE REMEDY. To keep at a chapter until it is perfect, this when you are writing it in the first place. . . . Never succumb again to the fallacy that it is pretty good now, if a little rough, and it will be easy to fix it up at the end. (April 28, 1958)

The pressure of rewriting made him view the short novel with a special fondness. "For weeks long books have been bogging me down. I mean the thought of doing them, all the effort and slow painful writing of years, stops me before I start" (May 31, 1940). Though short books like *The Sea of Grass* "enthused" him, he realized that what the reader wanted is "A BIG WORLD, A BIG APPLE THEY CAN KEEP NIBBLING AT for a long time. They can forget themselves and their troubles and enter this world" (May 24, 1940). Disastrously, two years later he would take *The Free Man*, which he had planned as just such a "big apple," and pare it to a four-part tightly plotted serial to fit the *Post*. The richness he had envisioned was not possible in the truncated form, and even the theme, appropriate during wartime, was not given the chance to be developed fully. Far later he commented in his journal:

> WRITING. It came to me last eve it's not what you feel about a book while reading it - it's the effect that stays with you afterward. This is what I should aim for. Plot, a story, are transient. Reality and formlessness as in life are permanent. The reader comes back again and again to sample, to make some puzzling point more clear. Once a plot story is finished, it is done, behind one, of no more interest than a mystery. But the other keeps alive in the mind, never quite solved, a more or less mystical testament to pick up again, to think about. (January 22, 1958)

6

Writing the Story

C. R.'s journal is a running graph of his up and down moods—what might be fashionably termed a manic-depressive cycle, not lasting the traditional period but rather an unspecified sequence of days or even hours. The troughs—the times of despair, discouragement, bewilderment (whether caused by ill health or writing problems)—appeared on the whole to be fertilizing times. "It seems I must get up to a pitch of desperation before the plot & story works itself into proper way in back of my mind" (April 1934).

When he came to the point of actually writing the story, there was no way for him to gauge whether or not the plot outline would work. Should he write the story in a quick first draft, "forcing" himself, or should he "revise, correct, rewrite my pages as I go - the day's work before going on. Then I have something to read without discouraging effort" (journal, December 1947). He settled for the latter, fearing a "loosely written" first draft that would be "a terrific and discouraging job to do . . . over." The longer novels were less rigidly planned. From his journal of March 1949:

> DEVELOPMENT of a chapter is first merely a setting down of the effect I want to make or an idea of contrast or a viewpoint. The second version includes a few ideas. Then I may do a third version with more ideas or action. In time the synopsis or outline will follow, but all the time it is growing.

He would also "sketch scenes that are hard to do - like an artist sketching a scene he will copy from later, improving, selecting. These sketched scenes must not be outlines, but emotional sketches" (journal April 14, 1934).

C. R. made a brief outline he called "Writing the Story" that seems to be an extension, at least numerically, of the outline on Plotting the Story (see Appendix B). It consists mainly of Major and Minor Writing Rules, not so much a series of helpful steps but of reminders—one more in the long series of admonitions to himself.

The first section of Writing the Story, #10, concerns the search for the right mood. Some six are listed, from "light dancing" to "matter of fact realism." It wasn't that C. R. would run his finger down the list and choose one or another; it was to impress upon himself that mood was all-important, that every word in the story or chapter must be bent in that particular direction.[1] Section 11 of the outline bears quoting:

IMPORTANT WRITING RULES. MAJOR

11A Compress much into a few vivid words
11B New word combinations, descriptions, phrases
11C Start each new paragraph or scene by picking up specific interest thread of the preceding
11E What is the current chief obstruction or interest in reader's mind? Ply it, embroider it in new way. This is to make use of energy flows already aroused in reader.
11F Conflict. Will against will, often little spoken. . . .

One subheading under Important Writing Rules, Minor, is another stern directive: "Rewrite till right. A revised story is a black eye to Reynolds [agent] & editors. Make it right before it goes out first time."

But the most important part of the outline is the admonition which precedes it: *First spend a solid day imagining yourself in the central character - try the scene with other characters* (italics mine). This idea appears in another form in his journal:

> REHEARSAL FOR STORY SCENES. I told V. that the mind was the stage and scenes should be tried on it while the writer himself sits down in the darkened orchestra pit and sizes it up while his mind runs through the action and some of dialogue of proposed scene and sees how it goes. It should be run through a number of times, the effect of the various lines and plot action tested and added to until he feels it is solid and right. Then he can sit down and write it fairly confidently.

A correlative note from a page of writing principles which C. R. sent me:

> Knowing human nature - what people would do or say.
> Projecting yourself into time, place, and people.

The same idea of projection emerges in a list of Story Principles Amateurs Find Hard:[2]

> 1. Author never analyzes. Character may.
> 2. Telling a story - writing everything to story line. All words adapted to story line - how things look in light of story line. If fear, then they suggest fear. If suspense, suggest suspense. If calmness, calmness. If sympathy, sympathy.
>
> 3. The above way of telling a story very difficult if not born to it. . . . A cause may be not enough selfless imagination or not being able to imagine yourself the other character. . . . must become wholly and completely that other character. . . . study & learn from others like that character . . . in real life.

Several factors probably helped C. R. avoid these problems. First, he was always profoundly interested in people. Second, fiction constituted an escape for him: from pressing problems, from times in which he did not feel at home. People of these earlier periods seemed to offer a constant stimulation and fascination. And thirdly, C. R. was a shrewd judge of people. Five minutes or a few words with a person and he knew everything about them. It was not a rational process but completely instinctive.

With the exception of Alexandria Morely in *The Aristocrat*, who was taken word for word, gesture for gesture, from a distant relative, most of C. R.'s characters were hybrid; part real people (two, three, or more persons went into their creation), part imagination. Concerning the origin of Lutie Brewton in *The Sea of Grass*, he wrote:

> We had next door to us in Albuquerque a doctor from Mexico and his delightful wife. The child of a Scottish sea captain and of the daughter of a Mexican shipyard owner in Mazatlan, she was as difficult to describe then as now, impulsive, intensely personal, full of gay animation, intimate fun, talk and laughter, quite lovely, with the faint sad melancholy of the Spanish waiting to appear on her face at any moment and as suddenly to vanish. Not that Lutie was drawn to life from her. The author's imagination played its part and when it failed there was another to count on, a former New Zealander, then living in Albuquerque, also curiously with some Scottish blood, and the picture of Katherine Mansfield in her youth. These two gave me the character I needed and in a pinch one or the other invariably came to my mind and rescue, for both like Lutie were exiles, uprooted from the place and culture of their birth, haunted by gracious memories of the old and repelled in some instances by the rude and uncongenial realities of the new.[3]

The name of Lutie was nearly as important as the creation of the character herself. My father had pages of names: modern, old-fashioned; first names, last names; foreign names. I remember the difficulty he had in deciding on the name Sayward for the trilogy's main character, a name discovered in the old records or histories he was so fond of reading. Most writers find their characters refuse to come to life until their proper names are found, and C. R. used several last names for Sayward's woodsy family until he settled on Luckett.[4] It was not until long after *The Trees* became a Book of the Month Club selection that he realized the name contained the word *luck*.

C. R.'s method of assembling lists of words (nouns, verbs, adjectives) to describe his characters[5] seems to have begun with "Smoke Over the Prairie" with a compilation for Frank Gant. But he also made character sketches which had the seeds of incident for the story. It is interesting to compare the following notes on Frank and Nettie Gant with the short story itself, outlined in Appendix A.

Frank Gant Don Francisco
(crossed out: James Gant and Don Jacinto)

> Not a tall man, but thick, powerful, held himself more upright than a tall man and made him seem tall - always thought he was tall and had to correct myself.
>
> Once I knocked on his door and he called Come In. I went in and found him standing in white bowl washing himself and was astonished at his thickness. He looked like iron, and his black hairiness. Was very much embarrassed, but he thundered at me what was the matter. I stuttered. He couldn't understand. One of the women might have come in. He didn't know who was there. He didn't care.
>
> I remember him with a wide black mustache and with a black beard at other times with the mustache. Gil, the Indian man, always shaved him. He said he wouldn't trust his throat to a Mexican.
>
> Whenever he would go places, he would throw coins and children, women and grownups would go after them. The

Mexicans called him Don Francisco, Amigo de los Pobres to his face but behind his back they called him El Rey and El Leone Prieto.

His interest was sheep and horses - sheep for money made - the life of a sheep was nothing - but the life of a horse, even a scratch on his knees of one of his Kentucky horses was everything. When he went to Santa Fe or Denver he loaded his two horse rubber tired buggy on the wagon and sent it ahead. It would have been injured on the rocky trail, but there, he would drive about on the streets with it in grand style. He could have hired horses and rigs there from liveries - fine rigs, but that didn't interest him. He wanted to show off his own.

My mother used to grow tighter mouth when he went to Denver - and speak about the women there he went with. She used to say it was no society like in Kentucky - vulgar, no religion, prostitutes, anybody. I wouldn't say anything but wished my father would take me to Denver but he never would.

He thought little or nothing of Juliana although she was like him - small, active, daring - used to ride and drive. She was a girl and I was a boy, and I was everything. Mamma used to send me to him when she wanted a favor. He never refused me anything except to take me to Denver. He said it was too far but I knew by mother's lips that there was another reason.

He disliked the Coddoms Juliana used to visit in town and call them the Goddamns.

He dominated New Mexico from a buggy or sulky. Men always came to talk to him, the governor and delegate from congress and others, to ask his opinion on things, what pleased him. His quarters were opposite from my mother's but they were in the parlors and only went in to my mother usually before they left to pay their respects briefly.

He drank endlessly - never affected - never more polite or angry. My mother called him an atheist - like the Indians worships sun and sheep and horses and the land.

Nettie Tankersly Gant

Not stout but like a great wrap, with bright dark eyes like a bird's in a quilted face. Because she came from the South, I thought all Southern people had dark eyes.

Not an invalid but acted like one - always in a chair - seldom left her room to eat at the table - had a heavy solid silver service just for her - it stayed in her room - the other things brought in on a huge brass tray with small dents all over it evenly. Her room always had an odor of being closed up, not musty as smelling of dresses and cloth, that peculiar smell which oppressed me as a boy and I was glad to get into the open air.

Strictly religious. Her Bibles always close but I never saw her read them. Very strict, especially on Sunday which she never called Sunday, always the Sabbath. Father never swore in the house. Whistling on Sunday not allowed or playing on the Vermont organ except hymns which Juliana would never play. Would object strenuously to Mexicans playing or singing within earshot on Sunday.

Something tight about her mouth. Mouth and eyes in such contrast to her face. She and father never got along well. She never said much - I can just see her eyes on him hard and her mouth set. [He] always called her "your mamma."

Never called on anyone although others came regularly to call on her. It was as if she were a queen and did not return calls. When a man once asked if smoking was distasteful to her, she replied, "No one has ever smoked in my presence," and he put the cigar away. She sat in her chair and they paid their re-

> spects to her as a queen. She always put a shawl over her when they came - a certain one - golden brown - there is no color like it - as if the sun were shining on it even in the dim room. I used to think it was a kind of sun of the place, an Egyptian or Persian sun.
>
> She seems much older than she was.
>
> She was the daughter of owner of great stock farms at Lexington and detested horses and horse racing which always seemed queer to me.
>
> Wants to see the R.R. come but does not tell my father. Perhaps it will bring an end to this lawlessness and bring churches. Everyone says it will - and people covering this barren land. Then I can go out and look at it.
>
> Portraits of her mother and father hanging up in her rooms.

What most interested my father in a character was power, with sympathy a close second. One could not exist without the other. In his Black Notebook II, a long section on characters lists Strength Verve Power Characters (power underlined twice), with psychological observations of the effect they had on other people. Another page is captioned Why You Like & Root For Him or Her, followed by Action Characterization That Makes You Root For Him (Very Important). Two examples on the latter page show the kind of women characters C. R. felt empathy for:

> A woman who in desperate scene & time refuses to hide with others in fireplace but stands out and gives them a piece of her mind - or loads guns, etc.
>
> A girl who calmly sings when [there] is danger & excitement all around.

Several pages of Other Characters - Types in Black Notebook II show either a power over self ("Calm outside - boiling within") or a contrast in relation to other people ("Child who advises & takes care of unstable parent" or "Contradictory type who talks against anyone but admires him privately").

If character was crucial, so was form. C. R. had another word for it: *arrangement*. Sequence and order, which taken together he considered the most important thing in writing, were part and parcel of it. A journal entry of October 4, 1945, reworked in Notebook 6, clarifies the term:

> ARRANGEMENT. . . . I think of it often when I am working - that arrangement is the most important and difficult art. In it lies development, contrast, effect, reality. (To the rushing writer in a mood it may come out right, but to me I must rearrange the thoughts, the incidents, the paragraphs to get *the consecutive rising effect I want*.)

Another journal entry (November 2, 1945) copied in Notebook 6:

> THE HARDEST THING IN WRITING for me is FORM, arrangement of all the thoughts and words for interest, beauty and emotion. Once I get it even in the rough, I can compress or enlarge it at great speed for the eventual form is there and I only cut or emphasize it. *Oh, that unknown eventual form! It is what I seek, endlessly work for, feel for, struggle for, patch and putter and almost give up to get*. What it is to be I cannot tell you. But once found, something in me recognizes it as the one sought.

From his July 1946 journal, when he had begun *The Town*:

> NOT RIGHT AND START A NEW VERSION. I am aghast at the numbers of times I must write this first chapter. But all this morning the things that I added lately did not seem to do at all and

> I went back to original first two pages, retyped them, wrote a third page and retyped that. This took me all morning and most of the afternoon. I also made up a new plan so that one thing will fit after the other . . . It is the *old difficulty of arrangement* because I try to fit together all the ingredients that have turned up for the chapter, not discarding any of them, and this is extremely difficult. *It is more like music. Which bar comes before which and what follows and precedes the melody and when it reappears, these are the most important considerations.*[6]

The final section of C. R.'s outline on Writing the Story, section 13, consists of one line: "New title with strength, lift, vividness, contrast." His notebooks have many pages of titles, light as well as serious.[7] He also formulated theories regarding titles. One was that "in magazine titles you provoke a mood; in a book, the trick is to pick one that suggests scope, a broad perspective." Another concerned the principle of contrast, using two words of uncommon strength and/or associations, such as *War and Peace* or his own *The Light in the Forest*. If possible, the unpleasant word should come first, so that the energy flows aroused by it enhance the pleasant word that follows.[8] Thus the violent, emotional word *war* in *War and Peace* increases the effect of *peace*. Reverse them (Peace and War) and the effect is negated.

Other ways to produce a vivid title are through the use of action or movement (Man on Horseback, Death Takes a Holiday); through emotion or an original word or idea combination (Fault of Angels); through silhouette, implying strong or vivid contrast (Man Against the Sky); or through alliteration. Original associations, such as The Song of the Rock, The Halted Earth, Enchanted Rubbish, Lost Sun, had appeal, C. R. felt, as did New Combinations of Beauty Words, Instruments, like The Silver Forceps or Gears of Gold. Unexpected pairings, with a strong element of contrast, such as The Winter Robin, The Magnificent Failure, Wild Hay, Sea Drought, Son of the Wind,[9] as well as *The Sea of Grass*, are drawn from several pages of such examples.

C. R. was often mystified by what made a novel sell. In a letter to me, discussing the title The Light in the Forest (which he had originally called My Enemy, My Son, changed because two other books with similar titles had been published that fall), he deprecated, "My titles are generally poor and this one will likely prove no exception. My best one, Always Young and Fair, made the poorest showing of all my books so perhaps a title isn't everything. I hope so" (August 1952).

Something inside C. R. demanded reasons for things. The relation between title and book sales both intrigued and confounded. One such speculation from his notebooks:

> A Woman in the Title. Kitty Foyle, Mrs. Miniver, Portrait of Jennie, all surprising sales far above expectation. My titles of Early Americana, etc. very bad. A woman in the title of Sea of Grass and The Trees would have sold many more, I believe. Women buy to read about themselves & men to read about women, but women know all about men. Women, however, are a mystery, always beckoning, alluring.

There were other considerations in writing the story not mentioned in the outline but appearing in Black Notebook II and his journals and his letters to me. They have to do mainly with such techniques as achieving suspense or getting across necessary information, or with vivid language. And they are short, crisp, and to the point. More detailed suggestions appear in the letters in Chapter XI.

> Compression & Action. I am learning that good gripping writing has picture of action & many things said in a few words. The latter especially stirs up a score of energy flows and concentrates them all in a brief record or time [?] which gives it the sharp story effect. And the action must be what the fresh reader with nimble mind is interested in. . . .

You need STRONG suspense and obstruction. You will make it restrained and convincing enough if you only have something violent underneath.

Suspense sentence: "Never had the air felt so choking as in the canyon."

At danger point, when sweetheart or main character's life is threatened, have story-teller think of them when they were very much alive, happy, etc., complete opposite of what is now facing them. . . . This increases reader's tension.

You never give suspense in what is going to happen, only in what isn't going to happen, or what you will get [the character] out of.

Summing it up. Break up, Introduce, or End Long Descriptive Passages by Dialogue that Sums It Up.[10]

Restraint, Keeping Back. Do not tell all. Leave much to be found out (1) to arouse reader to read on (2) not to insult his understanding (3) not to be too hackneyed. Something secret always kept back.

[Re Using Detail] You find you must have strong drama, feeling or emotion to carry your details, authenticities, phrase after phrase.

Reader cannot stand too much description or explanation at one time. Use it here and there when suspense has been aroused to carry reader's interest on and over it.

Blend description with action.

Action Rules.

A. Whenever you have trouble, always have contrast of no trouble beforehand.

B. In action seldom want thinking, but flashback by seeing, hearing, etc.
C. At crucial moments write in short sentences.

A Companion to Talk To. Someone close. [Illustrations follow from C. R. stories; this a way of conveying information to the reader.]

Motion, pictorial. Remember what Will Irwin said, that Shakespeare's charm was a series of pictures. Your best writing makes everything to be said visual, motion if possible, with strong emotion words like crush, batter, sweep.

Back to See, Smell, Hear. These are the vivid senses. Writing should be a picture, a scent, a sound, or all three with feeling in, the feelings we had as a boy. . . .

7

The Novel Notebooks

There were three important crises, or watersheds, in C. R.'s life. The first occurred with the move west, the second with the first sale to the *Saturday Evening Post* in 1934, and the third some twenty-four years later in 1958. C. R. removed half of the journal of that year from its binder, attaching a note begging that it not be read. Actually, that discarded section of journal is one of the most interesting. But the period it covers was extremely painful to C. R. He had written a novel about a woman with the gift of healing; it was titled *The Gifts* and was unlike anything he had written, both as to story and style. Although his agent was enthusiastic, neither the *Post* nor his publisher liked it. He grew close to a nervous breakdown. Irrational fears threatened him when he tried to go to sleep.

"Afraid of the night" is one of the phrases emerging from the journal at that time, and the period corresponds to the classic descent into the depths that Jung called "The Night Journey under the sea," part of the death/rebirth cycle from which the individual emerges with "germs of new possibilities of life."[1] It was a scarier, more irrational version of the periodic agonies of despair he suffered, that compulsive need to descend into the depths to get a grip on himself and his art.

Curiously, in the short novel which followed, *The Waters of Kronos*, the town to which the elderly John Donner wants to return lies under the waters of a large government dam. Through an interlude of fantasy, Donner enters that town of his childhood and, confronting both the boy-he-was and his father, realizes the bases for his fears. In those personal depths beneath the sea, C. R. had encountered certain mythic truths which form the symbolic level of the book. Art follows life, which follows myth.

Despite the extreme exhaustion that C. R. usually experienced after finishing a book, despite the depression of realizing "what a bitter disappointment and acid corrosion of the soul it was to have a cherished book turned down, despised, called crude and not worthy to have the publisher's name on it,"[2] the weeks which followed had "germs of new possibilities of life." *The Waters of Kronos*, *A Simple Honorable Man*, and *The Grandfathers*[3] were conceived the day after the *Post* turned down *The Gifts*. A little later that summer the idea came for *A Country of Strangers*. C. R. was then sixty-seven. His first novel had appeared when he was forty-seven. In those twenty years he had published ten novels.[4] In a little over ten years he would produce five more plus a book for children, as well as the novel notebooks for the third volume of his personal trilogy and *The Angry Saint*. His health was precarious; he seemed plagued by demons of undiagnosed illness and unease. But the ideas were flowing as never before. In an ironic way, *The Gifts* had made its own contribution.

For all of his novels C. R. kept what he referred to as a "novel notebook." This was not the same notebook in which he jotted down possible ideas for long fiction.[5] Rather it comprised the working notes for the novel at hand, kept in a two-ring, loose-leaf, cardboard folder, the notes carefully filed away when the book was completed, and the folder (usually a bright one from the five and dime) reused for the next novel. Drawing from those notebooks and from journals and letters, this chapter attempts to suggest three aspects of a novel's beginnings. From *The Waters of Kronos* notebook: the initial outline and examples of characters' feelings. From *The Light in the Forest*, the origins and changing outlines of the novel. And for *The Lady*, more briefly, the three sources which coalesced to form the story.

The Waters of Kronos

Because of its mythic element, I have attempted to suggest the unconscious climate in which the novel was conceived. There was another more conscious aspect of motivation. C. R. once told me that *Kronos* and its companion novel, *A Simple Honorable Man*, were his way of honoring his father and his mother. C. R. had been deeply attached to his mother (who died in 1925); the relationship with his father had always been strained, and he felt he had not fully appreciated the country preacher whose simple goodness had brought him no monetary rewards. The filial debt had been partially paid some eight years earlier (1950) in a *Post* story "Dr. Hanray's Second Chance." The story and novel have a great deal in common: the return in time to the town of his childhood (in the short story the town is not under water but destroyed by a government reservation); the meeting of the main character with the boy-he-was; and the discomfort of the father-son relationship. The character's realization of the father's solid worth is contained in *A Simple Honorable Man*. *Kronos* is about the search for the mother by a particularly troubled individual, who does not know the origin or meaning of the fears and depressions which afflict him.

The two novels were originally to have been one, called *The Good People*. With the plan of writing a short rather than a long novel (this just after the *Post*'s rejection of *The Gifts*), C. R. felt "an immense mental surge." But it was slightly more than another month (he had almost given up the novel) until the idea of doing it "the Dr. Hanray Second Chance way" came to him. "The new way moved me. I thought I saw and felt new depths and significance. . . . I felt pleased and relieved to have something good and solid to write, felt unafraid to show it to Alfred."

Kronos received the National Book Award, yet because of its painful sense of nostalgia, its desire to escape the present world to return home to the past, it is perhaps his saddest novel. In *Kronos* John Donner is rejected, as an old man, by each member of his family. The only one he does not see is his mother; at the novel's end he expects to see her, but the reader feels that the meeting will occur after his death. The question of returning home, and of the difficulties encountered there, also enter into *Tacey Cromwell*, *The Light in the Forest*, and *A Country of Strangers*. But nowhere in his work are the characters related to the author as closely as is John Donner, a writer of books. The deep sadness and bewilderment of the aftermath of *The Gifts* were transformed into deeper and more universal concerns.

Skeleton outline from the Kronos notebook:

I. (How to write it) (one page to each)
What people said, the common people
Symbols, Double talk, References
Bring in the Deep Things (Fate, destiny, doom, Hope, Earth, Evil etc)

II. Names
of specific characters
of people in town
place names for the town

III. [lists of nouns, adjectives, and verbs that fit in old days and recapture of past]

IV. Chapter outline - rough

V. Notes for revisions and corrections

VI. Conversations

VII. Family Sayings, Town and Country sayings to insert

VIII. The Key Suspense

IX. The Characters
His mother
His Dad
Boy's relation to and feelings about his youth and his Penna. Dutch background

X. Contents
incident - cruel, heartless
undramatic, humorous

XI. Feelings as boy, of childhood

XII. Strange realities of town
incidents, people

XIII. Other characters of novel - and conversations

As the novel notebook became developed, each character would have a section; so would each chapter, with plenty of blank pages on which to make notes as they came to C. R. In this way, out of jottings under the thirteen major points, the chapters themselves would form. It was a question of scene and incident coalescing in an almost organic manner. Especially in *The Waters of Kronos*, which contains so much of my father's emotional relationship with his childhood and family, he could collect from his journals both memories of that childhood and his feelings looking back. From the notebook:

(feelings of boys and old men)

Boy's eye, how it bores into holes, carvings, like an optic engine, runs up and down the grooves. A boy feels himself a tiny man invading crevices and . . . from quarter inch ledges, crawling around carved cliffs, through ornamental dark holes or making his way in the grooves of the carved leaves and flourishes.

Smell of wash water tonight gave me a sudden secure feeling as coming home as a child and feeling safe in all the soft reassuring family smells of home. It was a wonderful relaxing inner sensation. I went around the school yard and there was a big washing hung up and giving its odor on the evening air.

The wild sense and breath of youth from seeing in my mind a ripple in a forest pool.

Strangeness of walking. What a grotesque thing walking is, to be cut in two below the waist and moving about by putting one of these severed parts forward and then the other. . . .

Soft seductive smell of creek like warm smell of woman followed me on the road in evening, reaching out and touching.

Crying yawn. Older people used to do it. Now never thought I would. Each cry at a lower note, a sort of cry to heaven and earth of boredom and sleepiness.

Rainy day in summer, creek brown, warm to bathe in, rain running off the warm earth, the deeper muskier smells. Pleasure of a dry spot under some thick trees, game in the porch or attic, sounds of distant piano, the running gutter, the leaves and apples on ground from rain.

Oldtime sight of house back from street, especially at night with a faint golden light, seeming very distant, piercing the blackness and loneliness. . . . It gave me as a boy a feeling we don't have today of solitude, retreat, the long dark aisle the eye must travel to the light. . . . the mystic qualities of withdrawal, silence, independence, living one's own mysterious life. . . . people unafraid then of darkness and being alone.

Older Man's Thoughts

> The older man now thinks of the women he knew. To his surprise what rises in him, touches and moves him are flash memories of his mother, wife and daughter, of the former's love and hardship, of his wife's cheer through terrific troubles, of what his daughter went through - but particularly of their moments of happiness that came to him, happy with so little. He also remembered what other writers had said that old men remember the women they had passion with and those they regretted they did not. Now he found that such in his life lay quiet and clay in him. "They lied," he told himself. "Either they lied for their young men readers or they didn't know." No, the people he remembered were those who did something for the heart, not the viscera, the humble now that he must be humble, the brave now that he knew what it meant to be brave, those who were happy with so little. Their happiness lived, remained through the years, survived and was a living flame today. How could such small things have the vitality and durability to endure?

The Light in the Forest

In July 1951 C. R. wrote to the senior editor of *The Saturday Evening Post* to ask whether he would

> "be interested in a couple of short stories to be written to finance the six or eight months it would take me to do a short serial for the Post? It's to be laid in Ohio and Pennsylvania in the early pioneer period of THE TREES. It starts with an upright, likeable and capable white boy captive of the Indians returned unwillingly. . . ."

C. R. was writing Erdman Brandt in the hope of securing a green light for the novel, and thereby a promise that the *Post* would buy it. In 1951 my father had found himself more in debt than since the sale of *The Sea of Grass*. Although *The Town* had won the 1950 Pulitzer Prize, it had been three years in the writing and did not fatten our reserves. Fortunately, the sale of a short story to the *Post* saved the Pine Grove house from being sold for money to live on. But the need to write a serial was imperative. The two previous short novels serialized in the *Post* (*The Free Man* in 1943 and *Always Young and Fair* in 1947) had not been literary successes. All through the writing of *The Light in the Forest*, C. R. was chafing. The book was unimportant—it would not amount to a damn.

> October 27, 1951. DEPRESSED OVER MY SERIAL I can't see that it is anything. This morning when I picked it up, I was greatly disappointed. . . . It is only a narrative, all the same theme of conflict between son and parents, whites, etc. A story should have several different developments, a serial many.
>
> I AM DENIED MONEY to do better books and must spend my time working on something like this.

Dissatisfaction with the novel continued into January and February of the following year. On January 3:

> DISCOURAGED OVER MY OUTLINE & NOTES for part two of serial. Worked all morning but did little. Unenthused. Then at the very last moment before coming for dinner I thought to make boy's home place Paxton where the Paxton boys and the people in general would be hostile to anyone sympathizing with Indians, doubly so to a boy who wanted to go back to them. When boy hears, learns he is going to that place, a contrast and conflict are created waiting. He has heard about them, as have all Indians, murdering the peaceful Indians in Lancaster and other things. This lends itself to more possible incident.

In April he had difficulty writing the ambush in the story's climax.

> I WRITE END TO NOVEL INSTEAD. I hadn't intended to. While mulling over the above [river/ambush], a few brief ideas for

> end situation came to me. They came to me this way. I was so desperate that my river incident didn't pan out, I asked myself, won't the final ending, the tragic ambush and leave taking, work out either? A few lines came to me for it and I started to set it down. The action and story kept coming and I went on with it for four pages to the end.

The novel was finished in June, less than a year from its beginning. When on June 24 the telegraph office phoned that the *Post* had bought the novel for "seventeen thousand five hundred," C. R. was afraid it was a mistake, that it was only "seven five." Three days later: "There is something strange, almost fishy, about the sale of my novel." Only when the actual money came from his agent was he convinced. It was far easier for my father to believe in bad news than in good.

The following notes from the novel notebook are dated over a two-month period and show the novel's development and the problems which C. R. encountered. What appears to have caused the most trouble is point of view. He finally solved this by using several narrators, although True Son's is the point of view most frequently employed.

My Enemy My Son   Sep 27

> NEW PLAN from point of view of fellow prisoner, a little older and who had been captured later in life, so he has more of a feeling for whites and speaks English in pioneer vernacular.
>
> Talk much like in The Trees.
>
> Rebelling boy like [crossed out], a fiery Southern youth, fiercely Indian, impetuous.
>
> Narrating boy somewhat like Wyitt and Guerdon. Call him
>
> Read The Trees & The Fields to prime self for it.

Narrator does not feel so kindly toward Indians - understands torment of father who lost his several other children killed and scalped which True Son will not believe.

ON END when find that Indians did kill and scalp children, he delivers a blistering attack on Indian father. (But couldn't he see children's scalps brought to camp?) He instead thought it all right, part of Indian life, war.

OR IS IT BEST not to mention killing at all till later in book?

MY PROBLEM - the lack of sympathy felt by reader for a white boy unwilling to return to his race. ORIGINALLY I was going to have the home a miserable one to give more sympathy but then there will be none for the parents.

New Thoughts Oct 3

From the point of view of brother who enlists with Bouquet to try to get his brother only slightly more than a year younger - or someone who knew of family and watched him accordingly or was interested to see how this young patrician prisoner would be - or perhaps the son of a servant or tenant of the aristocratic family (this also provides more contrast and contrast of wilderness with this rich aristocratic family). Viewpoint character after his own brother or sister who is never turned up or found - instead this rich young Indian wastrel.

Problem of Being Along when He Goes Back: Boy, not being a brother need not be older, about same age. They become friends and when rich boy escapes to go back, other boy goes along, both loving the wilderness life although other boy is doubtful about liking living with Indians. However, he can do it also to keep an eye on him for the boy's parents but they should not be in on it or it is too contrived. He just feels he will be acting for them. But the main reason is that rich boy promises other boy he can find about his brother or sister who was never found - once he's there as an Indian and friend.

Boy writing story is and talks like Wyitt, Guerdon. Rich young boy has dignity, presence, intelligent argument.

Discussions & arguments between can bring out differences between Indians and whites.

Guerdon & sayward shrewd viewpoint and style of thot & writing.

A sister, which I, the viewpoint character, seeks among the Indians suggests a possible romance with True Son which is never developed.

True Son says that taking scalps is custom, used to it, not more than blood letting of whites.

T. S. declares against father having property - declares Indian idea of property, belonging to all, lets Indians pasture horses in young wheat field in spring.

Perhaps Just a Novelette for Post

My Enemy, My Son   Oct 9

Narrator should be brother so he feels brother's preference of Indians to him and his parents.

First he refuses to acknowledge brother at Muskingum Forks, then his [response] is the same to his father and mother. Prefers Indian brother who accompanied him and Indian parents. Narrator pities his father and mother. "What sort of a man is this Indian?" father asks. Mother holds with him patiently through all.

When he escapes, brother is sent back - or better, narrator wins brother's respect by saving his Indian brother who is about to be killed by Scotch Irish whites who have lost dead and scalped to Indians. True Son tells him he is escaping. Narrator says he will go along. Narrator taken back by Indians but they refuse to take brother - wasn't he a soldier against Indians with Bouquet? Take him prisoner.

Narrator gets word that his father is coming. Boy is sent out to call boat in. Narrator helpless is there to watch. Boy sees small brother or small sister and gives warning. Indians want to kill him. His Indian father says, no. Boy is white. He can go, but his brother will be kept. Indian father tells him they must kill each other when meet in battle some day.

Meantime they keep brother to torture and burn at stake. Several Indians take him to next village where he must run gauntlet, etc. Narrator goes along. Has promised not to help him free, if they let him go. In end he frees him and they get away. Brother says something that he'd be dead if he hadn't broken his promise. "Me Indian. No break promise to

But ANY VIEWPOINT BUT True Son's takes away something of freshness of white Indian son's alien feelings for white race and their customs. PERHAPS THIS CAN BE BROUGHT OUT ANYWAY by narrator brother in pity and understanding.

VIEWPOINT CHARACTER can also see feelings of Indian father. "I never liked them but I had to give in that I felt for the old scoundrel in parting from True Son" etc.

My Enemy, My Son   New Plan Oct 15, 1951

Boy's point of view.

Start with him at white camp, his feelings, his tears as Indians show tears for other prisoners they bring, his desolation when his Indian family go after camping nearby for days.

Boy cheered from depths when Indian brother calls to him the day they go, that night, has followed, calls cheer. (Shows feeling of brother for boy as well as boy for Indian brother.)

Indian brother follows him to Ohio and boy's feelings when he is left alone.

[above crossed out in notebook]

Stunned at meeting his stiff and well to do professional father at Carlisle - perhaps after others have been selected - several not identified by anyone - boy hopes he will be the same and that they let him go back - then his father comes

Resolves that night to kill himself - when he gets home
Stiffness between himself and father

Suicide all planned out - remembers how Indians take life - more noble to take it than live in dishonor and slavery. Then meets his small sister, dark, black hair and eyes, almost like an Indian. She is the only one he takes to.

His mother a lady, pained by this Indian boy, perhaps not his real mother but stepmother. His mother may have been killed by Indians.

His difficulties with table, silver, sleeping in bed, closed house, school

When scents of spring come from forest and stream, he cannot stand it. Tells girl only if she promises not to tell. She cries but keeps still. He runs back. Drunk on water, spring, woods.

His adventures stealing boat and making his way with Waggoners or in path.

His reception by Indian family. They have moved down along Ohio.

He is made to call in boat - hears his father is after him - he is in disgrace - Indian father tells him he must go - the others think he is surely white now that he has been back and preferred saving whites to them. One of them will kill him when he is not there to protect him.

Goodby - touching scene between father and son - "you must kill me some time as I must kill you."

Outline My Enemy My Son[6] Oct 19

1. Theme, with significance, importance, power.
   A son who refuses to respect or acknowledge his white parents but prefers the Indian parents who raised him and their way of life.

1B. Thoughts on subject by characters or writer.
   Racial discussions contrasting Indians and whites.

2. Freshness, Originality
   The theme itself is fresh in its setting.

3. Lift, Beauty, Feel
   Feel of parents for boy
   The feel of love for Indian home - the lift and beauty of woods, spring, water etc, nature to boys after they escape and just before.

3A. Characters with Lift, radiance, life.
   The boy's mother perhaps. The boy's Indian cousin, his irrepressible spirit. The boy in the woods, free etc.

3C. Beauty and feel of background, place.

4. Strong story, plot with violent obstructions and suspense and powerful climax.
   Needs stronger obstructions.

4A. Strong powerful unforgettable characters
   Violent Indian characters he admires - is with at climax.

Strong dour unforgiving white character who hates Indians in town.

4B. Contrast of characters and scenes.
Indian raised boy and his refined home and family - the refined white home and settlements after the Indian country and then the woods and Indians again.

5. Rough reality, especially to offset any mildness or sweetness.
More of this.

5A. Unsweetened common things of life and people

5B. Unsweetened talk

MY SON, MY ENEMY
OUTLINE   MY ENEMY, MY SON

1. EPIC AMERICAN THEME OF AUTHENTIC DUTY WITH FRESH IDEA: Son loves his Indian captor parents better than his own white parents & fights to stay with them:

THEME: Son against parents
FRESH IDEA: Instead of wanting to escape, white boys often wanted bitterly to stay with Indian captors
AUTHENTIC DUTY: Parents to get him back, son to resist and return to those he considered he liked best, as well as their life and teachings.

2. THEME FULFILLMENT. Parents get boy back again satisfied or he is permitted to remain with his Indian parents.

3. CHIEF POWERFUL, STARK, VIOLENT OBSTRUCTION TO THEME FULFILLMENT - out of which come other obstructions

CHIEF OBSTRUCTION: Son prefers Indian foster parents to white actual parents

OTHER OBSTRUCTIONS: He fights against return, is unwilling prisoner at home and runs away to return to Indians.

4. STRONG OPENING OBSTRUCTION OF CHIEF OBSTRUCTION THAT LEAVES STRONG SITUATION. The return of prisoners at Carlisle with many of them resisting. He just stares at father unfriendly when they meet.

5. THEME ACTION - DECISION & OBSTRUCTION ACTION TOWARD FULFILLMENT. Boy is taken home - resists father, mother, sisters, aunt - runs away with another captive back to Indians.

6. GRIPPING STRONG CLIMAX. BOY is sent out in Ohio to call boats to shore SEE BELOW [single-spaced page follows of conversation with Indian father and background of boy's experience with Indians. Includes "THE ONE WHO COMES with him East may be his Indian brother with whom he is inseparable and to part from whom is a great grief at the end. This time brother does not go with him. He goes alone."]

7. STRONG INDIVIDUAL CHARACTER YOU LIKE. Sympathy for boy who feels so for Indians, torn between them and whites, likes Indian way best.

8. RICHNESS, POWER, ATMOSPHERE, FAMILY. NOBILITY, SWEEP, BEAUTY, WHAT ENTHUSES YOU TO WRITE STORY. Rich appeal of free life in the woods, both freedom and wandering life in woods; No power; Atmosphere of Indians, woods, white house at that time; Family, both his own white and that of Indian parents; Nobility, of both Indian parents and his own; sweep of events of Indians being driven out of homelands by whites; Beauty of woods, Indian life.

MISC OUTLINE My Enemy, My Son

APPEAL. Not too grim but an idyl of life in the woods and nature as Green Mansions.

SOLUTIONS: Not easy

(Word comes that his father is in this boat)

1. That he is to call in boat on Ohio so all can be massacred. He recognizes his father and mother or thinks they might be and declines. He realizes his parents would not do that to his Indian parents. Rejoins parents.

2. He leaves Indian parents and goes on farther West, not taking up with either.

3. His Indian father sends him back. "We must fight on opposite sides. One of us will be killed."

4. He sends words to his father's boat not to answer call of help. Then he tells his Indian father if he kills his white father, he will kill him. Then he doesn't go to either, but goes West.

VIEWPOINT. At first I thought from both, but believe the son's viewpoint would have the greater sympathy and opportunity, and the parents' viewpoint would be implicit in it.

CONFLICT: Between boy and his father, boy and his mother, sister and brother, between boy and his Indian father.

CONTRAST: The white boy and his Indian relatives; the white but Indian looking and mannered boy and his white relatives. . . .

CHARACTER TO SCENE. The boy in his real parents fine white home and luxuries. Boy sleeps on floor of fine room. Boy's clothes he refuses to wear or does so rebelliously.

STRONG INDEPENDENT AMERICAN CHARACTER who has sympathy of reader but goes ahead his own way despite everything: True Son or Richard Matthew Nisbet. Had been taken at four or five, could talk English. Now thirteen. Straight, bronzed by sun on river, hair dark. . . . loved to hunt, fish. Fast runner.

What is interesting to note in this sequence is the gradual stripping down of theme and characters to the point where they represent the essential conflicts. Contrast appears on every level. In the following page, which is undated, C. R.'s manner of working as well as several themes important to the novel emerge:

> List of Strange White Customs to True Son
> Notes, Ideas - Freshness of his Viewpoint of Whites
> Notes, Ideas at House (his white father's)
> Notes for part 1, part 2, part 3
> Notes for different chapters
> Original idea titled: Good Eastern Pioneer Day Story, perhaps Short Serial
>
> The boy or girl captured by Indians when a very small child later taken to Carlisle in the return of Indian prisoners but unwilling to return. His white parents are strangers to him - his Indian parents he loves.
>
> Main part or all of story after they return to white home, from boy's point of view, how he longs for woods & camp & hates house & comforts.
>
> The freshness of viewpoint would be his viewpoint on what whites believe in & do, habits & customs - & how things we look up to he has contempt for or a different angle on.
>
> His escape & trying to get back, his adventures & the way he is treated.
>
> What finally brings his father & him together - perhaps his father's hunting.
>
> Significance: The Vanity & Folly of White Man's Things - house, gadgets - all expressed in a past day by the white captive who longs to return to Indian simplicity, who does run away to return.

A man encourages him - a successful business or professional man. He says all that was . . . a thin veneer of things that gave him no pleasure. . . .

And all he remembers how as he sits & waits is the glory of his youth in the woods. That is all & what followed little or nothing.

character above became 'Bejance, the slave

Filled with power & joy of youth - as deer overcoming gravitation - running - climbing
[then Outline of different days—followed by several handwritten pages of historical background of Colonel Bouquet]

The Lady

Jottings from here and there—from folders, notebooks, journal, and letters—reveal the very beginnings of the novel. It took nearly eighteen years for the unrelated ideas to mesh together into *The Lady*.

From a folder titled Western Story Ideas (undated):

Western Themes # 2 Women
She Never Smiled. Grave young woman who is thought to have killed man - Mrs. H's friend

Ideas To Develop Stories From

Climax. Horse race with old sheep like looking Comanche horse. [this grew into Critter, blended with Mrs. Cosand's horse]

From Maroon Notebook I, a page entitled "Western Stories & Serials" [undated]:

[the ideas each have their point ratings—Man on Horseback, for example, is 4 points]

> Mrs. Cosand and her horse (3 pt) } merged
> The Girl Who Killed a Man (3 pt) }

From RANCH-MOUNTAINS OLDTIME LIFE, Notebook 14:

> Mrs. Cosand's horse Dick. When asked how many children she had, she would say "Two. Baby and a horse." Dick was big black running horse, 1200 pounds. GOES THROUGH FIRE. Boy lighting dynamite to blow up rocks in meadow is scared, throws match, tall rush grass catches fire, spreads fearfully. Her child at school, some distance away. She saddles Dick. If anything can get through, he will. He goes right through fire and smoke. Three neighbor children, she and her boy get on and he brings them back. [More exploits of Dick follow - through blizzard, etc.]

From C. R.'s journal, December 1954:

> AN IDEA FOR MY Horse and Lady Novel tonight. I was listening to a long program on Hemingway told by those who knew him and H. himself spoke on the end. Something about courage and alchemy of suggesting more than you can say gave me the notion to make the horse the oldtime character of physical courage, who knows nothing else, and this in the end is what brings solution for the wiser and more civilized woman who restrains her hand from the second killing.

From a letter to Mr. Ralph Knight of *The Saturday Evening Post*, March 3, 1956:

> The serial was written from three kernels of happenings. Many years ago a gentle ranch woman - she was a good friend of our good friends - shot a man for the second destruction of

her garden. In another county at another time Judge Fountain and his young son disappeared, a mystery that's never been solved. Both of these things took place in New Mexico. Later a South Dakota woman told us about her beloved horse, Dick.

Most of the novel, however, is imaginative and fictitious. It took a good deal of reflection to let the three kernels fall into one hand-running story.

From a letter to Earl J. Cosand, March 23, 1957:

We met your mother in a trailer camp in New Philadelphia in 1938 and she told us some of her experiences with her horse Dick in the Dakotas. In my new novel, I drew on some of these experiences together with those of others and my own with horses as a boy. As a result what comes out in the story is mostly fiction but your mother's recollections were inspirational to me in writing the novel. . . .

8

Characters and Conversations

C. R. often said he had been lucky in where he lived. One particularly fortunate spot was Sandia Park in the mountains near Albuquerque, New Mexico, eight thousand feet high in the yellow pines. We stayed there several summers during the early thirties, one year until Christmas. It was here, in a rather charming cabin with a big fieldstone fireplace, that the material for "Early Marriage" came to my father. He very nearly refused it. The driver of the mountain laundry truck urged C. R. "to come and talk to his mother who, he said, knew Billy the Kid." My father wasn't interested in the outlaw—too many people had claimed to know him. But as he said, "you don't willingly rebuff the only laundryman who comes within twenty-five miles of your house." And so he called on Red Dow's mother:

> . . . there sat talking quietly to me from her chair a most authentic white-haired woman whose father had kept an early stage station at Antelope Springs when the Estancia Valley was a wilderness, and whose husband later on had run a general store at Ruidoso. Here, she told me, Billy the Kid had often hidden from the law, a friend of the family who took her small boy for rides on his horse.
>
> Her stories about Billy the Kid, while interesting, still left me cold, although not so cold as he had left many who had incurred his displeasure. On the other hand, what she told me of her life as a girl during the sixties in her father's dot of habitation on this wild and lonely land moved me deeply. Her father couldn't leave the station, and she and her brother,

> neither of them more than children, used to drive the wagon to Santa Fe for supplies. It was then a trip of several days. They would camp far from the trail at night, not daring to light a fire for fear of Apaches.
>
> She gave me such a picture of herself and her brother that they made their way into my next story. Under the name of Early Marriage it took me into the Post.[1]

The Ohio trilogy also had its roots among the yellow pines. Across the road from our cabin lived a retired engineer, who one day brought over two fat volumes of Henry Howe's *Historical Collections of Ohio*. Crammed with early settlers' stories and details of domestic and woods life, they fired my father's imagination, and *The Trees* was the result. Whether the volumes on C. R.'s book shelf were Mr. Clark's or copies my father managed to obtain I don't know, but they are heavily marked in pen and pencil. They also contain a great many photographs or daguerreotypes of early Ohioans which doubtless delighted my father, who collected photographs to get a feel of old-time characters.[2]

C. R. mined a great many sources for "color," as he liked to call his research material, going through early records and newspapers, writing curators of historical societies about such things as "just what the term 'square axe' meant in Ohio in 1800" or where he could find some "brief explanation of the . . . mineral salts made by early settlers from ashes and what these salts looked like and how they were handled to posts for trade."[3] To Anthony Wallace, Research Secretary of the University of Pennsylvania, he wrote:

> One of the handicaps of a writer is his difficulty in readily getting to the heart of material he's seeking. He knows it must be there somewhere. If the subject is not too long past, he interviews numerous old-timers. In either case, he searches librar-

> ies hoping for the rich and authentic material of some eye and brain who must have been on the spot observing at first hand.

In the early thirties there were still old-time Westerners around. In one of the dark blue notebooks, there is a five-page list of Characters to See: sheep men, cattlemen, former freighters, a well-driller, silver miners, ex-sheriffs, ministers, a granddaughter of the fabled Cerain St. Vrain, rangers, physicians, merchants, and ranchers and their wives—people in Arizona, New Mexico, Texas, and Oklahoma who were a living link to the days when New Mexico was still a territory.

How many of those characters C. R. actually saw, I don't know. Or whether he got an invitation to Floyd Lee's ranch "to hear of old dons who worked Navajo slaves in chains"; or talked to Charles M———who had "killed 50 men"; or called on Mrs. Crytz of whom the notation is made, "Don't jump when she barks—she'll talk for hours." But there were others he came to know well, like Agnes Morely Cleaveland,[4] who came from the powerful Morely ranching family and lived in Datil at the edge of the San Augustin Plains where, in *The Sea of Grass,* Colonel Brewton's ranch house stood. She introduced C. R. to Montagu Stevens, an impoverished English earl who had sunk his fortune in New Mexico ranchland but was able to show my father one of the three or four great rubies in the world, originally stolen, said Lady Stevens, from an idol.

There were dozens more, but the most important were Herbert and Lou Hardy, who lived just a few blocks away. He was seventy when my father met him, a former rancher and silver miner from Magdalena. Their wide hall was hung with long horns and old-time photographs, and Hardy, a banty-cock of a man, was a never-ending fund of color. When he went with C. R. to Socorro, Magdalena, or Grants, men crowded around to hear his stories, which were priceless, and hear him sing "Gypsy Davy and others including Sam Bass . . . quavering but delightful."[5] He also had the rare gift of knowing exactly what my father needed. Not everybody did. C. R. recounted talking with one man "who had been friend and companion to a famous early character." All that he could tell my father about his friend was that he was " 'about five feet eight, dark complected, and weighed around a hundred and sixty pounds.' "[6] On the other hand, probably half of the color that filled the three Western notebooks came from Hardy—often humorous, always authentic.

C. R. had started collecting historical material—that of Pennsylvania—as early as 1919. Besides the novel notebooks which contain a great deal of color specific to the particular story, there are six large notebooks (East and West) devoted to authenticities of characters, incidents, places, objects, talk. They represent forty years of collecting and form a unique, and perhaps the most complete, repository of such material in the world. C. R. tried to explain his fascination for this research: "My father, grandfather, uncle, and great-uncles were preachers. Their fathers had been tradesmen, soldiers, country squires, blacksmiths, and farmers, and I think that in my passion for early American life and people I am a throwback to these."

But there was something more. Although critics tended to consider C. R. a traditionalist, he was really doing something no writer had done before, and that is recreating life as it was actually lived in earlier days. Fortunate enough to have come west when there were still people who knew and could talk about those times, he became a link between the old and the new. Not only his novels but his notebooks were a vital means of preserving American life. This was not the art of the documentary nor of the historical novelist (a term C. R. detested as applied to himself) who, he felt, too often put modern characters into an old-time setting. He seemed possessed of the intuitive ability of projecting himself into past people, time, and place. Several articles dealing with "that early American quality"[7] attest to his understanding not only of how people acted but of how their very thoughts ran.

The notebook excerpts in this chapter fall into two sections. The first is a selection of *characters* and samplings of early Western color. The second is devoted to scraps of *conversations*, phrases, and old-time words. The excerpts are chosen at random from the three dark-blue notebooks of Western material. They have been picked not for style or literary value (C. R. typed these notes from hasty and often ungrammatical jottings on a pad) but for their glimpse into the daily life and people of the old West. They are highly visual, often suggest something larger than themselves, and are "seeds" for characters, incidents, stories. The value of this type of notebook to C. R. was not only the authenticity of the material but its ability to stimulate him or start his imagination working.[8]

Character Authenticities

Edwards was 21 years old before he ever had a shoe on his foot - always wore boots. Today at 40-odd can count his shoes on his hand.

Likes to get down & talk to you on his toes - not squatting - one knee ahead of other. Does it in home. Wife says "You're not out in the corral."

Man lost his leg in an Indian fight but could ride as well as ever, the only difference was he had to mount horse from right side, Indian fashion.

Boy promised mother would always be kind to dumb animals & he was with 1 exception - he became the greatest buffalo killer on the plains.

He would pull a bogged down buffalo out & leave it grazing contentedly, and then kill fifty that day for his skinners to work on.

Hat always on side of his head. And his character the same.

Outlaw would go no farther when a rabbit crossed the road - lived to be 80 and killed 60 men.

Man 75 years old lost one of his teeth and complaining about it.

Pushes hot red burning coals of pipe down with horny fingers from time to time.

Very strong. Would place his back to wheel of a loaded wagon, take spokes in hands and lift it. No one else could.

Cowboys could sit down & cross legs under them at roundup, plate on lap. Girls couldn't.

Character Incidents

When drunk he would go home & when wife lit candle & came to door he would shoot it out of her hand. She was used to it but other women said what they would do if they were she to stand for that.

Crazy character - starts over desert carrying a can of water that was leaking out through a hole. Hardy tells him it is leaking. "I can't help it," he says & goes out and never seen again.

Two women, one daughter of Confederacy, one Northerner, sew and argue together. Latter cuts finger & tries to hide it. Other says, "Don't hide it from me. There's nothing I'd rather see than Yankee blood."

Character Looks - Men

A man of older days. Short with a full jaunty beard, not long & flowing but sticking forward in a thick, cocky manner for such a small man. Walked with a hand behind him and when he came to dramatic places, he put both behind him. Walked with jaunty dignity - his large nose exactly at the angle & parallel to the angle of his beard.

Very narrow tufts of eyebrows like bunch grass.

Plain man. Something about the soil and plain people about him . . . a face that might have been a longish round rock turned up in a potato field but the eyes observed you fearlessly & shrewdly.

His nose runs straight down into his mustache from his forehead, a long powerful keel to his face. It gave you the impression it must keep on running down through his bristling thick mustache & beard. . . .

Characters Good, Interesting

Five brothers. First, oldest got drinking & getting drunk. He quit, then second. There was always one drunk at a time.

Horse character. Pegleg who had pouch made in saddle for his stump, and wild ride, could do anything another rider could.

Cowboy who had lost 1 arm - yet expert rope thrower, cigarette roller and gun shooter. All strength went into that one arm.

Characters (Western)—Men

Russian Bill, clean cut features, spoke four languages, liked to talk about literature, art, etc., political exile, son of countess.

No one knew where he came from, his family, his beliefs. He was close-lipped, mysterious, unapproachable. He avoided every word that would give away any of his secrets, although various means were tried to draw it out. Other men talked of home etc - when it came his turn, he shot a glass & made some cryptic remark, "That's all you'll get." Wrote his name three different ways.

"He was six feet 3" on one side & only six feet one on the other"

Lucky man who is never hit by bullets. Instead they only free his ropes. Charmed life.

El Zorro. A legendary figure. Now a beggar in the square, now a drunkard in the saloon. Might be 3 brothers look alike. Appear at various places at same time.

Chap who now has old well in Glorieta country. His young wife grew sick. After several days he threw saddle on his horse & rode off into the mountains. She died a day later. They held her 4 days, as long as they could, buried her. Went out to look for him. . . . Found him in mountains nearly starved. He didn't care what happened to him. He couldn't stand seein' her die and didn't want to go back where she had lived.

Old doctor on frontier confesses to new doctor when latter is sick he is not real doctor - only gave castor oil, quinine, or whiskey.

Uncle Billy Jones near Magdalena - makes up things as he goes - bright, never get the best of him. Kills wild turkey on rocks & it falls down. T———saw it was shot through the neck. "That was fine shot!" Uncle Billy shook his head. "Something funny here. Somebody must have been foolin' with my sights. I aimed for his eye." Looked and saw no sights on his gun.

Weisel, mounted N.M. police - eyes so nearly closed you couldn't believe he saw you & yet you knew he did. Bulky with a red birth mark the shape of the state of Texas on his neck. When he told you anything, he just held one eye toward you. But at emphasis or climax, he turned both eyes & they were like double barrelled shotguns.

The only one of a bunch of men who had never killed a man - looked down on - called tenderfoot, etc.

Hells Fire Hogan - sun blistered face - eyes bright like those of a squirrel - could dance till midnight - not big but alive & active.

Was to marry girl but she died before he came back. "Her memory is my bride," he says & never married.

Rawhide Bill. Expert at rawhide in making quirts, laces, hobbles etc.

Cap Skillman. Kentuckian in Texas, big blond giant with flaxen beard and hair. Had been Indian fighter, mail contractor & scout for U.S. troops. One fault drank heavy & shot up town. . . . Next day he [would] apologize & pay for it all. But if anyone else attempted to do it, he would disarm and thrash them.

El Soltario, the hermit priest of Santa Fe trails. Hair long and black. Born in Isle of Capri. Thrown out of church. Had beads and books of priest. Administered to dying men on trail. Always had look in his eyes of living - from Bay of Naples & Mediterranean - here in desert land. Spoke on delights of solitude. Would never break bread inside house but remain at door and take what was given - never sleep on a colchon but in his blanket on ground or with sheep and goats.

Romero - sheepherder who got his start stealing 5,000 sheep when his boss was murdered & he became one of principal men in state.

Sulky McCabe - No better worker when he was all right which was most of the time. Then he would imagine some-one or the world mistreated him & would not say a word for days, finally draw his wages and leave for good. In a few weeks or month would show up as cheerfully as if nothing had happened. And work better than ever before. Once came home unexpectedly and found him dancing by self on buffalo hide - was chagrined and much kidded.

The Unreconciled Rebel. Officer in rebel army who claims he has not yet enlisted in army of reconciliation in 1878 and does not propose to. Teaches school. Asks children, "If Yankee storekeeper mixes a quantity of wooden nutmegs which cost him ¼ cent each with the real ones at 4¢ each, etc."

"The field of Buena Vista is 6½ miles from Saltillo. Two regiments of Yankee Volunteers ran away from the field of battle at the same time. If one was travelling—etc."

Solomon Luna who ran New Mexico - dominated county from his buggy. Got life termers out of jail & put them as sheep herders. No sheriff dare touch them but if they ran away every sheriff would look for them in N.M., Arizona & elsewhere. As a result Luna had loyal and hard [working] sheepherders.

John Smith, a kind of king with the Cheyenne tribe. "Sooner reign in hell than serve in heaven." Exacted tribute from Mexicans before letting them trade & poured pumpkin seed etc. to ground if they wouldn't. Had Indian wife. Thought much of his baby. Had killed many. Yet sat in lodge & sang hymns with white visitor until the dogs would howl.

When drunk he claimed his name someone else & would not recognize anyone calling him by his real name. Talked of other man [himself] as a separate individual. "He's a gentleman," etc.

Baptist preacher who kept a race horse. Could be seen every day out with his sulky giving him a bit of exercise. In races horse was too good for anyone else to drive & he drove him himself. Never bet, however.

MISCELLANEOUS INCIDENT

The Ghost Riders. Cattle Missing. Some claim they saw them driven off in herds, no one driving them & yet when they got close, stray after - would be turned in as soon as he tried to leave the herd & yet no one was there to see them. Follows. Going in a direction where is no water & tries to turn them back. Horse violently shies. Follows. Remembers that Billy the Kid & ——— claimed they knew water up here - found it when pursued. Sees cattle go to this place and drink. Comes back & rides up & find water & cattle there as he claimed, but some believe was a lead steer or cow that knew the water and led the way. Much talk about it. Half believed, half disbelieved.

OBSTRUCTION SUSPENSE

Girl hears who shall kill whom. Indians threatened attack. All go to P.O. Put all children to bed. Mrs. C. lying on floor at foot of bed hears men in next room decide what to do in case savages were getting best of them. Planned who was to kill who of them, one woman & children. Heard friend of hers agree to kill her. She knows how Apaches hang babes on meat hooks & other indescribable cruelties.[9]

Witness at Killing. Boy only one who saw Clay Allison kill Chunk at dinner table in Cimarron. Chunk's head fell forward in soup plate. Clay finished his dinner. Other person at table pale. Can't eat. He disappears shortly afterward & no arrest or trial could be held because there was no witness. The danger such a boy witness would find himself in.

Ranch-mountains oldtime life

Got a black hat as a gift. Wouldn't wear a black hat. Wife used it as an egg basket.

Hardy says he stole calves, mavericked them, but he never killed a cow for its calf. He came on some where cowboy had taken baling wire and wrapped it around cow's mouth and then twisted it tight with stick. Cow smothered. Then took it off and cow had no marks on her. Looked like she came to a natural death.

[Texans] named the girls Billy, Willy, Jimmy, Johnnie, Danny, Benny etc. and the boys got just brands. J. L., C. C., G. B., C. D. etc. Ask any one of them what their name really is and they look at you in a surprised way and say, "CD" or. . . .

Misc. objects - Old Time

Presents in 1876 - cake basket, silver castor, tea knives
Sickle & Sheaf (newspaper) Enterprise
Silver watch, stem winder, 1880
Barometer carried on the stage by passenger all the way to Santa Fe
Notched penholder
Stagger knife (Schultz 69–70 Ko.)
The Blue-back speller & the dog-wood switch (Texas education)
Ray's Arithmetic
Moss Agate Jewelry   Wheeler & Wilson's Sewing Machines

Kansas wagons Hines Buggies Bain or Mitchell Wagons - N.M.

MISC. DOINGS, ACTS - Old Time

Sound of taking snuff

"What you leave on your plate is a sacrifice to Satan" (said to children who did not finish plate)

Click of flint & steel lighting pipe - 1848

Play backgammon 1848 in Indian village, on sunny banks, etc.

"Deuce ace," "double sixes." Light fire brighter to play by it. Indians watch, call players foolish.

Even the young ladies of wealthier people would watch from a secluded place when wagon trains went through. Could hear cracking of whips. Everyone was out.

Squatting down on ground making brands with forefinger in sand, asking whose brands this and that was he had seen on a cow or horse.

Business, Professions, Work in Old Days

Those in pioneer towns who had a living gathering & selling buffalo chips, part of which were cow chips. They would stack them up in large piles like haystacks and Clark says he can almost smell the perfume when the sun would shine on them after a rainy spell. Once such a pile caught afire from spontaneous combustion.

Quite common to see woman open a tailor shop in a tent. But instead of making new suits, her work was usually patching old clothes, knitting yarn muffs, mufflers etc.

Buffalo skinners. Some buffalo hunters each had two. Some Mexican, some white. British.

American consul at Santa Fe, 1824.

Young teamster who can write finds old timer who knows the trails. Gets latter to draw it in the sand. Other copies on paper. Makes maps & guides & approx. mileage & sells to emigrants on trail.

Cattle - Authenticities

"Cattle are almost as unreasonable as people."

Goodnight sold his cattle at Ft. Sumner for 8¢ a pd between 1866–70.

In old days nearly everyone killed other brands for own beef. K. tells me the story of L. bringing 2 beeves 12 hours late for barbecue and has to butcher in pitch dark which is done expertly - draw your own conclusions.

"Legitimate stealing" & illegitimate stealing.

Put wet blanket on calf's side and run hot iron over it. Will make a mark to look like it is branded. Sometimes even hair will drop out. . . . Later the brand disappears and can make their own brand.

TALK HUMAN OLDTIME

"Why them people spend all they have for to eat & never have a drop of whiskey in the house!"

"I got the start of the devil that time. The devil has always been against me and sometimes the Lord helps him."

Woman combing B———'s red hair.
"I'm feared they'll get your hair" meaning savages.
"If they do," joked B———, "it'll sure make them a bright light on a dark night."

Hated snow & when 4 feet tall: "I wish it was gunpowder. I'd get rid of it mighty quick. I'd touch it off and jump down the well."

"I'm afraid to sit on that chair. It might turn loose on me." He sits on the floor.

"She's my sister's kid. She's just about as low as that woman." Means that tall, pointing to preacher's short wife.

When food was praised at the table.
"Yes, it's good, what there is of it; and there's enough of it, such as it is. . . ."

"Tell me, doctor, what chance have I to live?"
"One chance in ten thousand."
"Begorrah I'll take that chance." (Is satisfied & got well)

"Let him have it - if it's a halter" (to hang himself)

"I wouldn't touch her chops" (kiss her)

"Some sense in a drum & fife, but these pianos and other truck I can't stand."

"Road goes smack to———, they say. I ain't never tried it."

"We wasn't much better'n Indians except we took an interest in religion and politics."

"I was used courteously."

"I want to live 1,000 years after everybody else except———."
"What do you want to keep him for?"
"To make whiskey for me."

"Thou, hussy!"

"Have to look through a collar the rest of his life" (getting married)

Hardy tells about father who couldn't stand son home from college with hair parted in the middle. Mother urges him to let him go. "Well, I will this time, but if he squats to pee, I'll lam him."

"I told her to go to hell (his sister). And I never did like her after that."

"You always want to shoot them in the right eye because that disturbs their aim."

"Where's your long-handled shovel?" Hardy asks when employer wants him to dig ditch. He meant long enough to reach from saddle.

"Knife slipped" when cutting ear marks on someone else's calf.

"Hair raise up and knock your hat off."

"I ought to know him. I run him down once with a horse."

"So dry you can't spit."

"Sure can hear the grass grow" (nice weather)

"Blow up at your house last night?"
"No, it stopped blowin about three and started to push."

"So gaunt he looked like he hadn't a gut in him."

"Not a dust of flour in the house."

"A mile and six bits" (1 3/4 miles)

"It came a flood"

"I would give more but my hand lacks the means"

Not first rate gentleman

TALK SAYINGS BELIEFS

"Sleep like a mouse in a mill," cosy place after a good meal.

Let every tub stand on its own bottom.

A green Christmas means a full graveyard.

Cat washing its face, company is coming. Last stroke of cat shows direction coming from.

RIGHT HAND ITCHES, meet a stranger - left hand, meet money.

WHERE THE WOLF HAS LAID, find his hair.

MUCH SQUEAL and less wool said the deil as he sheared his hogs.

WASH in May snow water to take freckles away.

TOUCH EVERY HITCHING POST for first mile to change luck.

THE WIFE, THE HOUSE and the gun may be shown but not lent.

CUT A CHILD'S FINGERNAILS before a year old and will grow up light fingered.

LITTLE GIRL blows dandelion & counts remaining seeds - times she will be whipped.

TALK STORIES RIDDLES

Down yonder stands a little house
In that house is a little cup
In that cup is a little sup
You can't get at that little sup
Without breaking the little cup — An egg

A girl in a red petticoat
A stick in her hand and a stone in her throat — A cherry

Thirty two white cows standing in a stall
Up comes a red bull and licks over all — Teeth & tongue

Talk, Speech, Writing, Oratory, Old Style

"Fear was a stranger to him."
"I want them off God's footstool" (telling them to leave town)
"A man deprived of life"
"He was poor and did not enjoy the luxury of carrying his his shoes to town" (had no shoes)

Toast for laying Cornerstone: "The public places in this street, a hotel, a theater, 2 churches and a burying ground. May we live in temperance in the first, enjoy amusements in the second, be duly prepared in the third for that which awaits us in the last."

His good nature gained complete ascendance over his anger.

Add to the sagacity of the lion, the cunning of the fox.
"The Exodus of the Eastern States"
"A speaking aristocracy in the face of a silent democracy"
(1790?)
I am sensible of
who passed for a man of parts
I lived with him a twelve-month

Talk - Rounds, Sayings

"Fire on the mountain
Run, boys, run."

"Gray eye, greedy gut
Eat the whole world up"

New Moon, true moon, fair & free
May I see my true love before you leave me

When the dogwood is white
The fish start to bite

Music, Dancing, etc. Call

Chase that rabbit, Chase that squirrel.
Chase that pretty girl clean around the world.

Swing him if you love him
And cheat him if you don't.

Pa Dutch Sayings & Sayings (from notebook kept for The Free Man)

Jolly single, sad engaged

It's not my fault bullfrogs have no tails

If it rains soup, he has no dish

If she will, she will, but she won't

You get wet only to the skin

Nowadays rabbits chase dogs (woman after a man)

Born in a thunderstorm, to be killed by lightning

If you've got to swallow a toad, it's best not to look too long.

A good grunt is half the job done

You can get used to everything, even hanging, if you hang long enough.

He has his faults on his back where he can't see them

He can lick his fingers to his elbow (thank his lucky stars)

Red hair, devil in it

At night every cow is black

If you hadn't climbed up, you wouldn't have fallen

When children are little, you have them in your lap, when grown up in your heart (grandmother)

Every peddler praises his pack

The cock closes his eyes when he crows. He knows it by heart.

First love never rusts.

He looks too deep in the bottle

Nothing is still nothing

Girls with fat cheeks have hearts of stone

Grey hairs don't weigh heavier than the rest

The rat with the shortest tail gets into the hole the soonest

Empty ears of wheat stand upright - full ears droop a little

The fiddle makes the feast

MISCELLANEOUS SAYINGS OLD-TIME, COUNTRY, SOUTHERN

A woman's name should be heard twice in public. Once when she marries & once when she dies.

A word and a blow and the blow first (hasty temper)

Bachelor's wives & old maid's children make the best people in the world

Break open a hot biscuit. If you cut it with a knife, you pierce Christ's side.

Christmas comes but once a year but when it comes I'll have my share.

A person will not be drowned that's born to be hanged (after rescue from water).

Come day, go day, God sends Sunday

He don't know where his behind hangs (said of proud person)

He died from shortness of breath

I'd know him if I saw his hide in the tanyard

C. R. at his daughter's Washington Square, New York, apartment. Photograph by Elliot Erwitt, 1949.

Above left, C. R. at 1617 Las Lomas Road, Albuquerque, New Mexico, 1950.

Below left, C. R. and his brother Fred, at 1421 Las Lomas Road, Albuquerque, 1952.

Above right, C. R., wife, and daughter, Pennsylvania, early 1950s.

C. R. and daughter, Rehoboth Beach, Maryland, 1953.

C. R. at his desk in the diningroom of 11 Maple Street, Pine Grove, Pennsylvania, 1962.

C. R. and wife at 11 Maple Street,
Pine Grove, early 1960.

C. R., wife and daughter at Pine Tree Farm, middle 1920s.

381

Obstruction Must Oppose Hero Driving For Their Fulfillment

Early Marriage. Notice how each trouble opposed Nancy Belle from their purpose which was to get married. Warning of extreme danger in going — no protection except a boy — first cabin burned by savages — sand storm, loss of horses & absence of boy — kept on even to cows.

Long Engagement Notice how trouble in the earlier version did not oppose Joanna in their purpose which was to consummate engagement in marriage — father's cattle dying from drouth (only Yancey's cattle dying would oppose marriage) — enemy leaves country (only Yancey leaving would postpone marriage) — mother dying from child birth (only if mother asked her to stay at home & raise Bennie would keep Yancey from marrying her).

OK

A sample page in C. R.'s handwriting from Black Notebook II.

9

A New American Style

In the summer of 1940, with *The Trees* just published and a new novel refusing to develop,[1] C. R.'s journal proposes, "Let me put words together in a new form." Some six weeks later, struggling for a break-through, he is again searching for

> A New Way to Write
>
> That is what I need. To let myself go & pour my feelings out - not like a Llewelyn or another but myself. God give me a new style, not artificial, but true. Life & the world are multi-fashioned. There must be many new ways to think, feel & speak. . . .

When these entries were made, C. R. *had* found a new language. But they serve to illuminate the close connection that style has with story. If he could just find a new style—or tone or voice—his journal suggests, then the novel would almost write itself. The flow of words and the line of the story were inextricably mixed.

"Story value" would be one of the more important elements of style for him. Also fundamental were compression, condensation, beauty, cadence and rhythm, and especially the cadences of common speech. Style was indissolubly linked with the language itself, the common vernacular used during the early days of which he wrote. Not only old-time words were involved, but the very thinking process of those early people. It was a subtle and extremely complex blend.

The entire period spent writing *The Trees* was a struggle to reshape his style. Already with *The Sea of Grass* he felt he had come to an impasse. He was dissatisfied with his "ponderous" way of writing. It not only exacted a "terrific strain," but seemed artificial to him.

> Sometimes I think my failure in writing, my inability to get things done except with terrific strain, is my late style. It is not I. I must get myself into a tremendous pressure to do it. . . .
>
> If all this be true it is possible that a short sentence, meaty, natural style may remedy it - let the mind function as my simple mind was intended, which is not the ponderous artificial top of the voice writing I affect.
>
> Even if my trouble is a lack of crowding thoughts, facts, meat in my mind - that is a lack of energy to float them - this natural short sentence style may help to correct it by coaxing those thoughts out of the shadows where, having been observed, they lie just off the tongue & pen. . . .
>
> Suddenly I see something. I have contended that the mind does not think in short sentences but in endless, involved ones. This is true. I see for the first time a reason for short sentences. They start from a new angle every few words, and this refreshes the mind. That refreshment is the energy that helps give vitality, energy to the reader's reading of the written word - hence to the writer. . . .
>
> A short sentence style constantly renewing the reader's energy from scores of different points is a rich style. It is like life itself ever drawing an endless variety & richness of things & stimuli from her teeming bag of non-alikes.[2]

The earlier romantic line he revolted against had qualities which, in themselves, were very closely associated with their subject matter. The sentences are long (the second sentence of

"Smoke Over the Prairie" runs to eleven lines) with rhythms that slowly wind back into the past for the nostalgia he wished to convey. In his self-criticisms, scathing as they are, C. R. seems to have forgotten the reason for creating what resembled a ballad-like type of writing: to give the essence of the event rather than the factual telling of it. But the energy expended in compressing and condensing to achieve this effect, as the 1937 journal entry complained, was tremendous.

It was partly as much to save himself as to enter into closer contact with spoken rhythms and talk that C. R. consciously pared his style. Yet he could never move away from the principles of condensation and compression; he simply used different methods to achieve them. He had always been fond not only of the early Anglo-Saxon ballads but of old verses, riddles, epitaphs, songs,[3] all of which suggested far more than their content. He also had a strong feel for the mythic and the way in which myth compresses emotion and experience. The opening sentence of *The Trees* has this mythic quality, rendered in a simple, almost colloquial rhythm: "They moved along in the bobbing, springy gait of a family who followed the woods as some families follow the sea."

Alliteration, repetition, and a rhythm that imitates the "bobbing, springy gait" characterize this sentence. The opening two pages of *The Trees* were the blueprint to which he returned again and again while writing the novel. It is worth noting that the opening sentence also has story movement; the words carry the reader into the work, and so explain what C. R. meant by "story value" being a necessary part of style. In 1938, struggling with the attempt to get the characters' thoughts into old-time language, he warned himself:

> YOU ARE WRITING THIS WRONG. IT WON'T DO
> YOU ARE TOO WORDY AND DIALECT-strained. . . . You must be DIRECT (compressed interest, not a word overlong, HIDDEN

> PLOT INTEREST) and simple beauty. . . . You try to get the feeling with words. What you need is STORY VALUE.[4]

Following this is a list of OTHER PRINCIPLES that forms a guide to showing the characters' thoughts:

> 1. Their natural viewpoint of enthusiasm for rude things "His three legged stools were steady any place you would set them. And still Worth hadn't enough. No such thing. He would work till black in the face splitting clapboards for a loft."
>
> 2. Sayward's rude fresh woman's thinking "A mortal person might put on a dress that was damp and the body would dry it, but Jary would never warm her bed again." THEIR MATTER OF FACT ACCEPTANCE and thoughts of TERRIFIC and TERRIBLE . . . and yet plain things of life birth, death, scalping. . . .
>
> . . . .
>
> 5. IMPERSONATING THE ELEMENTAL. Where was Death. Not until the sun was up would the dark wholly go away. The winter was sweet tempered.
>
> 6. SWEETEN drab thoughts and description with beauty. "He had one once with the fairest hair they ever seed." "A belly sweet and purring with hot mush made him sleepy."

On the following page:

> CONDENSE EVERY thing that is said into picturesque brevity like, "He come here with nothing but what he had on his back." Things were said that COULD BE REPEATED OVER AND OVER. The test is - IS IT A COMMON PHRASE?

By the next year he was still struggling with the style of *The Trees*. A thick folder with the outlines of the Ohio trilogy contains a sheet of blue paper folded in half with the following warning to himself:

KEEP THIS STANDING UP AGAINST BOOKS

I read MacKinlay Kantor's story of Missouri tonight, went back to chapter seven of my Trees and found it read the same terrible way. I picked up Lamb in His Bosom but that stood real and convincing as ever. That was the real thing. Kantor and mine were false.

My first chapter - I read only the first two pages - was more myself. It had integrity, reality. I must go back to that.

What Kantor and I Both Do

We go out of our way to use expressions of the time. Say a thing in the fewest possible words if there isn't a coloquial expression or word on the page. We think we do this to give it color and make it real. But the real reason is we don't feel those people and that life strongly enough so we use these expressions to make it convincing to ourselves. Say it direct, simple.

We say "Oh" and I say "Yes" and "no" where there is no emotion, just for color. Cut all these out.

What we try to do is give our own plot and action in native words to make it real. The plot and action must first be native, how they would tell it in Lamb in His Bosom, not straight forward, not for plot and suspense effect ever, but human, woman things, practical, how they looked at a thing because of the work it made, their tender woman's heart. Nothing but native action, talk.[5]

In Black Notebook I there is an undated page captioned "New American Style Possible." The idea came to C. R. "after reading The Devil and Daniel Webster that brings up America & many of its characters in one short story."

> What came to me to do was more than this - to stuff a great deal of early American I had read in Pa, Ohio or N.M. into one novel or story, just a stroke here & stroke there that would crowd a great deal into a little space as Donn Byrne did of the Irish or Benet in his Introduction to John Brown's Body - that would give the feel of Early America, not in beautiful language but the rough richness of those days - a rugged American speech. . . .

Samplings of this speech appear in the preceding and following chapters. Since "The Devil and Daniel Webster" was published in 1937, that would make it one more contributing factor toward the language of *The Trees*. But still another influence on his style, or more particularly on his rhythms, came from far earlier, and that was his habit of reading aloud to my mother and me for so many years. C. R. had, in turn, listened to his mother and aunt tell stories of their families. The oral tradition was thus strong in my father, handed down from mother to son. In hearing himself read aloud, he not only became conscious of story faults but of rhythm and cadence, of whether phrases "sounded right." Reading brought the category of *drama* close to that of *story*. Not only did each line have to advance the theme action, it carried within it that forward thrust which is part rhythm, part meaning. It is the ancient art of the scōp, the ballad singer or story teller, who holds his audience partly by the music of his voice.

In analyzing C. R.'s style, one notices that the narrative moves in the teller's rather than the writer's rhythm. The cadences change as the momentum of suspense increases. Here and there are long paragraphs, set up with counter rhythms, whose sounds echo the emotions the words convey. If the later novels appear to have a more simple prose, this is deceptive. *A Country of Strangers*, ending with a ballad C. R. wrote (following the Anglo-Saxon lament "The Wanderer"), is the closest of his books to the told story. The quotation from "Fates of Men,"

"Exeter Book," which prefaces the novel, has a quality similar to the prose, a directness combined with the mythic and mysterious element which early ballads possess. This elegiac quality is strongest in the two Indian novels, in *The Waters of Kronos,* and to a lesser extent in *Always Young and Fair*.

In a letter he once wrote to me (November 1938), C. R. advised, "I would get a book out of the library of the old English Ballads and study their phrasing for simplicity. They say things so directly and simply . . . powerfully because of their so called primitive or animal material, such as murder, death, unrequited love, jealousy, etc. You especially need this simple, direct phrasing. Cultivate it. I need it myself."

In the Maroon Notebook II are a number of examples of the "simple style" toward which C. R. was working. They are prefaced by a brief injunction:

> There should be no effort or effect except to say the facts simply. The facts should be strong and there should be an endless amount of things to say. Then write them simply one after another. Crudeness is better than sweetness and perfection. Short meaty sentences.

simple style examples

> "This is the barn," Adam Etzweiler said drawing a place on the ground. "This here's the house."

> A NATURAL SIMPLE STYLE TO ME WITH STRONG FEELING

> It came to me in White Deer Valley when Strong Feelings Came Welling Up.

> "Oh, such things as I know good of life. The moon, the yellow quarter moon, pouring down over White Deer Valley, over the stone church, over the sheds etc."

In deckertown. "You must know grass to live here. Grass along the street. Grass as well as houses. And unpainted houses. Black houses, but friendly inside."

On penny hill. "I could see myself going along here as a boy thirty years before, on the road that was almost unchanged. The roadside was grown up with weeds. No one had picked the black cherries. They hung thick on the trees. The road was so narrow I couldn't remember how two buggies could pass. So secluded it was that I could feel myself there as a boy in the late afternoon and dusk, trudging along, with the same shadows and cool layers of air coming in from the valley. The strangest feeling came over me. It was as if I could see the ghost of myself coming along, feel him. I could almost talk to him. My hair nearly stood on end."[6]

At the old parsonage. "Mother, do you remember how the lightning struck in the house while you and I were there alone? You had been down in the diningroom and when the storm came I called down the stairs to come up with me in the room Grandad always slept in and prayed in when he came. And father do you remember when I would not sing, Remember Yet, in the cemetery. Here we lived. Here we worked the pump handle and walked through that gate to feed Harry and carry him water. The same grove and house and orchard and stable and mountains walling all around. But where are you?"

The value of a simple style comes out in another self-deprecating entry in his journal:

The Hardest and Most Desirable and Effective Thing

To write simply

Going over my old journals tonight, March 3, 1938, I am stunned by my utter incompetence to have kept a journal. Liv-

> ing in the most interesting of backwoods valleys, with human and earthy drama, with woods and country life, going on all around me, I filled fat journals with drivel, writing like a sixteen year old theological student, giving my own highly spun and highly dull thoughts and observations, being opinionated, stiff, unnatural, making a great deal out of nothing. . . .[7]
>
> A little that is good came through. All of this is simply told, and the best of it what the natives thought, said, looked like or did. Even the simplest subject, when I noted the facts in a few honest words, had an interest and dignity. The people themselves were always literature. It was I who didn't know literature when I saw it and who didn't know how to write it in anything but drivel. . . .
>
> . . . I had always thought that to say things simply without exaggeration, sweetening or repetition should be easy - to write dazzling outbursts hard. Now I know the very reverse is true.

If C. R.'s journals continually cry out for "starker, truer writing" (November 1937), they also call for a way to start the language flowing. This was not so much tensing the mind as loosening it, and a good deal of his reading had this particular aim. Sometimes he referred to it as priming. From his journal of January 6, 1939:

> I read Growth of the Soil for a time to prime me. To read my own books would be best, for then there would be no chance of thinking or writing like another, not even being indebted to him for the reading. But I can't do that like the author of OF HUMAN BONDAGE. I am too disgusted with my own work. There are too many things I want to change. It won't do. The chief thing about reading GROWTH OF THE SOIL or KRISTIN LAVRANSDATTER is that the flow of words of the writer is in a feeble way transmitted to me, and this is the most precious thing I get, a kind of impetuous wordiness. My own flow of

> words is so slow that it just about stirs me to laborious word setting down.

Reading Virginia Woolf had a different effect on him. It is curious that he devotes more space to her in his journals than to favorites like Willa Cather or W. H. Hudson. From an entry of November 27, 1937:

> A LESSON FROM VIRGINIA WOOLF
>
> I started to read her THE YEARS tonight. The first page delighted me, the short sentences, the ease and interest and color. Here is someone that has something, like Cather, I said. But as I went on she became excessively dreary, page after page, chapter after chapter about nothing and meaning nothing. She is like one of those women who talk on and on and never say anything. Of course they tell what they saw and did and what they say is true enough and a whole cross section of facts and people and life, but it doesn't get anywhere. You have the feeling that you have been drugged and lived through all this and it is like living in a fog or a dream. The people are real people moving there you know but you don't feel them.
>
> But this wasn't the lesson. The lesson was that she picks up a pen and writes on and on and why in heaven's name can't I. Perhaps if I read her a bit and then sit to the typewriter I can write on and on and my people may be in a fog but what does it matter. In so many weeks I will have five hundred pages and there is a novel and it might even sell.
>
> Her chief merit, that I have found, is that she doesn't drip or strain as I do. . . . there is something in her going on and on. I should prime myself with her and write on and on and on.

Two days later:

I AM LEARNING FROM MRS. WOOLF

> She still does not get anywhere, but I am liking to read her. She says things with less waste than any writer I know. She is good for me. She does not mind beginning three sentences in a row with "he" or "she." She is natural. Above all she is cool, sane, so sane she is hard. The woman who sits and hears you and nods a few words to you and goes on to someone else and that is all she is affected, but what she says is shrewd and to the point. She does me good, but I want to say more, feel more, think more than she.
>
> Picking up my SMOKE OVER THE PRAIRIE and SEA OF GRASS, I am surprised to find the latter seems far the better. Too many "ands" and adjectives and straining here and plot there and hurdling, I should say, rapping a stick along the palings of plot and time exigencies. I see where I should have had conversation here and a word there and more solid stuff there. In EARLY MARRIAGE it seemed nothing until she started to dress in the early morning. Then it was very good and real for pages. The violent plot and suspense things don't belong, jangle out of tune, break the mood. The suspense should be underneath. Pearce and others called the story "restrained." It was not nearly restrained enough. MY FORTE IS COLOR, FEELING, SOUND, MOVEMENT.

On April 10, 1954:

> VIRGINIA WOOLF'S INTENSE passion for writing. This is the consuming interest of her book to me. [A Writer's Diary.] I am infected by her love and energy for writing and return to my pages with renewed life and freshness.

Although C. R. doesn't seem to care particularly for Woolf as a novelist,[8] certain similarities of taste might have attracted him to her writing. Things Greek and Shakespearean were her two passions; they were my father's also. He liked Shakespeare for his vitality, his commonness; the Greeks for their powerful themes, their stoicism, their tragic sense. He knew many of Shakespeare's sonnets by heart, although memorizing was not easy for him. In his anthology of world poetry, the Greeks are the most frequently marked.

C. R.'s special fondness for two lines from Shakespeare's "Sonnet 76" might be mentioned: "Why write I still all one, ever the same . . . That every word doth almost tell my name." Certainly, C. R. was conscious that his own writing sounded like no one else's. In a less conscious manner, he might have felt the closeness of the relationship between a writer's style and the writer himself. Style *is* the man, to bend the meaning of the phrase. And since style, as C. R. saw it, is composed of so many things (including the very tempo at which the writer's mind functions), it becomes a means of expressing the self. Many readers have commented on the integrity of my father's work, by which I think they mean the integrity of the man. As speech tends to characterize the speaker, so does the written word. Modern writers tend to hide themselves behind intellectualization (C. R.'s notebooks had many complaints against such). The refreshing quality about C. R.'s style is that he is so much in the open.

10

A Rude Thesaurus

C. R.'s search for a new American style would not have been possible without his obsession with words: Early American and dialect words; words that the common people, past and present, used in conversation; words which evoke a mood; words which describe the way a person spoke, acted, thought. "Get a page of words that will describe each character," he told me when I began the notebook for my first novel. "Adjectives, nouns, verbs—then when you want to describe how your character says or does something, you have it right there."

C. R. not only did this himself in his novel notebooks, but kept three thick $5\frac{1}{2} \times 8\frac{1}{2}$ notebooks with words under every possible category—words of Beauty, Emotion, Strength. Words expressing Suspense, Hidden Meaning, Significance. Violent, Harsh, Power Words, particularly western or old-time expressions. Words of Wildness, of Motion (to enrich the image). As early as 1933 he had written the president of the University of Arizona offering an "original course in modern fiction writing" with three book manuscripts to be used, the third of them "an original, classified vocabulary of writer's words." A first draft of this letter describes it as

> a new and extensive vocabulary. . . . classified into various moods and effects, a volume for which a great need has arisen in the last few years. The new effective use of words by modern writers has gone so far beyond thesauruses as to make them in a great measure obsolete. They contain most of the words, but not in new suggestive associations.

The need was no doubt a personal rather than a general one; C. R. was trying to sell an idea, and even in later years considered the possibility of working his thesauruses into shape for publication. Together with his intuitive sense there was a strong urge for organizing ideas, for trying to codify aspects of writing into law.

A note in his journal some twenty-odd years later touches the same theme: "What we need in a thesaurus is a wider range of associated words. Often I can't get near the real meaning I want but such a list would refresh the memory. Also words of all possible facets of thought connected with the word in question would be valuable for suggestion" (September 17, 1956).

Finding words that express character or mood is only one aspect of C. R.'s search. The story element, so important to him in regard to style, surfaces here in listings of words which convey aspects of narration such as suspense, action, movement, trouble, and so on. Latent or suggestive meanings are important here. When he was at work on *The Waters of Kronos* he wrote a critic friend asking for phrases which "could be taken on several levels, one of them of deeper implications."

Of greatest importance to his search for a "new American style" is his compilation of old-time words, expressions, and names of objects, listings which overflow into his east-west notebooks and the work sheets for his novels. No prior collection existed. Not quaint or antiquated expressions, they simply record the living speech of earlier days.

A student, Mrs. Mary Thurber, doing her master's thesis on C. R., wrote him:

> One of your greatest achievements, it seems to me, is the way you have captured the sound of the Early American speech and set it down on paper. You have written that you talked, first hand, to these pioneers in the Southwest. Did you follow the same procedure in the East, or did you have to rely more on written records?

My father replied:

> I spent so much time with oldtimer friends that their speech became quite familiar to me. Later when starting on the Ohio-Pennsylvania pioneers, I had something to draw on in my own experience. Pennsylvanians in some of the secluded mountain valleys still used a great many pioneer words. I had known them as a boy and young man. Of course, I didn't know nearly enough of them for a novel and spent a great deal of time making up a private, handwritten thesaurus of old-time speech found in manuscripts and authentic books of the period. It wasn't necessary to refer to it much of the time, but there if and when I needed it. I still have it, could not replace it, know no other like it, and should hate to lose this by-product of all the days and hours I've spent digging into old records. This and not my writing has been the most pleasant thing I've done, and I'm seldom happier than with old books around me, one in my hands and their peculiar smell in my nostrils.

The specific search for words of early life seems to parallel the beginnings of the trilogy. In August of 1937 his journal noted that he had "been making notes of common people's old time speech words." On Christmas day of that year, he "wrote pages of farm and forest life words and doings" in his note-books. The next year, in a letter to H. L. Mencken, he confessed to having "managed to gather a thousand or two of these oldtime Pennsylvania words and expressions. Some are dated. Some are not." He goes on to explain some of the problems in gathering living speech:

> . . . Living speech is easy enough to get today and was easy enough to get when I did things of the early West. Old men and women who had lived through those days were still alive to talk to. Of course, nobody who lived in the times I am writing about now is among the living. And, as you know as well

as I, most of the writers and editors of early America refined, "improved" and otherwise suppressed the rough, vigorous and very living speech of the people when they translated it into their formal manner of saying things for pen and print.

What I've been able to find out about early common speech I've had to get from two sources: one, the older generation of present day mountain people still living in segregated districts of Pennsylvania, the early dates of many of whose expressions can only be guessed at; the other, books, papers and manuscripts at the Pennsylvania Library, the Rare Book Room at Washington and private sources. Half of this material is accurately dated but. . . . Only the occasional author of a book quotes the rough spoken language. And only occasionally the manuscript writer forgets himself and lapses into the language he probably used himself when he spoke to the common people, perhaps to his own family.

To Dr. Bakeless, who had written C. R. asking him for his sources, C. R. replied:

In regard to the speech of early America, I wish I might be able to refer you to a list of sources. . . . Unfortunately I don't have any such list. My great aunt used many of the words. Her father, a country squire, wrote "a hunting" in his docket. In White Deer Valley and Clarks Valley I knew old timers who always said mind for remember and hireling for hired man. No contumely was intended. This ear has helped me separate the local and inventive from what I picked up in research and in going through what compilations I could find. . . .

I wish I could be of more help. I've made a rude, handwritten kind of thesaurus for my own use and refreshment of memory but it would be unintelligible to anyone else. Some day I may type it off and offer it for publication but I'll have to find a great deal more time than I have at present.

(June 1951)

There is an art to collecting early American words and phrases. If language represents a series of pictures, certain words, such as ribpole, bushnipple, gadd, butt, and whaup carry a vivid impression, whether or not one understands their meaning.[1] In one of C. R.'s notebooks was tucked a separate sheet with the following words and phrases:

> An old cocked hat with a feather in it
> The buckskin britches squeaked when he walked
> Racoon caps
> One had tied a cowtail on behind him and leather cap of horns over head and ran around like an Indian
> Flannel leggins
> Shoe with brass buckle for occasion
> Some men barefoot
> Coarse tow trousers almost like made of woven hickory bark
> Hickory bark for suspenders
> Leather bark
> Half silk and calico

It was not only colorful words which C. R. searched for but simple colloquialisms, such as "potatoes burn *on* me" or "like as not" or "down the road apiece."[2] For the Ohio trilogy he drew up pages of such words and expressions, some of them excerpted below:

Draw water Draw bucket
A bed set off the floor
Ellen yard (yardstick)
A paper of pins
Milk white sheets
Milk basin Oddments
Jimcracks Nicknacks
Post bed Cord bed
Pot stick Poking stick
Spider Trammel Piggin
To rench (rinse)

Bang up First rate
On the gaining side (recover)
All of (7) feet Set store by
No end to Up to Snuff
Fair to middlin' All fired
Something fancy Simon pure
Euchered out of Great shakes
Could catch a weasel asleep
Big gun Blue stocking
To pickaback Half a doze
Vomix To gape

Black churry brandy   A skinful (drunk)
Spoon victuals   Wash down
Braid the eggs (beat)
Sugar tit (for baby)
Swill   Pot licker
Light cake   Minced pies
Put you in mind of
Come in for (inherit)
Put a good face on   Gumption
Gander of   Dandle
Give her the mitten   Buss
Come about (happen)
Bound to   Buck up to
To rally (tense)
To arsle   Throw out a feeler
Turn up sheep's eyes
Mopy   Shifless   Out of heart
Bridesman   Cat gut scraper
Feel for   Hanker after
Bread basket   Crop   Craw
Gizzard   Horse bone (neck)
Scut (tailpiece)   Breech
Filled out plump and nice
Hunkers
Gimber jawed
Nothing for it (against)

Pioneer Vernacular Expressions for the trilogy notebooks were grouped under alphabetically arranged headings such as Clever, Superior or Important People; Love, Lady, Marriage; Human Parts & Descriptions; Like, Similes; Movement: Life & Fighting; Smell, Taste; Strong, Violent, Angry; Unpleasant.[3]

But C. R.'s most unusual and practical use of word lists were those he assembled for his novel notebooks. They became for him a means of developing character, for *expressing* that character through words which precisely defined the way a person moved, acted, thought, spoke. Those for Sayward of *The Awakening Land* fill several pages. In the gray cloth-bound thesaurus:

(nouns)	(verbs)	(adjectives)	
Coldblooded-ness	Could take it	Calm	Searching
	Hush	Cool-headed	Strong
Dead calm	Quell	Unruffled	Grim
Even temper	Lay	Practical	Stern
Tolerance	Forbear	Matter-of-fact	Brief
Patience	Allay	Impassive	Cruel
Peace of mind	Smooth	Hard headed	Harsh
Presence of mind	Could stand it	Like she was	Bitter
	Sober down	Steady	Without winking
Fortitude	Could endure	Mild Meek	Severe
Self control	Stand still - firm	Temperate	Hard shell

(nouns)	(verbs)	(adjectives)	
Self centered	Stand fast	Easy	Obdurate
Endurance	Stomach it	Tame	Even tempered
	Let well enough alone	Peaceable	Patient
	Master her feelings	Sober	Composed
	Compose herself	Moderate	Enduring
	Take it easy	Smooth	Level headed
	Live & let live	Restful	Placid
	Bear it	Immovable	Cool as cucumber
	Put up with	Unmoved	Long suffering
	Submit with good grace	Undisturbed	Untroubled
		At repose	
		Repose	
		Stolid	

From a separate sheet:

Sayward — Strong, Vigor

(nouns)	(verbs)	(adjectives)	Raw Rude
Backwoods	Brace	Firm	Simple
Clay	Breast the tide	Fixed	Unlearned
Soil	Buttress about	Lusty	Uncombed
Earth	Bear hunt	Elemental	Untutored
Land	Break a pack	Burly	Unmincing
Plowman	Endure	Calm	Backwoods
Railsplitter	Face	Collected	Mountainous
Bare legs	Forge	Broad shouldered	Pungent
Unbleached sheets	Go against current	Anchored	Sharp Tart
Buttress	Ride the storm	Muscular	Stinging
Hardihood	Stand	Rousing	Peppery
Life blood	Shoulder	Robust	Briny
Loins	Scorn	Rock-ribbed	Hardworking
Marrow		Stalwart	Plodding
Mooring		Salty	Strong willed
Rudeness		Stout	Peaceful
Sinews		Strapping	Forbearing
Thews		Stoical	Frosty
Whipcord		Tranquil	Short
		Unquenchable	Blunt
		Unflinching	Unsparing
		Sinewy	

(adjectives)	Without feeling and expression
Serene	Sober-eyed
Earthy	Strong-eyed
Freckled	Resolute
Home-made	Steady
Humdrum	Silent
Inelegant	Inflexible
Outspoken	Gruff
Plain spoken	

In general, the three word notebooks carry the same theme and flavor as his Novel and Serial Principles given in Chapter 4: significance, power, freshness, lift, beauty, feel, and rough reality. In Thesaurus I, beauty, emotion, movement, and strength contain the most subdivisions. Thesaurus II has a roster of slightly different categories, although the headings of Beauty, Emotion, Freshness, and Strength recur. The headings here are less abstract, more evocative, such as: Age, Air, Color, Couplings, Depth, Evolution, Fighting, Fireside, Gloom, Harmony, Harshness, Height, Horror, Intensity, Love, Minor Note, Peace, Places, Plants, Rain, Rocks, Shape/lines, Smells, Taste, Touch, Unwholesomeness, Villain, Water, Weather, Wildness, Youth.

Thesaurus III has to do with people, children, home, human behavior; love, marriage, nature, death. And of course there are compilations of place names, canyons, mountains, rivers; western place names like Chloride, Flapjack, Cactus Flat, K-town; eastern ones like Jug End, Apple Tree Corner, Quiggleville, The Three Chestnuts. If he couldn't find a mountain name he liked, there were the three-dimensional state maps he ordered from the army map service, fascinating not only for the local names but the way one could run a finger along a raised ridge and feel the mountain's shape. In a notebook my mother kept about C. R. in her last years, she listed the sky and mountains as what he most loved.

Dipping into the word notebooks is, for anyone who writes, an invigorating experience. As C. R. realized, they are crammed with "writer's words," a never-ending picture album with moods, images, small stories or incidents springing from the page. In the Pa Dutch Name Book which he made for *The Free Man*, "that girl with the round corners" is as fresh an expression as one could find. Here are others with a vivid folk quality about them, always related to common, sometimes violent experience.

From a page entitled Cognomers and Human parts:

High nosed (proud   haughty)
Busch knipple
The old rib (gaunt old maid or woman)
Dirt pig   Dirt slop
A weed-farmer
The little squirmer } children
The little dirt-rag sucker }
He wouldn't die for what he knows
Goose wing (feeble girl)
Tattle mouth
Dog legged
A wide stander
The over the Mtn people

From several pages of similes:

Smooth as butter
Sullen as a spider
Spiteful as a crab
He ran like Hain's mill
Always on behind like the peddlar's pack
Yellow as a quince
She makes a face like a cat in thunder
You stand there like a saw horse
She looks like she swallowed the vinegar barrel
As handy as a wheelbarrow in the kitchen
Ugly as ten weeks of rain
Dark as in a sack

Red as a rose dipped in redbeet juice
As full as seven in a bed
Old as the North star
Bad as gallows wood
Tough as a hog snout
Quiet as a sitting hen
Cheeky as a cock
Clean as if the cat had licked it
Bright as a saucepan
Breathing like a forge bellows

From Misc. Constructions:

He looks his eyes out
A good mouthpiece (talk)
Live you yet? (greeting)
Up to snitz
Oh, so so. So middling
Rump and stump (lock, stock & barrel)
My heart sobbed
The short end
Threw up to him
They had a crooked & straight
Yes, if I myself must say so
Well, so I was born
Tell me, once
He hung in his mouth
I got it in my book so
It's cold today towards yesterday
Give rain
So & so wants rain tomorrow
The money lays ready

From Names of Nature Things:

Fire in the mountain
Soldier's plume (in garden)
Adam & Eve (bear grass)

Earth berry (strawberry)
Oak cat, kitten (squirrel)
The summer side
The winter side
Star weather
Fire bird (firefly)
Clock flower (columbine)
Up Country
Down country

By far the most important principle underlying C. R.'s interest in words was the energy content of language. His theories on the human search for energy (inclusive of but much more basic than Freud's "pleasure principle") help explain the pages of Energy Flow words contained in the thesaureses—words rich in emotional connotation or tension which, in their own way, add to intensity and compression. Appendix C includes an abridgment of the chapter "The Energy Content of Language" from his Socratic dialogue *The Mountain on the Desert*, with its many examples of words and word combinations which raise or evoke energy and emotion. The choice of strong energy words accounts, at least partially, for the vividness and resonance of C. R.'s images.

A page from Thesaurus I:

Strong Energy Flow Mechanics

1. Words, to be effective, must belong in part to same group so their energy flow may be delivered to the sustained theme (dominant general cell group). Otherwise, they will waste their power, spread it among consecutively non-important minor groups which will become successively dominant.

Ex. "The Well of Loneliness" - "Well" is in the same group (as loneliness) because (well) is deep & one says "deep loneliness"

2. Fresh combinations as "a vast well"
3. See especially "Movement" words and use them,

C. R.'s use of a mechanical metaphor, as in cell groups which deliver a flow of energy if aroused, predated Jung's theory of energy contained within the archetype to be released by the user. To explain the principle in lay terms would be less helpful here than to examine certain characteristics that contribute to the energy content of words: wide association, sense of obstruction or predicament (i.e. "story" words), visual motion, physical tension, "lift," strong visual image. Occasionally a word will have opposite or polarized meanings which set up a strong contrast such as "vault" (listed under Energy Flow Verbs) which refers to jumping, the vault of heaven, and a tomb.

Two words chosen at random under the heading of Beauty, *bank* and *dike*, lend themselves to explication.[4] *Bank* is listed under beauty because of its association with the bank of a river or stream, the plants and trees growing there, the sense of coolness and refreshment; or sitting on a bank watching fish or dangling one's feet into water. It also suggests a sense of profusion (banked with flowers) or richness.

Dike, in contrast, is a word of protection and power. The power of the word derives from the implied image of a dam breaking and causing destruction which arouses the flow of energy in the reader. Thus it contains the tension between the idea of peaceful containment and the destructive element.

The following list of Energy Flow words is excerpted from some thirteen hand-written pages, with space left to allow additions as he found them.[5]

Energy Flow Adjectives	Energy Flow Verbs	Energy Flow Nouns
Audacious	Fan emotion	Jack in box
Alien	Flare	Jackanapes
Airy	Fight	

Energy Flow Adjectives	Energy Flow Verbs	Energy Flow Nouns
Alive & kicking	Flash	Life
Arrogant	Fling	Life of party
Astonishing	Frisk	Love of life
Animated	Flourish	Life blood
Awake	Fume	Lark
Acidly	Foam	Lightning
	Ferment	Lashing tail
Boisterous	Fizz	
Breakneck		Mettle
Bragging	Growl	Madcap
Boasting	Glare	Minx
Blustering	Grit	Mischief-maker
Barbarous	Glow	
Buoyant	Gambol	North Wind
Brusque	Grimace	Nettle
Blunt		Nerve
Brackish	Hop	Nip
Brief	Hurl	
Burning	Hum	Outcast
Biting		Outlaw
Blazing	Inflame	Outburst
Brazen	Intimidate	Oxygen
Bright	Incite	Ozone
Brand	Infuriate	Old Nick - Harry
Bold		
Bursting	Kindle	Quip
Bewildering	Kick up heels	
		Pepper
Challenging	Lounge	Pep
Cocky	Larrup	Panther
Curt	Let fly	Prank
Caustic	Lash - out	Plume
	Lunge	Punch
Dashing		
Daring	Leap	Raciness
Defying	Lord it over	Racket
Devilish - in eye		Rocket
Driving	Stew	Rebel - ion
	Seethe	Rogue

Energy Flow Adjectives	Energy Flow Verbs	Energy Flow Nouns
Expansive	Smash	Recklessness
Elated	Spurn	Repercussion
Exhilirating	Scoff	Riot
Exuberant	Swoop	Rawhide
Electrifying	Shoulder	Rascal
Excited	Shove	
Exasperated	Scoot	Spree
Enthusiastic	Splash	Sport
	Splinter	Shock
		Sap
	Tear along	Spark
	Thunder	Storm
	Throw up cap	Smack

Freshness has been mentioned as one of the qualities that appears both in Primary Writing Principles and in wordbook headings. A small separate loose-leaf folder holds some eight pages of "New Word Combinations," some of them model phrases, others original. The bulk are from Shakespeare, Wordsworth, and the Bible, the latter mainly from Genesis and the Book of Job. "Doth not the ear try words?" (Job 12:11) follows the heading New Way of Saying It on one of the pages. The word combinations appear to be a conjunction of contrasts—dry death, the Gentle Lady and the Moor—or words taken out of their usual context, such as "an astringent waist," "a plethora of skirts" (the last two C. R.'s). More of his original combinations beg for space here:

the good stepmother	the bold Virgin
dispatcher of the stars	deep summer
celestial traffic	the bell star
purr of the planet	the nebula's knot
slow sunshine	the short green wires of the pines
square-headed steers	the green loom of lawn—woven grass
unhurried oxen	
the glazed buttercup	the coco's plume (coconut palm)

11

Advice to Young Writers

From time to time C. R. flirted with the idea of teaching writing. In 1949 he had been invited to Bread Loaf as a guest, with the hope that he would join the staff. He enjoyed the conference and the people but was appalled at the procedure. "The teachers read stories and poems aloud to the student class, then asked for individual reaction and comments. That appeared to be the teaching so far as I could tell."[1]

For all his reserve in discussing his own writing, he continually found himself helping others. He had, I think, a strong altruistic streak. His being a severe (although accurate) critic did not help matters. Occasionally he would spend a great deal of time on a promising writer's work and never receive a word of thanks. Other times the advice was not heeded, and the writer went on to be successful on entirely different lines. His own attempt at teaching me to write brought on some of my most painful experiences. My father and I were extraordinarily close—so close that doubtless he felt I should at least write like him. If he had made a success at old-time stories, why shouldn't I? My father's mind—in spite of protestations to the contrary in the journal—worked very quickly. Mine plodded. He could not understand why I did not immediately get a point he was making; both his authority and agile mind served only to paralyze me. There would be scenes, tears on my part. Under his tutelage I wrote and sold two short stories to the *Post*, the second one featured. When the first one sold, my temperature shot up to 103. I was torn between being proud about the sale and mortified that my father had helped me with the story.[2]

Two journal excerpts comment on the problem which probably upset him even more than it did me.

> Never should I help writers. When I came back, Vene had done over the last several pages, the end, of her story. . . . But it wasn't right and I labored with her until one o'clock [A.M.] to correct, improve it. She rebelled, looked almost in tears most of the time, and this . . . confirms me in what I told her then. That she must do stories her own way, learn herself, follow her own veins of thought. If she is to write, she will write . . . A writer must be inventive must take great pains, and he will do this more for himself than for a teacher. Besides, I am a poor teacher, too temperamental. I am just a striving artist impatient with the work of those who do not strive as much as I. This has been hard on Vene, but good for me. I have been taught finally and completely, I hope, never to try to help anyone in writing - above all never to take a class in writing as I had hoped and which, I see now, would both exasperate and enervate me, occupy my thoughts and efforts, and there would be none remaining for my own work. (January 17, 1946).
>
> Feel badly tonight. This noon at lunch I mentioned to V that she could write four line poems to make use of ideas. She replied she couldn't, that no good poet did. When I mentioned Emily Dickinson, she had some excuse for her. She told me to let her poetry be, that it was one thing all her own and I shouldn't spoil it. H. sided with her. . . . It bewilders me because I read everything to them, ask for opinion, help. Last week I rewrote a chapter and edited another because of V's objections and didn't get angry. (July 25, 1954)

Yet his letters to me when I was in Europe in 1948–49, settled down to writing for the first time, have a sweet reasonableness that the personal confrontations never had. Since my mother had been ill much of my life, he had taken over the role of nurturing. The letters he wrote me were always warm and concerned. When I was away from home, letters from one or the other arrived two or three or sometimes four times a week; I responded in kind. Fortunately, the very fact of writing down criticism and suggestions for me bridled his critical impatience; more than once I have found in his journal that he wanted to advise me strongly on some point and refrained.

The following excerpts from his letters are not only wise admonitions to a daughter; the points he makes are universal whether it has to do with journalism or fiction writing. If my letters of 1948 and 1949 constituted a kind of journal for me, they were also a practice field. I lobbed ideas and descriptions and real life vignettes, and if I pontificated, my father gave me a well-deserved reprimand. The first letter dates from the time I was studying fiction writing at Columbia University. I have supplied my own titles from ideas in the passages.

good fiction is mostly animal November 20, 1938

> There were several things I wanted to talk to you about stories, things you brought up in your letters, but I remember only one. You recall that letter in which you mentioned a writer-speaker who said good fiction was mostly animal while a woman speaker denied it and you agreed with her. The name of the man was very familiar, that of the woman not so. They were both right but what the man said is more important because you can have good fiction without beauty but you cannot have any without the rugged primitive things of life. If you will think about Sigrid Undset's books or Julia Peterkin's you will see what I mean. Even Willa Cather meets the thing very squarely and so does Robert Frost. This rugged primitive element, taking people and things as they are, as Caroline Miller did in Lamb in His Bosom, will itself flower into beauty if handled according to life and balance. But to write about beauty itself is only swirling vapour and thin air. Beauty comes from life and people and only the fundamental things of life and peo-

ple stir up energy and emotion that can make genuine beauty. So the man was right.

the professional gets it off November 13, 1948

I urge you to try to write your articles fast as you did those three letters. The professional writes it and gets it off. The dilettante writes at this and that. The writing it through and getting it off and tackling another the next day is the biggest thing in writing.

go after facts November 22, 1948

If you had gotten down to work on stories, as you are doing now on newspaper articles, turned one out every two weeks and kept turning them out as Paul [Reynolds] so truly advised, you would have sooner or later arrived . . . by the method of trial and error, rejection and improvement. . . .

Meantime I think your writing newspaper stories the best thing that could happen to you, especially if you go after facts and concrete things, life as is, reality. It will give you a training you so much need and will give you something solid and real for fiction when and if you get back to it some day.

on story characters December 28, 1948

Your WEDDING DRESS story . . . was better written than any of your others, but it disappointed me that the next day it faded out. After some days the explanation came to me. . . . Sarah Ann is a weak character and her strong father and the strong dressmaker by contrast emphasize her weakness. . . . Now readers like people in life are drawn to strong characters. Mrs. G———used to say, "I'm interested in people who give me something." People read for pleasure, because they get something out of it. They are not drawn to weak characters in print any more than in life. In other words, if THE WEDDING DRESS is to be made into a story with a chance at sale,[3] the temper must be changed . . . giving the reader a strong Sarah Ann, making her father and Margaret [the dressmaker] the weaker ones, as foils. . . .

strength first and heart second January 2, 1949

I do hope that what I wrote you about the indispensable element for newspaper stories struck fire with you despite my loose and long-winded recital. Since then I find that what I wrote you was true to a greater extent than I dreamed at the time. The last issue of Colliers had three articles, one about the hard-boiled police officer in Berlin whom even the Germans respect. It was by Quentin Reynolds. Another about Mrs. Knox the grand old woman who still runs the Knox Gelatin Co. at 91 with her hands almost paralyzed by arthritis. And the third about a Chicago postman and the daily load he carries, the miles he covers and the good he does. The primary quality of all three articles was strength. . . . Strength first and heart second. When you have trained yourself to see these qualities and write them both in the same article, you'll go places. That's why I asked you if you tried to pattern a character out of your own mind. I never do, would never have gotten to first base if I had. The characters I write about are immeasurably stronger and more interesting than myself. That's why I am drawn to write about them, and try to picture and "create" them.

to keep the suspense January 30, 1949

Use or say nothing that does not contribute to the reality or suspense of the story. . . . to keep the suspense, keep setting down the little natural things that Sarah Ann does in the line of her duty and the story. You do not get suspense by saying the character felt great suspense. That utterly kills it. You get it by showing the great danger and obstruction against the character and then have the character quietly go ahead doing what he or she can, while it seems disaster will break over him or her any time. All those little natural things in the line of duty, provided they are said quietly, simply and are not padded or embroidered too much, add to the suspense. Of course, the character must feel some emotion, but it must be done with great restraint, suggested by what she does and the way she does things.

I am thankful that you are at last able to revise, work over, and improve. This is your chief requirement to success. . . . Do not be in too big a hurry to shoot the story to him [Paul] until you are satisfied it is the best you can do. It should not be over 15 or 16 pages. Pare paragraphs to essential sentences and sentences to essential indispensable words. . . .

strong suspense descriptions February 13, 1949

Your remarks about your difficulty with your garden story because of lack of obstruction or strong plot is a sign you are advancing. The one most important thing in a story is a strong obstruction, and should be the one thing you look for to start a story with. It gives both strength and suspense. Most of your notes [of travels] are sweetness and light. If you looked for and noted down descriptions of places affording possibilities of strong suspense, it would be well. The only such place in your letters that I recall is the passageway to the apartment of the Frenchwoman. . . . Do you get what I mean in looking for strong suspense localities and descriptions? If you will direct your inquiry from this viewpoint, you will find such places. The sweetness and light places can be used only with terrific suspense to offset their non-story nature, as the stark plot and sinister suspense and treatment of Wuthering Heights supported the idyllic descriptions of the moors.

use of detail February 18, 1949

A good plan in writing is not to use a specific name when you can't check or verify it, but to so write it as to get around the omission with clever innocence.

on revising February 18, 1949

You will get your best effects from going over and over a page, correcting in pencil until it reads to suit you rather than typing off an 'improved' version as you go. . . . I have tried the latter method and it never works out. My new 'improved' page is as poor as the old one. But if I read it over three, four, six times painfully correcting in pencil as I go, I can get somewhere toward what I want. Then I type that page off, being careful to stick to my notes rather than sudden inspirations, which almost never work out, and start correcting again, if it needs it, until it suits. Perhaps when I come back to it later on, it needs more of the same. This is the system under which all of my work of the last fifteen years has been produced. . . . I believe if you follow this method, your style will be stronger and carry the story more securely and simply.

arousing interest May 10, 1949

What you say about articles having a kind of plot is very true and if you study these feature news stories from the Telegram etc. you will see it. When I wrote for the newspapers we were taught to say the whole story in the first paragraph. If we could do it with vigor and originality, all the better. Then having aroused the interest of the reader, we went back to the beginning and told the story clean through. That first paragraph therefore should have something in it to make the reader keep on with it, to arouse his interest or excitement, to make him see how it turned out.

For that reason it is best NOT to tell all in your first paragraph, that is not to tell the solution, unless that solution is such a shock as to make him read how such a thing could happen. For instance if you write that "Will Carson, a tourist from Cedar Falls, Iowa, tried to beat the Near East Limited to the crossing on Mimosa Street in Nice," you would not tell in the first paragraph what was the outcome, if he escaped, but make the race very close and dangerous so the reader would feel sure he was killed and read on to see. But if he and six others were killed and their blood strewn along with their belongings for a mile along the railroad, you would end the sentence or paragraph with this gruesome fact which would make the reader go on for the details more than the most cleverly written omission.

a nose for news May 20, 1949

Well, you are a writer at last. If you love to hear a typewriter pecking away somewhere on the street or in the house, that is the final proof, or so I always thought in my own case, that it meant writing was in the bloodstream. Such a sound seldom fails to make me feel at home, congenial. Somebody hidden there in an unknown room somewhere is a nameless brother or sister of the craft. I try not to think it may only be a high school kid typing off a letter.

Your last one [letter] of the trip to Cannes one of your best, so spontaneous, full of life and meat. If that is a result of your writing a thing off at first draft, it's grand. I'm grateful I was led to write you about it. I wish I could as readily tell you how to scent a story, how to get a nose for news. The best way is a daily reading of news, seeing what is printed and why. That gives you ideas. You go and do likewise at first as best you can in your own way of writing, but the point and news value and mood of the story must never be tampered with. I think when you get back to America, you'll look at newspapers and magazines with an entirely new appetite, not to be entertained or amused or interested, but a kind of greed to see what the other fellows are doing entertaining, amusing or interesting, how they are doing it and how the editors are liking and rating it.

punch, punch, punch May 23, 1949

I sat there thinking that I had been making a mistake urging you to write well, that what you needed was plot, plot, plot - punch, punch, punch, no matter if it was old, although the fresher the better, and that if you wrote it right off like you have been doing lately on news stories, it didn't matter too much how far from literary it was written. So think about that story, get it all straightened out in your mind before you set down a word, the punch, punch, punch, nothing but plot and suspense.

imagine you are writing to someone July 3, 1949

As you have said so often, you get your best effects in your first writing. In this case it was your letter to us of the nun and her work. I could not feel her nearly as intensely as in your letter. Here are a couple suggestions that might be of value to you. First, when writing an article, imagine you are writing to someone such as Mother and me - try to make us see and feel it strongly - pile up one passionately vivid or pathetic or noble or sympathetic thing after another so that in your mind you feel you have us weeping or swept off our feet at the end. Second, never write it in the abstract but always in action - your visit - how you saw her the first time - how you saw other vital things as you moved along - how you were shocked by this person or that - and in the end how you felt as you left.

better for a reporter to be disliked July 11, 1949

Perhaps I will make a few comments on your Maugham interview now. I wanted it to wait for reflection and another letter, but the poor little things I wanted to tell you of our excursions around Penna do not fit very well along with Gide and Maugham and their worldly train. I think you did very well on your first major interview and that you will grow less awed as you go on and remain more of a reporter. I shall be greatly interested to see what story you got out of the Maugham visit.[4] I think Maugham liked you, am sure of it, but it is better for a reporter if he is not liked even disliked so long as he gets a story. Also the more you get in contact with these universe-sweeping planets, the less your tides will surge as you pass by. Then you can meet him on his own ground, and not be so humble or grateful for the honor so much as sound his mettle. I think when he called his best story RAIN, he was testing you. It was named something else. The play taken from it was named RAIN and in late editions the story is so called. But if you had come back at him with surprise that he called the story RAIN rather than the title he himself gave it, I think you would have touched off a spark. That is the sort of thing you will eventually get into as you feel your way. A time with Washington correspondents would be wonderful, to hear the questions, often outrageous, they ask leading figures including the president of the United States. They are so brazen and insulting in many cases that sensitive people like you and I need to be exposed to them for a while to become immunized so we can follow suit. For instance, I should like to have heard what Maugham had to say about a question concerning his celebration of the American Fourth, it being that day and it being well known that the American royalties etc. are supporting him outside of England. You might have badgered him into making an indiscreet remark which would have been hailed with glee by your editor and printed around the world. This does not change my code of being decent to decent people, but Maugham has taken advantage of so many people in his life. Carl Taylor told with anger how he would cater to people in the South Seas, live with them on their hospitality until he secured their life story and then drop them and bare the thing to the world. I should have loved to have heard his reply when you asked him if this were true. No doubt you would have then seen the arrogant look that the artist caught on the painting. I suspect his bounding after the interview was his relief at being let off so easy. It is far more of an ordeal for the one interviewed than for the reporter, or it should be.

on the theme novel March 18, 1953

There is a great deal of truth in what you say about MY ANTONIA. I think she learned more of following a theme in Death Comes to the Archbishop and Shadows on the Rock. Read the latter again when you have a chance. Just the same, I am not so sure that the themelessness of My Antonia isn't more of a true reflection of life in most cases than my themes which are written to get a point across and for which it is necessary to put together a composite character. Personally I like the theme novel the better. It has more depth and height, but I am not sure about breadth. Theme is often the author's not the real character in life. After some of Willa Cather's things one has a feeling not so much of fiction as of life. They could have been oldtimers in Albuquerque such as I knew. This is a great art if a formless one. In addition it is done with such great calm. . . . This calm is a little superior perhaps but it is often warm . . . is thoughtful, literary, judicious.

February 6, 1955

In a novel the mature writer has an idea separate from and underlying the general idea and story of the novel. Paul used to comment on mine by saying that he always discourages his writers from doing this as it is the most difficult to do. I think that most young novelists and poets feel they do this in their work, but mature readers do not find it, or at least not a true dual expression, first the imagery,

> ideas, movement, story for their own sake, and secondly the idea, movement, story of a deeper meaning.

The following are excerpted from letters to students and young writers.

on style (1935)

> One thing I would like to pass on is the profitable policy of a writer building up a strong style, saying everything as vividly, strongly as he can and still be true. The stronger the style, the more punch, and different ideas expressed.

on overwriting (1941)

> Let us take up the style first. It is strong, leaves a vigorous impression and has excellent possibilities. I would, however, work on your similes which I felt were too frequent. For instance, the first five lines of your second paragraph has three similes such as "like" and "as." It throws the reader off the movement and action too frequently. Often just an adjective or an adverb will carry the meaning and less obtrusively, and then when a strong bit of feeling turns up where a simile is called for, the punch will be fresh and unhackneyed. The second of what I call drawbacks is harder to remedy. It is the common bane of most beginning writers. They overwrite. By that I mean they make the writing of a thought, bit of action or situation or description stronger, often far stronger, than the piece of business itself arouses reader emotion. This is a very important bit of technique to learn. . . .

the study of good writing (1947)

> If I were a young man preparing to write today, I should surely go for the very great stimulus . . . of the older and modern classics. It is true that a man can read these for him-

self, but he doesn't as a rule unless compelled to, and it is not always helpful unless he has a purpose. Please forgive me if I say that I should blur my ear against the general academic note and discussion of literature, which is often confusing and sometimes fatal to a writer. He gets to believe that he is acquiring a knowledge of the art of writing when quite the contrary is true. He should understand that most students and teachers can discuss writing exhaustively, often wittily and profoundly, while few are able to read those technical secrets of the writing itself, to detect the many ways in which the writer succeeded and how he got his effects. Should a student find a teacher who is master of this art and still has not given up teaching for writing, he is lucky indeed. . . . Such a teacher would doubtless help the student to concentrate on writing. He would also encourage him to pick out one or two good writers whom he admired and from their work try to form a style, all the while practising to get as sharp and vigorous effects as his masters. In the end such a student would undoubtedly find his own individual style and effects.

So I would center on those courses that provided the reading and study of good writing. As to what general advice I might give a prospective writer, I might do no better than what I remarked to my wife the other evening before your letter came. We were driving across the Pennsylvania Dutch countryside, passing through a number of unspoiled villages and "corners." They looked good to me, fruitful, made me wish I were a young writer starting out. I recalled how when a boy of 16 working in Pittsburgh I resolved to make my way to China and become a writer of stories and novels of Chinese life as Rudyard Kipling was then doing work based on India. This was long before Pearl Buck. I never got to China, and this certain evening it occurred to me that today I should probably never try to go there but to some interesting countryside, village, town, city or professional center in America, whichever interested me the most. Here I should try to get to know the real people and collect from them a store of the most outstanding real happenings, tragedies, comedies and authentic details of their lives. This material I should make my own and use to reconstruct stories and novels faithful to the people and their background and yet done in my own way and along my own creative design.[5]

clear, fresh expression (1964)

I can't say sweet words about writing. Good writing is something to which my mind pays instant respect. I do not mean good English but the clear fresh expression of mind impressions. . . . To me good writing is to get the important down on paper so truly and competently that the reader sees and feels what the writer does.

on inspiration (1966)

You ask about inspiration. It is a word I never thought much about. It's true that I admired certain writers as a youth, especially the early novels of Robert Chambers before he turned to popular fiction, and felt the same way later about the work of Willa Cather and a few others. But if there was any effective inspiration it was the necessity to earn money first for myself and then for my small family. . . .

on the liberal arts (1968)

In answer to your question, if I were a high school student today I think I would view the future darkly but if I had the sense I had now I would do two things. One is get what certain education I could, not in a specialized subject but in liberal arts to know what has gone on in the past so that no matter what happened to the world or to me, I could lean on the lives, thoughts and sayings of the great souls of the past who went through upheavals of their own. In my own case I had to go to work after high school and only when my daughter went to the University of New Mexico in Albuquerque did I find what I had missed. I've always called what I learned from what spilled over from her courses to me at home my college education.

from a letter to Agnes Morely Cleaveland, Jan. 25, 1938

Now about the book. I still feel that born in New Mexico, with the chief engineer of the Santa Fe as a father, with Ray Morely as a brother, but chiefly with the Datil country as your back yard teeming with antelope, cattle, horses, grizzlies, English lords and lesser natives all living their lives as they damned pleased, and with the contrast of your Philadelphia and Stanford existence to open your eyes a bit sharper at home, you have in you grand possibilities for a lusty, firsthand classic of the oldtime life.

But you know me. I am a terrible crab. I am going to be utterly honest with you and tell you that I was badly disappointed with the first batch you sent me but did not want to hurt you by telling you. I thought you had been hopelessly spoiled to write your book by your life at Berkeley, as a clubwoman, political thinker and platform speaker. Your second batch was better and gave me back a bit of my original hope. But I am a terrific taskmaster for myself or anyone else in whom I believe and who is innocent enough to ask for my tyrannical opinions, and urge that before going a line farther, you sit down and see where you are going - and then revise and condense to that plan until what you have already written is right. Then you should have a measuring rod to write the first draft of the rest of it, and although you will seem to lose time at first, you will really gain in the end.

When we talked over your book at Berkeley, I assumed your plan would be something on the order of your earlier letters. . . . If there was one spirit pervading these letters, it was your passion for New Mexico, its oldtime life, land and people. . . . You once wrote me that when you crossed the border, it almost tore you to pieces. . . . When I say a passion for New Mexico, I do not mean that your letters tried to show that the life then was better than now . . . You took the attitude, here it is as it was then, as you knew and loved it, crude, rude, rough, earthy, even scandalous, full of lusty vigor, pungent absurdities, coarseness and humour, but fine in spots, too, and what ever else, tremendously interesting and American. That last word is the most important, the American of Mark Twain and Bret Harte and Abraham Lincoln.

I think this theme, plan, aim, purpose, call it what you will, would have helped to throw each thing you wanted to say into its proper perspective, which is the secret of all good writing. For example, in your book manuscript you devote three pages to the diary incident which in your letter you gave four or five lines. Which is right?. . . . The point was that someone gave you a fresh clean diary, that all through those years when just one evening's talk of the cowboys by the fire would now be priceless, you never filled a page because nothing ever happened important enough to put down. . . .

What I had hoped to be the great merit of your book was the sweep of brief and pungent expression of your country. You have so much to tell, so many incidents, stories, characters, illustrations of code, philosophy, morality etc. The moment they are approached from a platform and embroidered, their very nature, reality and effect are gone. But condensed to lusty and pungent brevity, every sentence all meat, followed by another sentence all meat, every idea and incident compressed into the picturesque economy of language a cowboy uses, each chapter packed like a chuckwagon out for months with twenty men, would provide a vigorous, hearty fare that would not merely show but BE the West as it was and which every reader would relive. And I especially urge the roughening and leavening of the narrative at every page with such things as the outlaw in the family - the boys who were not expert enough in obstetrics to bring in the right cow. . . .

Do this and you will bowl over everyone, especially the critics . . . publishers are always looking for a lusty, genuine chronicle in which the writer excites from beginning to end that quality which pays for its own publication - human interest.[6]

from a folder of miscellany:

If I were asked to say a word to younger writers, it would not be the same to all. To those who write with facility, fluency and spontaneity my word would be one of caution to saddle and bridle their wild horses so he can be guided where the rider and not always where the impetuous animal wants to go. To those who write more slowly, whose standards may be stiffer or dissatisfaction easier so that their thoughts and feelings are more difficult to set down exactly as they feel or think them, my word would be one of encouragement, to keep tirelessly putting their horse through his paces until he learns to perform the perfect act. In either case, let the young writer observe those on foot as he rides. To observe, meditate and express himself on life and man, that is the rewarder of him who rides and writes.

12

The Ever Writer[1]

Two sounds are closely associated with my father in my memory. One is the sound of him whistling as he came down the back alley from a walk. I would listen for it hopefully; even in later, less impoverished years the whistling had the same comforting effect. Work had gone well that day.

The other sound was the steady tapping of his typewriter. He typed with the second and third fingers of both hands, very fast, very purposefully. Like the whistling, the rhythm was a barometer of how well his writing was going. To him there was no pleasanter sound; it betokened both industry and accomplishment. His journal comments, "Vene's typewriter, the sound of it like that of a rain on the roof after a drought" (July 20, 1954). Once he heard it while in bed in the early morning and was dismayed to find only "a downy woodpecker busily tapping a tree" (July 26, 1954).

My mother and I too listened for his typewriter with pleasure, especially for the lulls which meant, we thought, that we could interrupt with something desperately needing attention. But silence did not necessarily mean he wasn't working, and intrusions could be disastrous. I remember waiting at his workroom door (always open—he did not like to shut himself off), looking for a sign of inactivity which meant I could intrude. C. R.'s mechanism was well-oiled; he clicked along mentally at a rate of speed that sometimes paralyzed me. Even if no activity seemed evident as I waited by the door, the minute he turned around, sensing my presence, his impatience crackled almost audibly. When words and ideas were boiling, his temper, correspondingly, would be at the boiling point.

Everything was sacrificed for his work. His was a silent breakfast that, visiting on weekends, I sometimes shattered by either coming down late or chattering away. A look of great pain would come over his face. When he wasn't worrying about my mother, money, or me, his mind was on his writing. But except for talking about plot when he found a snarl, he tended to keep his work to himself. "Don't tell it, sell it," was a maxim I heard often. "I Must Keep Stories More to Self," a journal entry is headed (February 28, 1934):

> I forget continually & talk about my plots & stories - especially when enthusiastic. It is good I feel to test them out on V & H for they turn me from many poor & cheap ideas. But when I talk too much & when not necessary, *I spill the leaven & cannot make bread*. Kept in me it adds & accretes, working automatically.
>
> [italics mine]

An excerpt from a New Year's Day entry (1941) shows how deeply engrained was the work ethic:

> . . . the biggest thing that happened to me this day was reading Andrew Lang's translation of the poem of Leonidas about old Platthis who warding hunger from the door and driving sleep morning and evening from her plied her loom till in her eightieth year. I raise this and her up before me this first day of the new year and hope it may be an omen, that I may work hard day and night and do my work as she did hers.

At times my father's work seemed a burden to him—"a burden to think of writing, of phrases, of putting it into words to set down" (June 8, 1946). He envied the antique dealer who can "get hold of a beautiful piece of work without having to design and create it" (March 7, 1952). But let him feel blue or depressed, it was his work that cheered him. A Quiet Room to Write Filled with Books and My Things gave him a sense of "quietness and power" (November 8, 1944). Journal entries in the nineteen fifties are titled The Blessing of Work, Work is My Happiness, Work My Delight. He liked the "wonderful feel" of his "thick manuscript" in his hand, not for its contents but for "the knowledge that I have done it." He had made something "out of nothing" (March 25, 1945). The same image appears in a comment after a dinner at Alfred Knopf's, who had just accepted *The Town* (September 18, 1949):

> WRITING, PUBLISHING & SELLING. I felt it keenly at the time, but it did not come clearly in words to me until later, that from Alfred's and Paul's talk it seemed so pleasant, interesting, and even easy to be a publisher or agent. Many books come to them in the course of a year. If this one didn't sell, another would. And all they had to do was prepare and offer the book to the trade. But I, the poor author, had first to spend several years slaving alone to make it out of nothing, or almost nothing, and if it was destroyed by locusts or drought, it was not just a season's crop like the farmer's, but might be of many years, as was this [*The Town*].

C. R. needed sales to survive. He cringed at criticism; he was almost as embarrassed by praise. In 1950, just after *The Town* was published, he wrote, "If a mail like the above (full of good reviews for The Town) disturbs me so I get only a little work done, so I have to go out and water the lawn to calm myself and get hold of my work in my mind, what would real success do to me?" When good reviews came in, he could not bear to have my mother read more than a sentence or two from them at a time. A Review Reaction from a review of *Always Young and Fair* by John Marquand in the Book of the Month news:

> H read the first few lines from Marquand "this graceful and sympathetic tale . . . the medium in which Henry James so often worked. . . . & Mr. R follows that master's footsteps with selective skill & certainty." "Don't read any more," I

> begged & sprang up. "I have to wear that off" & for a long time walked back & forward through the house.

And yet when in a strange town, my father would go at once to the library to see how many of his books were in circulation. His was a private relationship between writer and reader; critics intruded. But readers seemed to grasp what he was trying to portray, telling him how real his characters were, how the action rang absolutely true. But even then he would not allow himself to feel praised. "For me to believe my work good as my kindest readers tell me would be dangerous as would be justifying it academically. My awareness and even despair over many of my shortcomings stirs me to try to do better, reach higher" (March 19, 1961).

I have my father's desk in a special room I built for his manuscripts and files here in the west, with the balsam pillow still fragrant in the drawer. A long pheasant feather is laid against the bookshelf on the back of the desk. Here are his own books (with marginalia), several volumes on Shakespeare together with the complete plays and a small paperback of the sonnets slipcovered in leather; two books on Greece by Edith Hamilton; Keats' letters; Kilvert's *Diary*, two poetry anthologies, several small volumes of his favorites, W. H. Hudson and James Barrie; Crowell's *Handbook*, and the usual dictionaries, Roget, and Bartlett. England, Scotland, Shakespeare, the Greeks—these were compass points to C. R.'s own particular directions.

Underneath his typewriter table and chair (now under mine) was "Pegasus's Saddle Blanket," a bright Navajo used saddle blanket he bought from an Indian in Albuquerque. Characteristically, he claimed it was to "save the floor" when he worked.

Growing up as the child of a writer whose weight rested on the saddle blanket of the Muses' winged horse, was bound to be different. In some ways it was a secretive world. When we moved west, my father did not want it known that he was a writer so that, when asked what my father did, I would remain mute. This was during prohibition, and later my father was amused at what a neighbor judge, whose daughter was my friend, must have thought. Because of his work hours and my mother's need of quiet, there was little social life at home. But this supposed lack of freedom was offset in many ways. During those depression years, the three of us were very close. The simplicity of the situation helped enormously—our one path to survival lay in my father writing stories that sold. Everything was bent to that effort. The smallest pleasures were intense, such as a ride in the sand hills, or an occasional candy bar, cut in half and then each half in thirds, so that the treat lasted for two meals. Or a Sunday drive to Bernalillo, eighteen miles north along the Rio Grande bosque, for ice-cream sodas—always vanilla with chocolate ice cream—at the main-street drugstore. They were ten cents each.

Another of the joys was custom-made bedtime stories, which my father told me until I was thirteen or fourteen, when my mother thought it ridiculous that I should be storied to sleep like a small child. I had no trouble in believing that my father was a born story-teller. I was a rapt audience, and every night, from as early as I can remember, he spun out stories like "The Staircase Pine" or "The Wooden Woman."[2] Some time after we moved west, the stories turned into serials; he was always careful to end that night's installment on a perilous note. Being young and unwise, I never wrote them down. But I remembered one which became a poem called "Black Eggs," probably because I begged so often for it, and because one night he told me the story in the farmhouse cellar, where I usually accompanied him because he would feel "presences" there and was uneasy. The cellar was dark and dirt-floored, the furnace fired with great chunks of chestnut from a blighted grove halfway up the mountain.[3]

And there was a heightened sense of life simply from the fact that, with a writer in the family, our imaginations and powers of observation were kept sharpened. When we went for our ritual ride late in the day, my mother and I were pressed to find a fresh way of observing what we saw. "Put it into a phrase, or better, two words," C. R. would encourage us. This would result not only in seeing something new about the object or scene but in compressing it to give more power to the image. My father was always interested in the picture, packed with associative meanings. The exercise was a game for us—the oral practise of writing which, I suspect, he engaged in silently all the time.

Still another joy was talking over ideas for stories, but mainly novels. One novel often discussed the last two years of his life—*The Angry Saint*—I was certain would be written. I was wildly enthusiastic over the idea, a deeply philosophical one concerning the problem of human suffering and a saint's revolt against God for His apparent cruelty. It did not seem possible to me that C. R. would go before it was written. Only a notebook of ideas, scenes, and characters remains of it.

And there are other tantalizing fragments. He had begun the third volume of his "personal trilogy," as he called it, the first two volumes of which were *The Waters of Kronos* and *A Simple Honorable Man*. Curiously, every time he worked on it he became ill. It was to be a fictional rendering of his own life titled *Search for Meaning*. But it seemed almost impossible for him to write overtly about himself. As an antidote, he sketched out four Pennsylvania Dutch children's stories to follow *Over the Blue Mountain*, each with a color in the title: *The White Horse, The Red Ark, The Yellow Summer*, and *Through the Black Daylight*. He was also making notes on a book of fables which would satirize modern politics and mores. Of these, several rough drafts of "The Littlest Lion" remain. One satirizes, among other things, the psychological myth that all great men or heroes are secretly burdened with guilt and fear. The littlest lion asks, "Do I need to be frightened? Can't I let myself go. Can't I once say BOO and roar?" "No," comes the answer, "you must sympathize and cry with the little frightened ones and tell them what good reason they have to cry, then they will not be so frightened."

If sympathy with weakness and loss of heroic models bothered C. R., so did the concept of the welfare state. Another draft has an old lion pointing out how well off lions in captivity are, that they eat enriched food, get vitamins, have a roof over their heads.

> "There are always lions who are never satisfied," the old beast continues, "who talk about the good old days when we had to run for our food and sleep out in the open, when we had to be in the rain and had no running water. When we had to crawl through the grass and dash into a band of zebras." "But wasn't it fun to dash into a band of zebras?" the littlest lion asks, and adds, "I think it would be nice to run through the grass and go wherever I like."
>
> "You are ungrateful and unpatriotic," answers the older lion.

In the early 1950s my father wrote to me (April 28, 1953):

> I only hope you will always think of me and try to convey to others my work as that of a serious artist trying to express his ideas as honestly and painstakingly as he can. How much of all this I can accomplish I don't know, only that I have planned, scheduled, even mapped out, more than I at my age can ever do, and my moving about, when not for the benefit of Mother's health . . . is to find a place where I can work and get ahead on these books that are on my mind night and day to be written, and my hope and prayer is that enough money might come in from my serious work so that I can remain on it and not turn aside to write more salable books to finance others.

C. R. published a total of fourteen novels, three collections of short stories, three philosophical books, and a tale for children.

He was neither a nineteenth-century man living in the twentieth nor what he termed a "modern"; that is, "a man who is far more important personally than any subject in which he is interested and never, however lightly, lets his audience forget it." My father was far too humble to make himself more important than his work. But he is there in every page of it, a quality which delights me as I pick up one of his stories or novels and begin to read.

Notes

Chapter 1

1. Thirteen recurred significantly hundreds of times in his life (including a daughter born on March 13). From his June 13, 1936, journal, when he sent out the ms. of The Sea of Grass:

> Story Mailed 6 13's
>
> Ms took 13 air mail stamps. Today is 13. There are 13 letters in title of story & in the name of its author. I was born on the 13th & when I looked up I found that the first installment had been mailed on March 13.

On May 18 his journal noted that "Page 65 was not only 5 times 13 but 13,000 words." On February 6, 1938, his journal records:

> MY THIRTEENS AND THE THIRTEEN STRIPES
>
> Last evening . . . it came on me suddenly that thirteen was the number of stripes in flag of the early United States. The discovery that this number, so significant and recurring in my own life, was significant also with the early colonies blinded me for a moment with hope that my work with Early Americana, especially my passion for early day people, life and ideals might mean something some day. Particularly it gave me some of the confidence I so badly need that my feelings for early America might be of some importance after all, that my writings might be meant for something and perhaps myself. We can only work, wait and see.

2. Actually, this was not his first sale to the *Post*. "The Sure Thing" appeared there in 1917. But "Early Marriage" was the first in a long series of stories for the Curtis publications

3. O'Brien was of the Boston *Transcript*.

4. C. R. always said he got his college education when I went to the University of New Mexico. He read everything (nearly) that I did; at the dinner table we discussed ideas encountered in class. He had always read voraciously, and had gone through all of Shakespeare's plays by the age of sixteen.

5. The letter continues: "When I was deepest in gloom at Cleveland, ill and about to be fired, I wrote 'Brothers of No Kin' and 'The Laughter of Leen. . . .'"

6. From a letter to a student, March 10, 1959.

7. Part of the answer to a questionnaire written for the Philadelphia *Record*.

8. "Newspaper work taught me a great deal. The story had to be written whether I felt like it or not. There was no waiting for inspiration, for something that violently interested me. In fact I had to let out things that interested me personally but had no place in the story as such. I had to meet a deadline. A great many stories had to be written every day, some short, some long. I had first hand experience with all kinds of people. It was necessary to get information, material and sometimes pictures from them. A good reporter learned to tell when a man was telling the truth. Too much newspaper work might have been fatal to me. I had just enough." From a letter to Mary Thurber (doing her M. A. thesis on C. R.).

9. From autobiographical notes.

10. C. R. was briefly with The Literary Bureau in 1912. The Pagets took him on in 1915. Brandt & Kirkpatrick, later the well-known Brandt & Brandt (Carl and Erd Brandt; the latter became an editor for *The Saturday Evening Post* and a close friend of C. R.) handled his work until 1931 when he went to Marguerite Harper who specialized in pulps (see next chapter). In July of 1932 he went to Paul R. Reynolds.

11. This is not an exaggerated estimate. Paget, in the quoted letter of February 8, 1916, said, "What I am saying I am basing upon careful judgment and calculation." Considering the cost of living in 1916–17, magazine rates were unusually high. By 1917 C. R. was receiving $250 and $350; by the mid-twenties he would get $400 and $500. In 1931 his first stories to *Liberty* would bring $600; later the depression forced them down to $400.

12. From letters from the president of the Atlantic Paper Company, the General Manager of the Slingerland Printing Company, and the Glidden Company, 1921 and 1922.

13. Edward Bok was the editor of *Ladies' Home Journal*; his autobiography, *The Americanization of Edward Bok*, was famous in its time. Sinclair Lewis was then assistant editor of *Adventure*.

14. Many of these magazines were short-lived. *The American* folded in 1933; *The Forum, Munsey's Magazine, Everybody's, People's Magazine,* vanished in 1929 and 1930. Several stalwarts, such as *Liberty, The Farm Journal, Country Gentleman,* and *Woman's Home Companion* were gone by the end of the 1950s. All had been C. R. markets.

Chapter 2

1. C. R.'s nervous condition, which doctors were unable to diagnose, led him to attempt to find both its causes and cure. Two semiscientific/philosophical books were published in the twenties: *Human Vibration: the Underlying Mechanics of Life and Mind* (1926) and *Principles in Bio-Physics* (1927). A third, *Nerve Energy Management,* was completed before the move west but never sold. In 1928, C. R. wished to devote his time fully to his theories in order to help people suffering from the same type of ailment. He had received a good press for the first volume (Luther Burbank, William Lyon Phelps, Stewart Edward White), and in 1955 Knopf published *The Mountain on the Desert* which attempted to explain C. R.'s theories in Socratic dialogue.

2. C. R. published some fourteen stories during this period.

3. From the story "The Singing Texan" (*Blue Book*):

Climb down and listen, all you boys
That know the Lone Star yell.
I'm going to turn loose Martin Barr
And how he went to hell.
Ole Martin threw a wicked loop,
Was Texas born and bred.
Wherever sundown caught him at,
That place he made his bed.

Old Martin worked the Texas brush
For steers that tried to hide.
He worked till he was ninety-two
And then the ole wolf died.
The neighbors came to hol' the wake
And drink around his bed.
Ole Martin sat up, took a drink,
And this is what he said.

I been to see the devil, boys
He said, ain't hell plumb hot?
I tole him t'was a little cool
Beside what Texas got.
He asked me what I wouldn't give
For jes' one drop of rain.
I said I hadn't seen the stuff
Since Texas was a plain.

The devil got a little mad.
His pitchfork jabbed my head.
I tole him it felt mild beside
A Texas cactus bed.

He dipped a pan of red hot coals
And made me drink plumb that.
But after Texas chile, boys,
It tasted kinda flat.

4. A notebook page dated October 1, 1931, had a bitter note on "Miss Harper's Letter & Our Reaction" (see footnote 10, Chapter 1): "Universal theme must not show feeling or sentiment but be according to modern characters who don't show feelings or sentiment & are bravado, clever, smart, flippant, make faces etc. . . . flippant above but good underneath. True modern character all through." (This applied to smooth papers.)

5. From the opening of Notebook 6: "H told me tonight of the priest reading Death Comes for the Archbishop a sixth time and saying he was not done with it yet. Why, I asked myself, do I not write of things that move me - of what I feel in church. It should be from someone in power as Willa Cather's bishop and Cronin's priest.

"I am so eager to write of Pennsylvania as I know, feel & love it. What I know & love will be much easier to write about. Including a novel of Pennsylvania Lutheran church that will do Dad and Pa-pa proud." (The latter would be the novel about his preacher-father *A Simple Honorable Man*. Three other novels and an article for *Holiday* show his deep love for the state.)

6. A series of earthquake tremblors (Albuquerque lies on a fault) happened in December 1930, and February 1931. Beds careened, pictures danced on the wall. A February 8, 1931, journal entry describes the jolt as if a boat "keel suddenly with a terrific crash hits an unbudging rock."

7. The second house we rented in Albuquerque where my mother almost died in November of 1930.

8. A second quotation, likewise heavily marked in his anthology of world poetry, is cited in his journal when he was "stunned" by the poor reception of *Always Young and Fair* (6/29/47):

> AT BREAKFAST REPEATED from translation of Horace something I tried to memorize some years ago & couldn't. Yet today it came to me perfectly word for word.
>
> If hindrances obstruct thy way,
> Thy magnanimity display,
> And let thy strength be seen.

But, oh, if Fortune fill thy sail
With more than a propitious gale,
Take half thy canvas in.

Chapter 3

1. From his journal, October 2, 1943.

2. The "passive plot" would be one in which the characters are not actively involved in the obstruction. In a Black Notebook II entry he remarked of this story: "Notice how troubles in the earlier version did not oppose Joanna in theme purpose which was to consummate engagement in marriage - father's cattle dying from drouth (only Yancey's cattle dying would oppose marriage) - everyone leaving county (only Yancey leaving would postpone marriage) - mother dying from child birth (only if mother asked her to stay at home & raise Bessie would keep Yancey from marrying her)." This entry is titled "Obstruction Must Oppose Hero Directly For Theme Fulfillment."

3. Similar plotting difficulties are examined in several pages titled "Plotting Record - Helpful Experiences." An example: "Today November 5 after working vainly on 'Buckskin Vacation' for 5 weeks or more, I realize the trouble as usual is lack of plot. My plot lacks Rosalie in a strong, unfavorable situation at beginning - lacks a reason for reader to root for her - lacks an important reason why she goes home, vacation not being enough. I saw in Early Marriage outline that Nancy Belle was rooted for by reader because 'she insists on keeping appointment of her own wedding despite everything.' I asked H 'what is a more important reason for her to insist on going home or in addition to vacation?' & we worked out going to keep appointment at 4th of July Dance & Barbecue with her army lover who has arranged to have furlough at this time. We will see if this works out" (Black Notebook II).
C. R. made the reason even more important by a secret marriage being arranged. Rosalie takes a stage to join wagon train—it is held up by buffalo migration, a strong obstruction—and she arrives home too late for the dance. Coates has had a short furlough and is gone, but he catches up with her on the way back and they are married in the wagon train scene.

4. The next page in Black Notebook II is titled WRITE ONLY POWERFUL EVEN VIOLENT EMOTIONAL SYMPATHY OBSTRUCTIONS and continues with examples of openings from his own short stories and several novels by other writers. Several of the examples:

> A bitter feud in rough Western town about to break out again and kill the young Piatt just old enough to fight and in love.
>
> THE SQUARE PIANO

> Indians, terrible Apaches, are waiting on trail young girl must take with her younger brother to her distant wedding.
>
> EARLY MARRIAGE

> Rough cowmen and Indians, terrible Kiowas, have killed or chased out every family at spring now being homesteaded by young wife and baby, her husband being away [i.e., it is the husband who is homesteading—he is away to file claim on the land].
>
> NEW HOME

> Just but adamant father refuses to let his only daughter marry R R engineer with whom she is desperately in love and she is deadened and lifeless as a result.
>
> SMOKE OVER THE PRAIRIE

> Boy about to leave as buffalo hunter after wedding finds that Comanches have killed and mutilated all parties to the wedding and that his own parents are missing and only a handful of them left to guard tiny remote settlement.
>
> EARLY AMERICANA

> Boy in foregoing story must kill girl if Indians successfully attack, sooner than let her be taken and tortured by Indians as was bride.
>
> EARLY AMERICANA

> Having a baby and think you will die in wagon, alone on prairie at new homesite, with dog howling under wagon.
>
> NEW HOME

5. In his foreword to *Great Short Novels*, editor Edward Weeks says, "We quite overlook the originality and the delicate art which makes for compression in a short novel like *Thais*, *Death in Venice*, or *The Sea*

of Grass. . . . This short cut across time can be approached in a variety of ways. For instance, in *The Sea of Grass*, the best short novel that has yet been written about our Southwest, Conrad Richter encompasses the whole magnificent struggle between the cattle barons with their ranches 'as big as Massachusetts with Connecticut thrown in,' and the nesters who would invade them from the East. This struggle consumed roughly twenty-five years. Richter has not the space in which to build up the story year by year. Instead he tells it to you in the person of young Hal, a nephew of the great ranch owner. Hal sees what is happening in his recurring visits to the Cross B. His trips home happen to coincide with the high spots in the conflict. But why not? That's what a novelist is for."

6. July 26, 1934.
7. This would be used in chapter 5 of *The Fields*.
8. Used in *The Town* in the story of Rosa Tench.
9. Discussion of love stories between C. R. & Wife (in section of Love Obstruction):

> H.: "Editors like stories that show the man selfish enough to think he can leave girl and forget her (perhaps telling her their affair was just friendship). But he can't stay away and comes back in desperation."
> C. R.: "Best feeling love stories are those that bring in obstruction <u>after</u> they love - one or both, reader feels, can't do without the other and yet obstruction has parted them. Or obstruction can be there from the start but they love despite it, perhaps not intending to go so far, but it carries them on and on.

Chapter 4

1. Obstruction characters: those whose actions or personality form an obstruction to themselves or to others.
2. Italics mine.
3. Used in *The Town*.
4. Used in *The Waters of Kronos*.
5. *Ibid.* His father does not appear in the photograph.
6. Experienced by C. R. at Three Arch Bay, California.
7. Actual words, "And see the children sport upon the shore." Ideas used in *A Simple Honorable Man*.

8. Examples from the notebook: Artistic and fastidious Foster Whitman cooking in home and hotel (from story "The King Was in the Kitchen"). Society woman staging prizefight for charity.

9. Color: C. R.'s term for material which adds "color" and authenticity to the scene (compare with phrase "local color").

10. From Black Notebook II: "The contrast of things of old days in story with present in which reader lives, the latter of which need not be mentioned. Log Cabin so convenient as in New Home. [When cabin finished, Sabina thinks how convenient everything is - which automatically contrasts to modern-day houses.] Takes 5 days for 200 mile journey."

11. Additional misc. contrasts listed in notebook: animal and man friendship. Manner of telling story, as letters and telegrams which contrast different writers' opinions and character right after each other. (Black Notebook II)

12. The note continues: "but she still loves and believes him despite all disgrace and tears he brought her. She grows lower in respect in town and countryside until climax of No. 2 happens." C. R. was working on this story in Hollywood for MGM.

13. Additional notes applying to the principles discussed in this chapter appear elsewhere. B. I (mainly model quotations from C. R.'s work and others') devotes nine pages to Contrast. Pages of Obstructions (see Chapter 3) occur in both B. II and Maroon Notebook I. There is little specific on form but a great deal on style, which will be considered in Chapter 9. B. II has four pages on new ways of telling a story (which would contribute to Freshness). From that notebook:

Something New New Plot, Way of Telling It

<u>Several lives listed & joined by one thread</u>
(living on same street, married to same husband, in same hotel etc)

<u>From one character to another by cause & effect</u>
(the one who rejects in love is rejected by another & so on)

<u>Story told from new angle, viewpoint</u>
(from telephone operator, child of divorced parents, child or wife of crook, etc.)

Story that keeps you wondering who is who & why
(reader does not know even after end if hero is villain or hero)

The Same Character in Relation with Different People
(a man in successive scenes with his mother, wife, daughter, kept woman and charwoman at office - Fanny Heaslip Lea)

Story Brought Out by Question & Answer Method

Taking Opposite Side of An Old Theme

14. July 26, 1934: Get Back to My Good Outline Book.

December 16, 1945: "Working On My Writing Principles. I feel again the keen pleasure & eagerness in working over my black writing book, re-reading it, swearing to follow it.

"My Black Writing Book. I have discovered it again. I am enthused over it again as I was at Tucson the first time . . . which preceded breaking into Post. I must never put it away."

15. The "Grant" refers to land east of the Sandia Mountains, near Albuquerque, one of a group of large land grants made to early Spanish settlers by the government of Spain. Each had a special history; the Maxwell land grant, in northeastern New Mexico, was especially famous.

16. Used in *The Light in the Forest* and *A Country of Strangers*.

17. "MUST BE ONE sustained action and time for the Post. This eliminates being governor some day in his old age and having an Indian wife and halfbreed children. Instead, for the Post, there should be a certain definite and completed sequence as a trip to Oregon. . . . It should also, for the Post, have his marriage to his first love rather than some Indian woman" (M I).

Chapter 5

1. Written for the Philadelphia *Record*. A correlative note from his January 2, 1940, journal: "I am an erratic, irrational, slow and split-level being who gets anywhere only because of a dogged, persistent

sense of what I want to do in the background that keeps ruling this out and trying again until it suits."

2. My father had been a botanist in the Pennsylvania farm days. Ferns, grasses, and trees were his specialty, and we always carried various field guides on trips, jammed with penned notations of where certain specimens were found—a condensed guide to our travels. C. R.'s books were apt to shed pressed ferns, flowers, and four-leaf clovers.

3. From a letter to me from Florida in 1954: "I've been taking my typewriter out in the car mornings. I drive up Lake Park on one of the deserted paved roads or park along the lake in the shade of a friendly salt cedar and get to work. Your putting your typewriter on your knees gave me the idea. I do the same and have been doing fairly well. . . ."

4. Characteristically, he kept his manuscripts, notes and notebooks in an enormous heavy filing cabinet in the kitchen. His journal makes fun of his "LITERARY BANK: I told her [H] yesterday morning I felt like a fraud going to my fireproof safe-file and taking out my manuscript to work on for the day, like a banker bringing out the cash and currency to [with] which to conduct his day's business" (June 24, 1954).

Chapter 6

1. From his journal (January 5, 1934): "I am learning mood - the sense of the appropriate - everything that doesn't keep up mood seems unreal. It may be real in life. In a story it must sustain mood. If it breaks it, it is unconvincing."

2. This grew out of C. R.'s difficulties in teaching me how to write. The Principles has the subheading "as found out by Vene" and the third paragraph under section 3 speaks of that curious relationship between a writer and his or her character: "Of course some of her inner self enters and motivates the character as the soul enters and motivates a human mortal, but it must be so pure & so concealed that the identity . . . is never visible or to be detected."

3. Preface to the Time Reading Program Special Edition of *The Sea of Grass*.

4. In the short story of Sayward's death, "The Rawhide Knot," published in the *Post* before the novel was written, the family name had been Hewett, perhaps connected with the cutting or hewing down of trees.

5. See Chapter 10.

6. Italics mine in the three journal excerpts.

7. Some of my favorites (probably the early thirties) are Aunt Tom, The Wrong Mistake, Excuse My Star Dust, and Twelfth Nightie. None of these were used for stories.

8. See Chapter 10 and Appendix C on the energy content of language.

9. All but Fault of Angels and Death Takes a Holiday were original.

10. Several pages of illustrations follow in his notebook.

Chapter 7

1. Carl Jung, *Contributions to Analytical Psychology*, quoted by Maud Bodkin in *Archetypal Patterns of Poetry* (Oxford University Press: London, 1963), p. 52.

2. This was a very subjective reading of Knopf's letter.

3. From the journal: "This morning I find in the journal of 1952 the good suggestion of another, THE VALLEY, with M——— K——— living calmly through her family and the abnormalities going on around her and finding a husband and home for herself. It would be done, I suppose, from our point of view as visitors in the valley." The novel was finally done from Chariter's point of view (main character) and was the first novel my father really enjoyed writing, partly because of the Clarks Valley and Pine Tree Farm background, partly because he could freely indulge his sense of comedy.

4. The ten include *The Mountain on the Desert*, technically not a novel but rather a fictionalized philosophical journey.

5. From his journal, February 3, 1957:

> Start a Novel Book
>
> I found myself getting out my "Writing Book" to start a Novel book [for] which I could see most of my story examples of writing would not rank enough to enter.

> I spent nearly all evening on it, including . . . strong, solid types of stuff that I would like in my novels. . . . I feel this Novel Book keenly - solid, unsweetened, authentic, real - the only things that tonight in my cloyed state of reading appealed to me, stirred me.

6. This outline follows that of Primary Writing Principles given in Chapter 5.

Chapter 8

1. Article in *New Mexico Magazine*, March 1957, titled "New Mexico Was Our Fate" and reprinted in *The Spell of New Mexico*, ed. Tony Hillerman (University of New Mexico Press: Albuquerque, 1976).
2. One notebook contains many pages of photographs of old-time people, usually "strong faces," from Wyatt Earp to Roald Amundsen. He also kept folders of photographs which gave a sense of the character of the person or of the place.
3. From folders containing letters of research for the trilogy.
4. At my father's urging, Mrs. Cleaveland wrote the highly successful *No Life for a Lady* and later *Satan's Paradise*.
5. From "New Mexico Was Our Fate" and a letter to Matt and Helen Pearce, November 1, 1953.
6. "New Mexico Was Our Fate."
7. Title of an article in the *Atlantic*, September 1950. See also "Individualists Under the Shade Trees" in *Vanishing America*.
8. A 1935 journal entry: "Such Keen Delight in Work Tonight . . . went through my black book of characters & authentic color, not western, and it moved me strongly. I am deeply enthused in my work of such things, especially the Old Time Feelings & Thoughts and the characters in this book. So real & rich & of life. I am pleased with my job, if I can only use more of these things and less action, obstruction & suspense! Like old times."
9. Used in short story "Early Americana."

Chapter 9

1. *The Free Man*, abandoned in favor of *Tacey Cromwell*.
2. Journal, December 30, 1937.

3. Journal entry of December 20, 1937: "GETTING A PASSION FOR OLD VERSES, SONGS. Tonight I added several to list and a number of epitaphs in verse. I could hardly lay these typewritten pages down. This collection seemed the most interesting and valuable thing in my book."

4. Other journal entries take up the same theme: "I must be simpler, much more detail. My plots are good enough perhaps. It is the writing that dresses them up too much, strains too much for effect. There should not be too much effect aimed at at all . . . the writing is too artificial, sketchy, soaring, overdoing the effects I want to make. I NEED MORE SOLID, STARKER, TRUER WRITING. . . ." (November 22, 1937).

In Maroon Notebook II a page begins:

> "Early Marriage"   My Guide & Standard
>
> In later stories I have been growing literary and high faluting & involved, almost pompous.
>
> I should be more simple & direct, more real & clear in my writing, to carry along story vividly. The average reader especially dislikes poetry, rhetoric, grandiloquence. He wants to lose himself in story.

5. This exhortation appears in a thick folder with the outlines of the trilogy (*The Trees, The Fields, The Town*)—its date is corroborated by journal entries, including that of April 16, 1939. The "books" would be those in the bookcase forming the back of his desk. *Lamb in His Bosom* by Caroline Miller won the Pulitzer prize for 1933.

6. Used in *The Waters of Kronos*.

7. Journals from the years we lived at Pine Tree Farm, 1923–28. They are not the way C. R. describes them but rather Thoreauvian in quality, with the feel of woods and field.

8. He did care enough about her to suggest that I try to follow her when I started a novel of my own in 1957, that she was "my sort." Woolf appeared to have the same effect on both of us (although in different ways): loosening our writing. I would go on to do a book about Woolf (*Virginia Woolf: The Inward Voyage*, Princeton University Press, Princeton, 1970), never dreaming that I would come upon these passages about her in my father's journals.

Chapter 10

1. In a letter to M.M. Matthews of the University of Chicago Press, who asked about these words in the trilogy, C. R. wrote: "Some of these terms came from Penna. and Va. sources as well as Ohio. Many such terms travelled far. For example, plunder, meaning personal belongings, I found used by my old-time ranch friends in New Mexico in the 1930's. I also found it with exactly the same meaning in Pennsylvania nearly 200 years earlier, during the French and Indian Wars and particularly during the Great Runaway on the Susquehanna in the 1770's."

2. These are two from a long list including As lief, overly, High time to, The livelong day, I used to could, All his born years, What fur?, It's a good sight better, Couldn't come it (do it), By rights, Directly (soon).

3. Expressions under these particular headings:

CLEVER, SUPERIOR OR IMPORTANT PEOPLE. His Nibs. Highfalutin'. Give himself airs. Blue stocking. Great folks. Big wig. Euchared out of. Run through (waste). Too deep for. Kick up a dust. Have a mint of money.
LOVE, LADY, MARRIAGE. Pop the question. Sweet on. Set cap for. Wench. Hussy. Spark. Keep bachelor hall. Sheep's eyes. My love and my dove etc.
HUMAN PARTS & DESCRIPTIONS. The horse bone. The hams. Scolding lock. Gut. She filled out plump and nice. Fleshy. The spitting image of etc.
LIKE, SIMILES. Slick as an eel. Ugly as sin. False as a gypsy. Gray as a bat. Wide as the barn door. Stiff as steelyards. Sure as death etc.
MOVEMENT: LIFE & FIGHTING. Touch and go. Kick over the traces. Rip and tear. Make high jack. Go it night and day. Fisticuff. A hitch with etc.
SMELL, TASTE. Stink weed. Lilac smell. Tickle palate. A nip of etc.
STRONG, VIOLENT, ANGRY. To sull. Dander up. Crosspatch. High words between them. Not on speaking terms. Put out. Give him jesse, etc.
UNPLEASANT. Maggoty. Turn the stomach. Smell to high heaven, etc.

4. Excerpts from pages of Beauty:

Altar
Arm, white
Approach to
Aspect

Burns with clear flame
Bowling green
Blade
Bosom
Bank
Boundary
Band of
Breath
Box Bed
Bough
Branch
Blessing

Chiaroscuro
Contour
Curve
Chastity
Chain
Curtain
Clasp of
Cloth
Cloud
Chaplet
Crown Corona
Canvass
Casement
Coverlet
Communion with
Chalice
Carpet
Call of

Drapery
Drop
Dance of
Dike

Fillet
Fleur de lis
Fragment
Flame
Fountain
Finger
Face
Form Figure

Goblet Gem
Garment Gold
Gesture
Garland
Gleam Glint
Guise Glimpse

Halo
Hill
Hand
Haunted by

Inscription
Island

Jewel

Laden with
Likeness of
Lobe
Limb
Land of Faery
Line - lineament

Leaf
Luster
Lamp
Lattice Lace
Lancelot

Mosaic
Morsel
Masthead
Maidenhead
Mane
Message

Orbit

Niche
Nook
Net
Nuance
Nakedness

Pattern
Posture
Path to
Pigeon
Pageant
Pedestal
Patina
Polish
Purity
Plumage

Queenliness

Ribbon
Repose
Recess

River
Rod

Sanctity
Shade
Shape
Stream
Spire

Spray
Sprig
Symbol
Seed
Source
Setting
Sweep
Skein

Sword

Touch
Token
Taste
Tinge
Tincture

5. There were also lists of words for different character types, such as Strong Hard Character. Excerpts from this list: (verbs)

Anchor
Avenge
Affront

Bark
Blow up
Batter
Bare teeth
Benumb
Bite off
Break teeth in
Bang
Butt

Clash
Collide
Crash
Chill
Chop off
Cleave
Corode
Cuff

Defy
Deride
Determine

Elbow
Encounter
Explode

Fix eyes
Flay
Freeze
Frown

Growl
Gripe
Grasp
Grudge
Grit

Hoot
Hate
Harden
Hurl back
Hammer

Insult
Imbedded
Invite

Jostle
Jeer

Knot

Lash
Lunge
Loom up

Mock
Mortared
Maul

Narrow eyes

Petrify
Plunge
Pummel
Punch
Push aside
Push out lips
Poke at
Pound

Rankle
Rasp
Rawhide
Ride rough-shod over
Ram
Roar

Scourge

Show teeth	Spurn	Thrust
Skin	Scoff	Thump
Spit	Set jaws - face	Thunder
Snap - fingers	Shock	Tear
Steel	Slam	
Stiffen		Upthrust
Shove	Trample	
Shoulder	Tread - on	Whip - out
Splinter	Twist	Wound
Snarl	Taunt	Wreak

Chapter 11

1. From a letter to Storm Jameson, May 21, 1949.

2. August 28, 1949, my father wrote me that he was reading a biography of Sibelius and quoted how "Katarina who inherited her father's love of music once wrote a song which she left on the piano. Her father picked it up and made a few improvements but instead of being grateful, Katarina was furious. Mrs. Sibelius sought to comfort her, saying that her father must have approved of it or he would not have bothered to touch it, 'Yes,' Katarina cried, 'but it is no longer mine.' "

3. The story, much revised, did later sell to the *Post*. Several of my father's letters mention the problem of weak characters. December 18 he wrote that no story "can be written about a weak character save perhaps by an expert who does it on purpose and with great strength himself for a certain end. Characters you pity or sympathize with are never weak characters. The minute a character shows weakness, the reader or observer loses sympathy. The ones people feel the most tremendous sympathy with are characters in dire straits, facing great odds, who go into them without complaint, as if they accept their fate and take it." Another letter compared the plight of my heroine with that of Nancy Belle in "Early Marriage": "Only the last days while trying to work out a climax for the story [The Wedding Dress] do I see why it is so hard to do it. You did not plan it so that Sarah Ann has a duty. She merely goes for her wedding dress. There is nothing else she must do. Nancy Belle goes hundreds of miles through a hostile

region for her wedding. That is her duty action. . . ." (January 9, 1949).

4. Two newspaper stories came out of that visit, one to the European edition of the New York *Herald Tribune*, one to the Christian Science *Monitor*. The Tribune story was rather satiric and included his saying, "I've always been interested in people but never liked them. When I'm through with them I put them into a drawer." The *Monitor* article, written to atone for the *Tribune* piece, was warm and sympathetic. I sent Maugham a clip and he replied on his pale blue crested stationery that "One of your innumerable fans" had already sent him a copy, which was surprisingly gracious.

5. From a letter to Eldon C. Hill, Associate Professor, Miami University, Oxford, Ohio, August 4, 1949.

6. See footnote 4, Chapter 8.

Chapter 12

1. This phrase comes from his journal (September 30, 1944): "THE EVER WRITER. "I told V, who is reading, to succeed she must write day and night, be ever interested, thirsty to be writing." Cf. the chapter "The Ever Hunter" in *The Trees*.

2. These were from the *Junior Book* which he wrote and published (see Chapter 1).

3. This was published in *New Letters*, Summer 1984, Vol. 50, No. 4, p. 46.

Appendix A

The First Outline and The Complete Outline

The letter X in the outlines refers to the story "Early Marriage," Y to "Smoke Over the Prairie."

THE FIRST OUTLINE

I. Universal American theme of authentic duty with Fresh Idea.
   Theme X. Marriage in Old West.
   Theme Y. The coming of the railroad to the West.
   Idea X. The long and dangerous marriage journey in old days
   Idea Y. The railroad means destruction of powerful old freighter baron.

II. Theme Fulfillment
   X. Nancy Belle and Stephen safely together married.
   Y. a) Juliana married to railroad engineer; b) Frank Gant's preservation of his power and freighting.

III. Chief powerful obstruction to Fulfillment - out of which come other obstructions.
   X. Chief O. Apaches off reservation in path of marriage journey.
   Other O. Warning. Find friend's cabin burned and horror in water. Sand storm. Horses lost or stolen. Find river swollen in their path.
   Y. Chief O. Railroad threatens to come in and ruin him.
   Other O. - His wife's antagonism. Juliana's lifelessness. R. R. sues for 80 miles of his choice land. Sends him on false alarm to his sheep. Not invited to celebration. Celebration train overtakes him.

IV. Strong Opening Obstruction of chief Obstruction that leaves Strong Situation.

X. No traffic on trail for several days. Something wrong.

Y. His wife demands if he has had R R engineer murdered.

SQUEEZED—

X. Not speaking of it. Uncle Gideon doesn't come as promised. Father can't go. Nancy Belle must go with younger brother. Warned by two not to go.

Y. I am made to hear it. Juliana comes in.

V. Theme Action - Decision and Obstruction Action Toward Fulfillment

X. Nancy Belle insists on going to her wedding. Her preparations of trousseau. The wagon. The journey day by day.

Y. Frank Gant refuses to let Juliana marry R R engineer doomed to failure. He ignores her runaway marriage and coming of the railroad and prepares to fight for his land in court.

VI. Gripping, Ringing Climax to Top It Off.

X. The boy and girl swimming their wagon across flooded river, and then the frontier wedding.

Y. Frank Gant, powerful baron, races ruthlessly with the celebration train that has Juliana and hated son-in-law on board.

VII. Strong Individual American Character you Like or Admire and Who Goes his Way despite All.

X. Nancy Belle, gentle but strong-willed Western girl who will go to her marriage despite all.

Y. Frank Gant, strong baron of frontier, influential sheepman, land owner, merchant and freighter.

VIII. Richness, Power, Atmosphere, Family, Nobility, Sweep, Beauty, What Enthuses you to Write Story.

X. Not much richness and power.

Atmosphere of the post, of marriage and trousseau and journey.

Taking leave of her family, last night in house, goes with brother.

Nobility of her womanhood and boy's manhood to go overcoming obstacles.

Sweep of country and journey.
Beauty of young marriage, memories of home, feeling between brother and sister.

Y. Great Richness and Power of old-time frontier baron.
Atmosphere of establishment, house, life and R R
Family of his antagonistic wife, lifeless daughter and son.
Nobility of his manhood fighting R R to bitter end.
Sweep of R R coming in and his country.
Beauty of Juliana's runaway marriage, of boy's memories of grand establishment, of country.

The Complete Outline below expands on character, contrast, and basic themes, and stresses the natural aspects of the action.

THE COMPLETE OUTLINE

1. Name the epic, significant American theme-idea of real people in their native environment, life and work.
   X Marriage journey in the old days.
   Y Railroad coming into the Western territory

1A. Man in authentic duty pitted against frontier, desert, mountain, or against civilization etc.
   X Frontier, Indians, solitude, sandstorm, flood.
   Y Civilization's railroad coming to destroy his freighting business and baronial splendor.

1B. Containing or touching such universal themes as:
   LIFE EVENTS, INSTITUTIONS. Birth, childhood, youth, love, marriage, death, spring, summer, fall, winter, day and night, festival, holiday. The land, the forest.
   CHARACTER Courage, sacrifice, integrity, manhood, womanhood, motherhood, pioneer self reliance.
   HARDHEADED business stuff to Post, woman stuff to L H J.

2. Theme fulfillment. (Purpose of chief character).
   X To reach Gunstock on wedding day and be married.
   Y1. Juliana to marry her lover, Vance Rutherford.
   Y2. Frank Gant to continue in his baronial power and living.

2A. Decision to do it.
   X. Nancy Belle insists she will go despite danger.

Y1 Mrs. Gant demands of Frank Gant that her daughter marry Vance Rutherford.

Y2 Frank Gant declines utterly to let daughter marry a railroad man, tells Guero there will be no railroad and scorns Vance Rutherford's advance information that railroad is coming.

3. Chief powerful emotional obstruction to theme fulfillment.

X. Apaches off the reservation.

Y1. Father opposes Juliana's match with R R engineer.

Y2. Railroad coming to destroy Frank Gant's freighting business.

3A. Step up obstruction, squeeze it, make it thicker, more at stake by having more dependent on it.

X Father cannot go and Nancy Belle must go alone on dangerous journey with younger brother.

Y1. Juliana walks around like dead person.

Y2. Juliana runs away with engineer and now railroad coming in to ruin him is engineered by daughter's husband.

4. Outstanding power character who takes center of stage and runs away with story.

X. Nancy Belle, quiet, resolute, quality

Y1. Juliana, quiet, in love.

Y2. Frank Gant, powerful, indomitable, unyielding, sincere.

4 A. His or her power to be shown dramatically by plot.

X. Nancy Belle's quiet will, courage, going ahead as a matter of course in her dangerous journey.

Y 1. Juliana's submission to father but love for Vance.

Y 2. Frank Gant's indomitable, uncaring, bathing with Apache chief, lathering horses, righteously refusing Juliana's and mother's requests, taking his bloody whip with which he had lashed herders deserting their sheep.

4 B. Why you like and root for him and her.

X. Because Nancy Belle is quietly determined to go into danger to be at her own wedding.

Y1. Juliana's love for Vance.

Y 2. Frank Gant's sincerity and strength and everything against him.

4 C. A Woman interest

X. Nancy Belle

Y. Juliana, also her mother.

4 D 1. CONTRAST CHARACTERS

X. Nancy Belle's gentility and quality compared to rough frontier father and silent brother.

Y. Frank Gant, strong powerful, against quiet son, gentle Juliana, demanding wife and the Eastern engineer, Vance R.

4 D 2. CHARACTERS CONTRASTED TO SCENES AND EVENTS.

X. Nancy Belle, gentle bride contrasted to rough journey in wagon, horrible danger from Apaches and to flood.

Y. Frank Gant overheard praying in agony. Juliana, lifeless, dispirited coming to radiant life in boy's room elopement night.

4 E. OTHER CHARACTERS NOT TRITE AUTHENTIC DIFFERENT

X. Nancy Belle's father, brother, Stephen, Ignacita, warning family on the trail, friend whose cabin is burned, Uncle Billy Uncle Gideon, preacher and guests at wedding.

Y. John Gant, clerks at store, Vance Rutherford, lawyers, sheep herder, crowd at celebration train.

5. AUTHENTICITY. NOT FICTIONALIZED BUT NATURAL AS COULD AND PERHAPS DID HAPPEN.

X. Nancy Belle being married, going on journey, meeting hardships that do occur and getting married on the end.

Y. The railroad coming in as it did and making freighters no longer necessary on Santa Fe trail, with race as happened at Las Vegas.

5 A. Test natural fit of Theme Fulfillment and Obstruction

X. To go to Gunstock and be married Apaches naturally to be met.

Y. Frank Gant's will to continue his power as leading freighter etc. is naturally disrupted by the railroad coming.

5B. What are the root causes that make situations natural?

X. How Nancy Belle's father brought her gentle mother to

this wild Western place. How Nancy Belle and her brother were brought up to regard it as matter of fact. How Uncle Gideon was coming to let father go. How she and Stephen had met.

Y. How Juliana met Vance. How mother favored railroad. Why and how father could oppose railroad utterly and yet sincerely etc.

5 C1. RICH AUTHENTICITIES OF COLOR AND ATMOSPHERE FOR CHARACTERS, LIFE AND STORY SCENES.

Authenticities of

X. The post, the Putmans, the trousseau, the journey, horses, Apaches, sand storm, flood, wedding.

Y. Authenticities of the Gant Mansion, his vast business and power, the Gants separately, the railroad, Capitan.

5 C2. COLOR CONTRASTED WITH EVENTS AND CHARACTERS.

X. Nancy Belle's room in contrast to rude post. Her calmly packing her gentle bride's trousseau as Ignacita repeats horrible dangers on the trail. Nancy Belle and young brother alone in desert, in Apache infested country etc. Beauty of home after she left it in darkness and when trouble came.

Y. Frank Gant bringing Juliana dresses from St. Louis.

6. NAME THE LIFT GLOW EMOTIONAL EFFECT ON THE READER NOBILITY Courage, keeping word, not giving up, Fighting to end, Doing it for another. FEELING, heart and sympathy. WARMTH, home and family. BEAUTY. Glory, enhancing. POWER (People like to be taken out of their drab lives). Strength, Verve, Wildness, Control, Riches, Position.

X. Courage of Nancy Belle and brother. Duty. Nobility. Keeping word. Family feeling. Warmth of home. Beauty of country and thinking of Stephen, wedding and new home. Wildness of country and Apache danger.

Y. Not giving up. Fighting to the bitter end for what Frank Gant believed right. Glory of those baronial days. Heart and sympathy for Juliana. Family and home. Beauty of those days boy remembers and Juliana coming in to say goodby. Power, verve, strength, wildness, richness, position.

6 A. ESPECIALLY COLOR AND FEELINGS OF FAMILY, FAMILY LIFE AND INTER CONTACTS WHICH IS YOUR FORTE.

X. Household of Putmans. Meeting between father and she that night and when she says goodby. Nancy Belle and brother.

Y. Gant household. Meeting between four Gants. When Juliana gets dresses, runs away, supper table that night, office etc.

6 B. DOES SOMETHING GOOD COME OUT OF IT?

X. Nancy Belle is married and all is well with her at least.

Y. Railroad comes to territory. Wife satisfied and Juliana and Vance can come home to visit.

6 C. DOES IT CONTRIBUTE TO COUNTRY, TO AMERICA?

X. Nancy Belle and Stephen married and go to new ranch house to ranch and raise new family.

Y. Railroad comes to territory, bringing people, schools, civilization.

7. SOMETHING NEW FRESH SUBTLY DONE (Can be theme, idea, plot, way of telling it, hero, story scenes, life.)

X. Presenting Indians and danger in a new way without showing them or even referring to them.

Y. That the railroad coming destroyed such previous transportation kings as Gant who believed sincerely in his methods.

8. COMPRESS STORY INTO CONTINUITY OF BIG DRAMATIC OBSTRUCTION SCENES.

8 A. <u>Plot and write straight to hard-to-do conflict situations.</u>

X. Nancy Belle and father discuss whether to go.

Y. Meeting between four Gants. At table when Juliana has gone. Vance Rutherford beards Frank Gant in store. Nettie and Frank Gant meeting when he returns from sheep alarm and he gets whip to go to town.

8 B. OPENING OBSTRUCTION.

X. Strange that there is no traffic on trail. Silent. Something wrong.

Y. Wife demands of Frank Gant if he has killed Juliana's lover.

8 C. WHICH BRINGS IN THE AMERICAN THEME

X. Nancy Belle is taking the trail 200 miles to be married.

Y. Frank Gant is accused of [by] wife because Juliana's lover is engineer for hated railroad.

8 D. Squeezed. step up of opening obstruction.

X. No one speaks of silence on trail. Uncle Gideon doesn't come. Father can't go with girl. She must go with young brother. Warned by Ignacita and lone travelers not to go on.

Y. Nettie Gant makes boy come in and hear conflict instead of staying outside and guessing. Juliana comes in voluntarily because it concerns her, pale, silent. Stiffness between Frank and Nettie Gant. Hint at killing brought in.

8 E. Character decision & obstruction - action toward theme fulfillment which leaves greater obstruction.

X. Nancy Belle insists upon going & starts.

Y. Frank Gant refuses to let Juliana marry a railroad scoundrel.

8 F. Greater obstruction that is left.

X. Nancy Belle has dangerous journey ahead of her and leaves next morning, grave and shaken. Boy sober.

Y. Juliana looks at father with eyes of dead person, goes around lifelessly, refuses presents he brings her.

8 G. Further great obstructions natural to theme fulfillment.

X. Nancy Belle and brother find cabin of friend just burned by Apaches. Sand storm engulfs them that night. Horses gone next morning. Nancy Belle stays alone until late following night while brother goes for them. Coyotes maddening.

Y. Juliana elopes with man her father refused. Now the railroad coming in to destroy his freight business is engineered and built by his daughter's husband. Frank Gant hauled into court to lose 80 miles of choice land for railroad right of way. He loses while he is called away on faked call. Goes to town when he returns, with whip to meet officials who did this to him.

8H. Gripping, strong, if possible ringing and exciting climax

THAT TOPS OFF STORY AND ITS EMOTION. UNEXPECTED IF POSSIBLE.

X. After overcoming all hardships thus far, Nancy Belle and brother find Rio Grande swollen by floods and blocking path.

Y. Frank Gant, deeply angered, races deadly with celebration train on way to town to horsewhip officials and wins. Juliana on train.

8 I. NEW REAL LIFE SOLUTION THAT LIFTS, IS NOT TRITE SWEET OR PERFECT

X. Nancy Belle is married surrounded by frontier friends and brother.

Y. Frank Gant is killed on crossing by the train he has beaten.

Appendix B

Plotting the Story

This eight-page outline, handwritten, is dated August 23, 1934. At the very top of the first page is noted: "check every word like 'authentic duty.'" Black Notebook II.

O. Name the significant, epic American theme-idea, of real people in their native environment, life and work.

O A Man in authentic duty pitted against Frontier, sea, desert, mountain, air, cold, snow, flood, lonely desert, wild land.

O B Life Events and seasons.
Birth. Childhood. Youth. Love. Marriage, age, Death. Breeding. Children.
Spring. Sunshine. Cloudy. Afternoon. Night. Winter. Festival - Holiday - Xmas.

O C Life Institutions.
Home Family. Friendship. Partnership. Brotherhood, Science, Fellowship. Feud. School. Father, Mother.

O D Character.
Courage. Sacrifice. Integrity. Manhood.
Womanhood. Motherhood. Power.

O E Timely Theme.
Pioneer self reliance.

O F Western Theme [this section crossed out]
Grass. Water. Horse. Sheep. Sheriff. Trail.
Herd. Drought. Guns. Bad man.

O G Misc. Salable Theme [this line crossed out]
Business to Post [Sat. Eve. Post]. Hard-headed, practical, man stuff that Post likes.
Women's interest to women's magazines.

1 Theme Fulfillment. Name it!

2 Theme Action. Name it!

Early Marriage: marriage journey

New Home: home protection against I [Indians]

Frontier Woman: journey across plains

What pioneer character does from beginning to end toward theme fulfillment & against obstruction.

2 A Decision to do it.

3 Powerful Obstruction to Theme Fulfillment that grips you, stirs up powerful emotion to give energy flow to interest.

3 A Faced by present trouble
other obstructions

3AA To life & happiness

3AB Love separation

3AC Conflict

3 B Faced by future trouble. Suspense

3BA Danger to life & happiness

3BB Love separation

3BC Mystery. Things happen not explained to reader.

3 C What is much at stake to thicken issue? Not thin. Step it up. Does it greatly matter? Much dependent on it.

3 D Squeeze it. Great Justification.

3 E Model plots to consult.

3 F Very important! Obstruction must clearly matter to hero & each one matter harder, stronger. Check this!

4 Authenticity. Naturalness.

4 A Test absolutely natural fit of Theme Action, Fulfillment and Obstruction - must be natural as Marriage Journey, Marriage Ceremony & Indians & River of Early Marriage.

4 B Go to [crossed out] natural root reasons for situation & character.

4 C Mood dare not be broken even by something real.
What is mood here?

5 Outstanding Power Character who is the center of stage in such drama as shows his or her power characteristics

5 A His or her power that fits plot

5 B Why you like and root for him and her

5 C Contrast characters

5 D A woman interest
5 E Other characters
[most of section 6 that deals with principle of Contrast is crossed out, including contrast of character, of scene, of Present with days or places where things are different—included below are two sections not deleted]
6 C In Manner of Telling Story
Letter & telegram stories contrast characters, their language, viewpoint, actions & scenes constantly against each other.
6 E Twists, surprises.
7 Something new, Fresh, Subtly Done
New theme idea
New plot, way of telling it
New hero, heroine
New story scenes, life background
8 Name the lift, glow that is emotional effect on the reader. Does something strikingly good come out of it? Will it sell the English magazines? Should contribute to West as frontier home, woman, bringing first piano there rather than playing it [i.e., the bringing of the first piano to the territory in "The Square Piano" is part of civilizing the frontier—playing it would have no thematic importance.]
8 A Nobility
Courage Keeping Word
Sacrifice Doing it for another
Not Giving Up Fighting to end
8 B Feeling Heart Sympathy
8 C Warmth Home Family
8 D Beauty Glory Enhancing
8 E Power. Makes story stronger, more vivid.
People like to be taken out of their drab lives
Verve Strength Wildness Primitive
Calm Strength Control
Richness Position
8 F Lightness Humor
[between sections 8 & 9 is note to "Pay more attention to Obstruction-interest & follow this"]
9 Make out & try on H & V. Synopsis of Obstruction-Interest

Action compressed to Big Dramatic Scenes that serve to portray character and background as you go along.

9 AA Obstruction interest, preferably with suspense mystery

9 AB Begin with brilliant [?] punch line

9 AC Beginning Theme action (Elaboration of obstruction toward theme-fulfillment, taking advantage of Reader's energy already stirred in obstruction).

9 BA Increasing Obstruction-Interest

9 BB Increasing Theme action (Elaboration of Obstruction)

9 CA Climax Obstruction - Interest, desperate, seemingly unconquerable

9 CB Climax. Theme Action (Elaboration of Obstruction)

9 CC Something happens in climax different & more than expected

9 D New real-life solution that lifts -
not trite, sweet or perfect

9 DA Bigger solution than expected

9 DB One of troubles brings solution

Now Imagine yourself for a solid day as the central character living with the other characters. . . .

[Note: this outline is continued in Maroon Notebook II with points 10 through 13, the heading changing from "Plotting the Story" to "Writing the Story."]

Appendix C

The Energy Content of Language

Chapter excerpted from *The Mountain on the Desert* (pp. 69–91), a Socratic dialogue about the human use and transference of energy. The terms are metaphoric, the philosophical meanings universal in implication. The main character is Michael, a weaver in the mountains of New Mexico, who embodies C. R.'s views. His interlocutors are Carl, Dennis, Milt, Mohammed, the blind poet R. V., and the narrator.

"I would say language is self-expression with sometimes the added purpose of communication. The chief purpose is to release energy to the speaker. Even when intended for the listener, words are meant to make him react in certain ways to provide energy relief for the speaker. This energy purpose influences the speaker's choice of words and language. He learns that certain words and combinations of words bring certain energy effects in both himself and others. So he uses words accordingly. Am I saying anything you understand?"

"I'm not sure." The blind man's face was attentive but restrained.

"I mean," the weaver went on, "that the real measure of language is the energy content of words and their arrangement. You know the tone of voice of one speaker may relax you while another may annoy or excite you. The tone is providing you with more energy than expenditure in the one case and less in the other. There are races that speak with a very strong burr like the Scotch and some of the Russians. Anyone who hears them feels the energy required by the speaker to form these words in his mouth. Even though unconscious, there's more physical effort and accomplishment in the speaker than in the words of the soft-spoken races. This effort arouses more energy flow in the speaker and more in the hearer. You mightn't understand him, but you feel the increased energy."

I saw the first gleam in the sightless eyes of the student poet.

"Please go on," he requested.

"Like the voice and tone," the weaver obliged, "so the words a man uses and the way he places them together control energy responses in the speaker and listener. The powerful speaker or writer is an instinctive master of processes to release energy flows in his hearers or readers."

"Are these the same release processes we know?" Carl asked.

"Yes, but in language there are additional processes. One I call merging. A word usually sets off more than one cell group and the energy flow of each are merged. In a brand new word, the merged energy may be thin and slight, say that of the meaning, look and sound of the word and the experience. However, in more common words like 'boy' and 'girl,' each experience with them in person or with the words or pictures representing them, adds a bit more rate-flow. In time when either of these words strikes our eye or ear, it sets off its particular accumulation of merged flows in us. It's like turning a switch so that a circuit of mingled lights, most of them very faint but contributing by weight of numbers, others brighter, flash on at the same time, forming a certain sensory flow from the energy and rates involved."

"How about words that have several different meanings?" R. V. asked.

"Different meanings are often given a word originally to animate it with more energy. For example, the first student or teacher who called a translation of Caesar or Vergil a pony felt the extra vitality of the merged flows when he first thought of it and again when he used the word aloud and students laughed. What gave it the increased energy was the secondary meaning which in this case was the mental conception of the student not having to labor on foot but riding easily on horseback. In the course of the history of a language, a word acquires many new meanings, and most of them are given it for increased energy purposes."

Michael considered, and went on.

"Once a word carries several meanings, then each of them contribute some energy flow when the word is used. For instance, the word 'boy' may suggest a waiter, a servant, a redcap, a child or even a highboy. A word like 'air' may set off the various notions of a wind, a tune, the human spirit, a manner and other things. The particular meaning the speaker intends usually dominates but energy from the subconscious quickening of the other meanings is also present. All of these merge for a moment."

"There are words spelled differently that sound alike," Dennis mentioned.

"Yes, they'd hardly be affected by writing, but they might in speaking. More important, I think, are words with a resemblance in sight or sound to other words and yet with a distinct meaning. When such a word is used, the cell groups of both meanings are invoked and their flows merged. The garden plant 'salvia' may have energy echoes of 'saliva.' Also, a part of a word may have its own individual cell groups which reinforce the rate-flows of the larger group. Such as 'cow' and 'coward.' "

"I've always felt 'coward' an interesting word," R. V. said.

"As a matter of fact," Michael pointed out, "we can never be quick and sensitive enough to detect all the merged energy content of a word. Each word is a chord, sometimes minor, sometimes major, of rate-flows compounded of cell groups established in our experience."

"You begin to excite me," R. V. said.

"Up to this time," Michael went on, "much of our merging has been more or less unconscious. Now let's look at the conscious merging of energy flows. For example, the word 'man' sets off its own certain compound of rate-flows. If you add the word 'big' and say it was 'a big man,' you set off a secondary compound. As one word closely follows and involves the other, the rate-flow of 'big' is merged with that of 'man.' Now if you add the word 'dangerous,' you reinforce the energy flow of 'big man' with the considerably more energy associated with 'danger,' making it stronger and more vivid. How about giving me other examples, well known ones in poetry or something like that?"

It took us a little time to get on the right track.

" 'Wee sleekit, cow'rin', tim'rous beastie,' from Burns," R. V. suggested.

"Good!" Michael beamed.

" 'So red the rose,' from Omar," Mohammed said.

" 'A brotherhood of venerable trees,' from Wordsworth."

"Isn't this just description?" Carl asked.

"Description is one name for reinforcement of rate-flow," Michael explained. "But you can describe or reinforce too much. Too many words spread the energy too thinly over each word and as a result the energy effect in us is dulled. There's a point of diminishing returns. We'll get to that later. Right now let's look at different kinds of energy reinforcement. We've had reinforcement with the spoken word. Now let's reinforce with implied or unspoken words. Can anybody tell me what I mean?"

We couldn't. He went on.

"Let's take the same word 'man.' This time instead of calling him a man, let's call him by his occupation, say, 'a tanner.' Now I don't mean the phrase 'this man who's a tanner.' That's too long. It spreads the energy of both meanings, man and tanner, over too many words. When we simply call him 'the tanner' we first imply a man, touching off the energy of this conception, then reinforce it with energy flows from our experience with hides, vats, bark, leather and so on. We've doubled the released energy without adding any more words to dilute it. All these several energy flows are joined in one word, making it stronger, brighter. The same thing happens when we refer to a man as a mule driver or a sailor."

We were getting interested now. I think he felt it. He hitched forward.

"The inventive hunger of man for more energy flow from his words didn't stop there. He found out a long time ago that if instead of saying 'sailor' or 'mule driver' he called them something like a 'tar' or 'mule skinner,' he could give his words still more energy so he and the hearer could feel them more keenly. What happened was that there was now energy from three general cell groups, those of the man, sailor and tar, all merged and concentrated in one word, giving it power."

"How about personal nicknames?" asked Milt, who was never slow.

Michael nodded his quick approval.

"Here we have man again striving for more energy in his speech. Call a man Skinny, and the flow he sets off in you is reinforced by those of leanness, skin and so on. If he's big and you call him Shorty, it adds the flows of bigness and shortness. If he once stole a sheep and you call him Sheep, the energy flows he invokes in you are reinforced by those of a sheep plus the act and consequences of stealing it."

"You mean slang has a scientific basis?" Mohammed asked.

"The slangy and purist are after the same end—increased energy power in their speech," Michael assured. "They use the same psychoenergic processes basically but with different sensitivity and inhibitions. For instance, before slang, man was more of an artist and reinforced his words with energy flow from poetic conceptions. He called a pedestrian a foot traveler and a boat a wave traveler. To the modest energy flows of tramping he merged those of feet and traveling—to those of a boat, those of waves and traveling. Can you give me any more?"

We thought a while.

"'Watcher of the skies' for astronomer," R. V. suggested.

"'The fruit of the lips' for speech, from the Bible," this from Milt.

"'Harvester of the sea' for fisherman," R. V. said again.

"'He who walks alone' for a leper," Mohammed suggested.

"'The bear who walks like a man' for a Russian," Michael gave.

"Aren't these metaphors?" Carl asked.

"Psycho-energically," Michael said, "a metaphor is a descriptive phrase with a secondary meaning whose function is to reinforce the cell group representing the first meaning with additional energy so it can glow more brightly in the mind. All metaphors aren't necessarily poetic or dignified. The expression 'top drawer' is an example. When this is used in connection with an object, the cell group representing the object and the grade of its quality are reinforced by energy flow from the mental vision of a top drawer in a desk or table. How about giving some more energy reinforcements of the type called metaphors?"

"'Castles in Spain,'" R. V. said.

"'Burn the candle at both ends,'" this from Milt.

"'Put the cart before the horse,'" Carl suggested.

"'Upset the apple cart,'" Dennis said quickly.

"The last three," Michael commented, "are especially effective because they're what I call fantastic or topsyturvy. An unusual situation like that sets off a good deal of new energy flow in the hearer or witness. This secondary flow merged with that of primary idea illuminates it with more energy, makes it more vivid. Any more?"

"'Born with a silver spoon in his mouth,'" Mohammed said.

"Still fantastic," Michael nodded.

"'The grapevine route.'"

"'Give an inch, take a mile.'"

"'Apple pie order.'"

"'Father Time.' 'The sands of time.'"

"I hope you're seeing what's happening in you psycho-energically with these metaphors," Michael said. "With Father Time, the energy flow from the picture of an old man with a scythe is merged with that of your ordinary or primary conception of time. In the phrase 'sands of time,' you see the sands running out of an hour glass, and energy flows from that are added and merged to those of ordinary time."

"I can't say that I get much of this consciously," Milt confessed.

"No, the most sensitive of us may not be aware of much," Michael said.

"How about poor metaphors?" R. V. asked.

"A metaphor must have points of energy transference in itself and also with the group it stands for," Michael pointed out. "Otherwise, the energy isn't merged economically. Take the old example, 'The ship of state stood on its feet.' The descriptive words in this sentence don't belong to the same general combination of energy groups in us. A ship has no feet, so there's no common transfer point. This means the energy is eaten up, never merges to reach the primary group and illuminate it. We say it's a mixed metaphor. On the other hand, we may say, 'The ship of state rode the rough seas.' Now 'ship' and 'rough seas' belong to the same combination of cell groups in us. The energy can be merged inside the group where its transfer is efficient."

"I think I see," R. V. murmured.

"The crude speaker tries to force energy between unconnected groups in the hearer's mind," Michael pointed out. "The effective speaker takes advantage of natural transfer points. Somebody awhile ago gave a phrase about trees and brotherhood."

" 'A venerable brotherhood of trees,' " R. V. repeated.

"Good. 'Brotherhood' is in the same general family group as 'venerable.' Brothers may have a venerable father. As a result energy is merged and retained in the sentence. It would be psycho-energically less efficient to say, 'a brotherhood of sawn trees' or 'a brotherhood of profitable trees' or 'a brotherhood of beautiful trees.' The metaphors are mixed or poor. What we mean when we say this is that the groups of the individual words are more or less unconnected in our nervous system and the energy can't be easily merged."

"Can you give us another example?" Milt asked.

"Well, let's take the title of a book, Tolstoi's *War and Peace*. Peace being closely connected with war, the cell groups are strongly and naturally connected. Peace comes out of war, war out of peace, and one is often on the lips during the reign of the other. So 'peace,' a mild word, is directly reinforced and strengthened by energy from the very powerful and violent word 'war.' "

"Doesn't contrast have anything to do with it?"

"By contrast I suppose you mean unlikeness. Offhand I'd say that effective contrast in words calls for more than unlikeness. You need the transfer of energy from one object to another making the words and phrase more vivid. A common point for this energy transfer is an important psycho-energic requirement. For instance, rabbits are unlike war, but if we said 'War and Rabbits' or 'War and Lambs,' nothing much happens, except to someone primarily interested in rabbits or sheep. There's little connection between the two cell groups involved. There's no place to transfer energy. That's to say, the phrase has little power or contrast."

"You surprise me, Michael," R. V. declared.

"I hope so. The technique of energy transference is important. Its efficiency depends on how direct the energy may be transferred. Take for instance the phrase 'beat back the woods.' Its not so strong a phrase in my opinion as 'beat the woods back.' The strong energy flow of the word 'beat' is passed more directly to the quieter energy group standing for 'woods.' You see and feel the action more vividly. It's much the same with 'Blow the man down.' Energy is merged more directly with 'man' than in 'Blow down the man.' "

"That brings up something," Carl broke in. "What's more effective—the adjective before the noun like we say it in English or after a noun like the Spanish do it?"

"It all depends, I think," Michael reflected. "Order of words is like arrangement of plot in novels. Its chief purpose is to arouse energy flow to bathe and bring to life what is being said and done. These energy flows keep the reader interested in what's going on. Otherwise we might go to sleep. The mystery book gets its effect much the same way. It often sets off a violent deficit cell group at the beginning in the form of an unexplained or unpunished murder. This group goes on spending energy and bathing unimportant, often banal, incidents with that energy until the group is finally relaxed and dismissed by the revealed identity and arrest or death of the murderer. Reveal the murderer at the start or half way through, and you'll have to supply some other form of energy release to keep the reader from laying the book down."

"Tell us more about this!" Carl said.

"On the other hand," Michael went on, "you may hear a long anecdote about someone who isn't named or whose name you didn't catch. The details aren't exciting and you're not much interested. You scarcely listen. On the end you learn it's about a friend of yours or at least someone you know. You ask then if it can be told again. If you had known it was he or she at the beginning, the large cell group in you representing this friend or figure would have been very active supplying energy to the things told about him, making them interesting and vivid."

"You spoke awhile ago about the diminishing energy of too many words of description," R. V. reminded.

"I meant chiefly words that get in the way between energising words and those to be energised. As a rule, they absorb more energy than they contribute. Also most word energy flows subside quickly. If several words are interspersed, by the time you get to the word that should receive energy transfer from the earlier word, the energy flow has trickled off and the effect is lost."

"Then the best language is brief?"

"Not always. I would rather say that ideas have more energy and power if the words representing them are compressed. It's rather hard to do. Poets and cowboys, men who live alone and have lots of time to taste words and think about them, are best at it. They and geniuses. For instance, I remember a phrase from Shakespeare, 'full star.' "

R. V.'s face kindled.

" 'That full star that ushers in the even,' "he quoted.

Michael nodded.

"It's a good example we haven't touched on up to now. I mean the energy management process of compression. Given the same amount of energy to spend on two phrases, the fewer words of the shorter will naturally be more energised. Let's examine this phrase, 'full star.' First, the hearer's or reader's energy flows established with full moon are merged with those of the star. But that isn't the main source of the phrase's energy. If the poet had said, 'That bright star with a brilliance like the fullness of the moon,' it would have been the merging of energy alone. By compressing the allusion of twelve words into two, you get a concentration of energy that makes the two words sparkle. This is the psycho-energic process of compression."

"I think I see," R. V. exclaimed. His unseeing eyes were turned on the weaver with an intense deference. "How about another of Shakespeare's phrases, 'dry death'?"

"Excellent. The energy rates and flows of dying on land plus those of implied dying in the water are all compressed into two words."

"How about 'old night' from Milton?" Milt asked.

"A milder example. There's not so much energy to be merged and compressed into two words."

" 'The lark at heaven's gate' from Shakespeare again," R. V. said.

"One of the best. The old master seems to have the highest batting average. A great deal more energy than appears is compressed here—the energies of the bird, its singing in the sky, its flight to the very gate of heaven, which word itself carries a great many energy flows of life and death."

" 'I am alpha and omega, the beginning and the end,' " from Milt.

"Very good," Michael said. "There are nine or ten words. But into those nine or ten are compressed about everything we know—birth and death, life, creation and destruction, and above all, the Powers That Be."

After a moment Michael asked if we would drive him to the San Pedro Mountain. We got out of the cars where the mountain dropped away beneath us. We stood overlooking a large wasteland laced by dry sandy watercourses.

Michael pointed out points of interest, making no concession to R. V., who seemed to prefer that kind of treatment, standing with the others, his sensitive face alive with feeling as if he perceived something beyond sight.

"You see all those arroyos?" Michael asked. "They're dry or seem to be. But you don't have to dig down far in their stream bed to find water. Underground moisture follows all their twists and turns. It comes from past rains and snows. That's the way with words. You don't see the energy flow, but it's there if you dig underneath. It's established from past emotions and experience."

"What are the best words to use in writing?" Carl asked.

"Well, there's still another source of energy in words and phrases that we haven't touched on as yet. I'm sure the power found in these particular words and phrases has been noticed by the bright men who write English text books, although the psycho-energic causes may have escaped them."

"What kind of words do you mean?" Carl asked.

"R. V. wasn't with us the other day," Michael answered. "Perhaps the rest of you will excuse me for repeating how ancient man detected danger and game by means of his senses, principally sight. As a result, strong energy flows are associated with our senses. Visual energy release, being the strongest, usually dominates consciousness. So, other things being equal, word pictures release more energy in the reader and hearer than words of the other senses."

"Are you by any chance speaking of imagery?" R. V. asked.

"Imagery is your name for the visual energy-release process."

"A lot of Shakespeare's power is supposed to be from imagery," Carl said.

"Well, let's see. How about giving us some examples that release energy through the eye?"

Carl couldn't think of any at the moment, but R. V. could.

" 'Proud-pied April.' "

" 'Like the dyer's hand.' "

" 'Lady, by yonder blessed moon I swear, that tips with silver all these fruit-tree tops.' "

" 'Sit, Jessica. Look how the floor of heaven is thick inlaid with patines of bright gold; there's not the smallest orb which thou behold'st but in his motion like an angel sings.' "

"Excellent," Michael praised. "I think you can see what R. V. and Carl call imagery and what I call words that release energy flow established through the eye. So much for poetry. Let's see if the common man found any energy released by slang or colloquial imagery."

It took a few minutes to understand what he wanted. Then we all contributed.

" 'The double cross.' "

" 'The blue stocking.' 'The blues.' "

" 'A dark horse.' "

" 'A feather in his cap.' "

" 'The lame duck.' "

Michael beamed at us.

"Good enough. Now we come to another phase of the eye process. You remember when we were over at Celso's we found out that if the object seen is moving, it releases more energy than when standing still. Well, it has the same effect in words. I wonder if you literary young gentlemen can give me specimens."

We discussed it awhile.

" 'Winking Mary-buds begin to ope their golden eyes,' from *Cymbeline*," R. V. started us off.

" 'If I take the wings of the morning and dwell in the uttermost parts of the sea,' from the Psalms," this from Milt.

"There's another from Shakespeare. From *Hamlet*," R. V. said. " 'Nor do not saw the air too much with your hand thus.' "

"I know a few from Omar Khayyam," Mohammed mentioned. " 'The moving finger writes' and 'Yon rising moon that looks for us again—how oft hereafter will she wax and wane!' "

"I can think of several from the Bible," Milt said. " 'My cup runneth over,' 'The walls of Jericho came tumbling down,' and 'Flee as a bird to your mountain.' "

"There's more from Shakespeare," R. V. said. "Why, man, he doth bestride the narrow world like a Colossus, and we petty men walk under his huge legs and peep about,' from *Julius Caesar*, and 'Tomorrow and tomorrow and tomorrow creeps in this petty pace from day to day,' from *Macbeth*."

"I can't think of any literary gems," Dennis said, "but I can slang. How about, 'I ran into So and So down town'?"

"Very good," Michael declared. "Notice how much more energy is released by 'ran into' than if you said, 'I happened to meet So and So down town.' 'Ran into' implies collision, accident, complications."

"Oh, I know plenty of those," Milt said. " 'He flew off the handle,' 'He blew his top,' 'He got a big kick out of it,' and 'He kicked like a steer.' "

" 'Like a bat out of hell,' " Carl said. " 'Go fly a kite.' 'Jump in the lake.' "

It went fast after that.

" 'Off his trolley.' "

" 'Fall between two stools.' "

" 'Stars fell on Alabama.' "

" 'Swap horses in the middle of a stream.' "

"Now let's skip it," Michael said, pleased with his own contribution. "Let's try words that release energy through the ear. R. V., how about the bard?"

" 'Hark, hark, the dogs do bark,' " Carl grinned.

"I can't think of too much sound in Shakespeare," R. V. confessed. "Not at the moment, anyway. There's 'I'd rather be a dog and bay the moon,' from *Julius Caesar*, and 'Full of sound and fury signifying nothing,' from *Macbeth*."

"There's plenty in the Bible," Milt said. " 'The morning stars sang together, and all the sons of God shouted for joy.' "

"I read one last night in Scott Fitzgerald," Dennis said. " 'Planets in chime.' "

" 'The bells of St. Mary's,' " this from Carl.

When we came to slang, there were still fewer that we could think of.

" 'Oh, for crying out loud!' "

" 'Before you can say Jack Robinson.' "

Michael shook his head.

"It doesn't look like common man released too much energy through ear-words. How about energy flow from taste and smell words? In poetry or slang, it doesn't matter which."

"'A very ancient and fish-like smell' I think from *The Tempest*, and 'Something is rotten in the state of Denmark,' from *Hamlet*," R. V. said.

"'I smell a rat,'" Dennis said.

"'A land flowing with milk and honey,'" Mohammed said.

"'Wet your whistle,'" Carl said.

"'The fathers have eaten sour grapes, and the children's teeth are set on edge,'" Milt said.

"'All the perfumes of Arabia will not sweeten this little hand,' from *Macbeth*," R. V. suggested.

Michael was plainly pleased.

"Now we come to the last of the senses. Energy released from words of feeling."

"'A thorn in the flesh,'" Mohammed said.

"'He that toucheth pitch shall be defiled,'" from Milt.

"'And then the lover, sighing like a furnace,' from *As You Like It*," R. V. said.

"I think R. V. gave another sample of feeling a little while ago when he said, 'full of sound and fury, signifying nothing,'" Carl said.

Michael nodded.

"Many lines have energy flows from words of more than one sense. How about giving me a few?"

We thought for a while.

"'Bell, book and candle.'"

"Eye and ear and perhaps feeling from religion," Michael analyzed.

"'Here's mud in your eye.'"

"Eye, movement and feeling," Michael said.

"'A bee in his bonnet.'"

"Ear, eye, movement, feeling. That's a good one."

"'Spitting image.'"

"Eye, taste and feeling."

R. V. had been silent up to now.

"I can give you one from Milton.

> 'A thousand fantasies
> Begin to throng into my memory,

> Of calling shapes, and beck'ning shadows dire,
> And airy tongues that syllable men's names
> On sands and shores and desert wildernesses.' "

"Very good," Michael nodded. "Eye, movement, ear, feeling and plenty of them."

"There's a phrase I want to ask you about," Milt said. "It's from *The Lost Chord*. I always thought it a powerful one. 'Death's bright angel.' "

"I think that brings us to a new classification." Michael spoke thoughtfully. "First we had simple unconscious merging of energy flows in one word. After that we had conscious merging and reinforcement by using secondary words and phrases. Then we had stepup of energy flow by compression. Finally we talked about energy released by sense words. Well, now we come to energy reinforcement of lines by shock words and conceptions. 'Death's bright angel' uses such a shock word. The words 'angel' and 'bright' are themselves pretty strong, but when used in connection with such a power-rich word as 'death,' they're bathed in energy to make them fairly glow."

"What if she had said, 'The bright angel of death'?" R. V. asked.

"Reactions in different organisms vary. I think to some of us the phrase would have been less powerful and perhaps more beautiful. The word 'death' coming first carries with it such painfully high and uprooting rates that to me it drains energy from the words 'bright' and 'angel.' If the latter words were to come first, they'd have enough energy of their own to glow of themselves for a moment, and the word 'death' coupled so closely after should make them brighter. At least it does in my nervous system."

We repeated the words to ourselves and agreed with him, all but Mohammed, who said he liked it better the other way.

"Isn't 'death' a deficit word?" Dennis asked.

"It is indeed," Michael agreed. "To most people, especially soft modern people, it's so painful that when it's associated with a contemporary or a friend, we often say, 'He passed on' instead of 'died.' Sailors used to say 'Davy Jones' locker' instead of the painful words 'drowning' or 'burial at sea.' As words become overburdened with high expenditure, most of us try to escape by using less deficit-burdened substitutes. The word 'consumption' became too distressing, so we started saying 'tuberculosis.' Then that became loaded and we tried to disguise it with 't.b.' Now 't.b.' has become distressing itself, so out here some of us don't say 'He has t.b.' but 'he's a cure chaser.' It avoids the deficit rates of 't.b.' and substitutes the sense-motion flows of 'chaser.' "

"I guess that's why we don't say 'graveyard' any more," Carl said. "First we changed it to 'cemetery' and now we're changing that to 'memorial park.' "

"Just the same," Michael pointed out, "despite the pain and distress, deficit words carry strong energy flows. The energy simply doesn't measure up to the greater spending or need. Take the word 'dead.' Its energy flows put it in a lot of popular expressions. 'A dead beat,' 'dead pan' and 'a dead stick landing.' Can you give me any more phrases with shock words?—clean ones, I mean."

It didn't take long for us to catch on.

" 'Blood and iron.' "

" 'The gentle lady and the Moor.' "

" 'The viper in his bosom.' "

" 'Lightning never strikes twice in the same place.' "

" 'Stealing the other fellow's thunder.' "

"How about 'thunder mug'?" Carl grinned.

"I can give you a long one from Addison," R. V. volunteered.

> " 'The soul, secure in her existence, smiles
> At the drawn dagger and defies its point.
> The stars shall fade away, the sun himself
> Grow dim with age, and nature sink in years.
> But thou shalt flourish in immortal youth,
> Unhurt amidst the war of elements,
> The wreck of matter and the crush of worlds.' "

Michael looked at him with admiration.

"What would we do without you, R. V.? This technique is the opposite of compression. We might call it enlargement with vigor and power. Let's state the idea of Addison's simply. We might say, 'the soul survives and is eternal.' Compare the effect of that on you with Addison's strong energy flow words—'the drawn dagger,' 'the stars shall fade away,' 'the sun himself grow dim.' What's the rest of it?"

" 'The war of elements, the wreck of matter and the crush of worlds.' "

"Splendid. The energy from these powerful words, phrases and conceptions bathe the lines and us with brilliant light and power.

Good poetry is full of energy flows. In fact, ordinary words in great poetry are like dark inert stars lighted by the passing bright stars of energy words."

"I can give you more from Shakespeare on that," R. V. volunteered. " 'Lilies that fester smell far worse than weeds' from the Sonnets. And this line that some think is one of the most beautiful ever written. It's from *Macbeth*. 'There lay Duncan, his silver skin laced with his golden blood.' "

Several of us had comments on that.

"Some words are beautiful that aren't strong or shock words at all," Milt declared. "Say 'morning' and 'home' and 'window.' "

"If a word is beautiful and moving to anyone, there are strong rate-flows attached to the word for the person involved. For instance, 'morning' calls up the strong rates of 'night' which it dissolves. 'Home' is most beautiful to somebody in whom deficits have been aroused by the suggestion of being away from home and family. 'Windows' carry a lot of energy flow among prisoners, the bedridden and housebound who look longingly out of windows. The word also associates the absence of a person or ship at sea looked for. More than that, it implies being shut up by walls. Windows are a break through for the eye and spirit."

For a long time that morning we stood in the sun on San Pedro Mountain, looking down on the network of dry arroyos. Michael talked eloquently. This was only a glimpse, he insisted, of energy in language. Before we started for home he came back again to Tolstoi's title *War and Peace*.

"There's something else in these words. I hope to talk about it later on but I can't resist mentioning it today. I mean something more than that certain contrast which is energy transferred from a strong word to a milder one. The phrase 'Viper in his bosom' has contrast and so does 'The gentle lady and the Moor.' But neither has what I mean. I won't talk more about it today except to say that it's the most important process I know. It's the establishment of strong energy flows which keep on after the painful things that made them have passed. Do you see what I mean? Take Tolstoi's title again. The violent and painful flows of war are released in peace. Take 'the lion will lie down with the lamb.' The violent flows of the lion are released in the lamb. Take 'Out of this nettle, danger, we pluck this flower, safety.' The painful flows of 'nettle' and 'danger' are released by and in 'safety'. . . .

Bibliography

A. The Writing Notebooks

The notebooks fall roughly into three categories: those concerned with writing itself, those containing "color" or story material, and the thesauruses. C. R. marked the notebooks on their spine with either an Arabic or Roman numeral or with a capital letter (with the exception of Maroon Notebook II), and they have been titled accordingly. The numbers appear to follow no set sequence, and those excluded from this list, numbers 1, 4, 5, and 10, are novel notebooks and so uncatalogued. Also not included is Notebook E with ideas on energy used in *The Mountain On the Desert* and number 7 which is a personal notebook. Number 3 could not be found. Except for the three thesauruses, which are $5\frac{1}{2} \times 8$ inches and three-ring, the notebooks are the traditional $8\frac{1}{2} \times 11$ inches and two-ring. The contents vary between hand-written and typed, usually on both sides of the page. In the margin of material C. R. especially liked he would write a large O.K.

Black Notebook I. Mostly a commonplace book with "A Collection of Examples of Good Writing." Title page includes "Remember what Will Irwin said, that Shakespeare's charm was a series of pictures. Your best writing makes everything to be said visual, motion if possible, with strong emotion words like crush, batter, sweep." Entries have page classifications such as Reflection, Contrast, Comparison, Emotion Technique, Association with Something Alive, Impersonation, Compression, Character Misunderstanding; Enhancing, Nobility, Beauty; Motion, Pictorial; Strength, Power, Vigor; Authenticities That Play the Lift Mood; Scotching the Reader. A number of entries original. Includes page on "New American Style Possible." 187 pages.

Black Notebook II. Contains admonitions to self, writing theory on Obstruction, Theme Action, Theme Fulfillment, etc. First story outline. Complete outline. Contrast, Conflict, Theme. Model and Original Obstructions. Love obstructions. Suspense Mystery. Model Plots to Consult. Authenticity That Lifts. Character Types. Strength and Power Characters. Twists, Surprises, Complications. Something New, Fresh. Gripping Involvements That Grow Deeper. Beginnings with Obstruction Mystery. New Real Life Solutions - Not Sweet, Perfect. Secondary Important Things. [Outline of] Plotting the Story. Early Test Outline. 260 pages.

Maroon Notebook I, marked 9. Notes for article ideas, including "A Writer's Preface" and "Essay for Writers." Ideas for short stories and "A short tract book." Miscellaneous Records. Programs for several years, incl. 1936–43. To Do Now or Soon - Present Pressing Things to Write. More ideas for Articles. Resolves to Self. Ideas for "Post Stories of Early Life." Western Post Stories # 1. Short Novels #1 [including Man on Horseback]. Short Novels #2. Fable series [including "The Littlest Lion" and "The Cat & The Birds"]. Original Short Stories # 1. 128 pages.

Maroon Notebook II. Story Principles. Misc. Writing Rules. Novel and Serial Principles (Freshness, Lift, Strong Under Obstruction, Strong Original Real-Life Obstructions, Model Obstructions, Major Obstructions, Oldtime. Rough, Uneven Reality of Life. Unsweetened Incidents of Common Life. Unsweetened Dialogue. Action of Life, People). Journal excerpts on writing. Simple Style Examples. Outline of Writing the Story (10 through 13). Name the Story's Theme-Mood. Model Titles (Serious, Light). Titles (Light Original). Novel-Serial Titles. Four pages of notes on Lawrence's *Seven Pillars of Wisdom*. Notes on historians. 59 pages.

Notebook 2, yellow cloth-bound. "Note Book of Stories & Novels to go over daily & add notes, ideas." #1 Short Stories perhaps for Post. Misc Short Novels (The Curse of Teresa, the Palestine Novel, Shakespeare Novel, The Farm). Short Novels #2 (The Man Who Was Born Again). Possible Post Eastern Stories # 2 (Another Pigeon Flying Story, The Green Patch, A Modern Pa Mining Story). Notes on Pine Grove characters. Notes on Augusta [to be used in *The Aristocrat*]. Misc Story Ideas. Ideas in Brief for Strong Salable Stories. 87 pages.

Notebook 6, light blue cloth-bound. Things That Move Me - To Write About. Affirmations. Quotations on My Work & Working [excerpted from his journals]. Build Success with Your Own Type of Story. Authenticity. Find Myself. Suggestions for Making Yourself Write. Misc Writing Notes. (Criticism of several of his own novels). Writing, Said by Others [quotations about writing by other writers—includes smaller inserted sheets]. Southwest & Desert Quotations. Misc Quotations [includes smaller inserted sheets]. Misc Biblical (Significant, Strength, Trouble). Misc Not Biblical [these and some of Misc Biblical on smaller inserted three-ring sheets]. Fate Novel Quotations. 239 pages, 91 smaller inserted pages.

Notebook 12, maroon-bound black. Original Stories # 2. Strong Pioneer Ideas Applicable Today. Short Novel (idea). Story or Chapter Idea. Articles. (Articles on modern America. Articles on early America.) Early American Vs Modern. Working versions of poems "When the summer's light is spent." "The Hills of Pedernal." Poetry Ideas. "Sonnet I." "Christopher Street Ferry." "The Bridge." "The Cathedral." "Sonnet II." Short Poetry Ideas. Music I like. Book for Vene to Write. (Notes for revision of the) Hound's Tale. Mystical Ideas for Stories or Chapters. Legend Story Series of America. (Other ideas for stories, chapters, novels.) (Other article ideas.) 128 pages.

Notebook 15, brown with green stripes. My Biographical Pluralogy of Novels. Volume 1 of The Seekers. [24 pages follow with ideas/notes incorporated into *The Waters of Kronos, A Simple Honorable Man,* and *The Grandfathers.*] Notes for The Dutchman. Tetralogy. The Fighter. Things to Attack. Volume 2, Body and Soul. Death and Life (Volume 3). Vol. 4. The Wife. Notes on the Pennsylvania Dutch. Article ideas on the Pennsylvania Dutch and Germans. Thoughts on Modern Writing. Fate Serial - Novel (The Hand). Reincarnation Novel. Notes on Ego. The Dominant Eighth. The Master. 256 pages.

Notebook 16, light blue cloth-covered. Title page: NOTEBOOK OF LATER AMERICA 1880 or 1890 to PRESENT OTHER THAN SOUTHWEST especially Pine Grove, country and Pennsylvania Dutch as H. & I knew these. Cities also.
Childhood authenticities. Character Authenticities (Younger Woman, Girl, Misc., Older Man, Older Woman, Young-Older Woman, Town, Young Man, Youth, Family). Church Authenticities - Cemetery - Preacher. Country Mt. Authenticities. Common Life People, Incidents. Dad & Mother [used in *A Simple Honorable Man* and *The Waters of Kronos*] and notes for book about them. Furnishings. Hex-

erei. Houses, Buildings. Lady & Woman's Things. Misc Color. Music Color. My Thoughts & Feelings. Night Authenticities. Party Authenticities. Pa. Dutch. Talk Pa. Dutch. Sea. Sky Weather. Small Town Life, Authenticities. (Some character sketches). Stories to Tell. 283 pages.

<u>Notebook A, light blue cloth-covered</u>. B to R. [Eastern - Old Time] Books. Character Authenticities. Character Looks: Men. Character Looks: Men & Boys. Character Looks: Girls, Women. Characters. Church, Religion, Preacher, Missionary. Church, Preacher, Funerals. Church, Preacher. Children. Girl & Boy. Court Case, Jail, Judge, Lawyer. Dates. Doctor & Family Doctoring. Dress: Men and Boys. Men and Boys Clothes, Dress, Hair. Dress, Hair - Women & Girls, Jewelry. Farms, Fields, Country Life. Food, Cooking, Teas. Fort, Blockhouse, Stockade, Army. Furnishings. Girl & Boy Authenticities. Guns, Swords, Ammunition, Arms. Hotel, Tavern, Drinks. Houses & Gardens, Buildings. House & Cabin Life. Hunting, Wild Animals, Wild Fowl. Hunting, Trapping, Fishing. Indian Talk (Names, Signs, Objects, Manners, Thought). Indians & Indians with Whites. (Misc. Indians). Letters. Love, Marriage, Courting. Misc. Characters (Men, Women). Misc Oldtime Authenticities, Objects, Incidents. Names (Girls, Women, Men's First, Last). Names, Spots. Newspapers, Magazines. Oldtime (and Later) Thoughts and Feelings. Oldtime Thoughts, Sayward. Misc. Oldtime Thoughts. Oldfashioned Authenticities, Thoughts; Places. River, Stream, Lake, Canal. (Expressions, words for this area.) River, Stream, Canal, Boat, Bridge. River, Boat, Canal, Flood. 396 pages.

<u>Notebrook B, light blue cloth-covered</u>. S to W. [Eastern Old Time] Schools, Books. Songs, Verses, Hymns. Subjects for Talk. Talk Character. Talk, Conversation. Talk Human. Talk Oldtime, Human, Different. Talk, Oldtime Quotations. Talk, Sayings, Beliefs. Talk, Stories, Riddles. Tame Animal, Dog, Horse, Pet, Cow, Oxen. Topography - Trails, Settlement Names etc. Town Street Life. Town, Settlement Life. Town, Street Incident. Trader, Post, Business Man, Goods. Wagoners, Trail, Pike, Stage. War, Anti Slavery, Revolution, etc. War, Talk and Memories of War. Whites with Indians. Woods—Country Doings, Life Business, Country-Forest. Woods—Country Life, Adults, Family, Boys, Girls. Woods, Forest. Work, Business, Profession. Words - Country & Forest Life. Words and Phrases. Cabin Life and Around It. Hunting - Wild Animals, Skins, Geese,

Game Birds, Forest Birds. Settlement Life, Farming. Portius Wheeler's Legal, School Teaching Talk. 301 pages.

Notebook 13, A-G, dark blue cloth-covered. [Old Time Western] Buildings, etc. Buildings, Ranches. Business, Profession, Work. Cattle Authenticities. Characters To See. Character Authenticities (Men, Men & Women, Women). Character Incidents. Character Looks (Man, Men & Boys, Women). Characters Good, Interesting (Men, Men & Boys). Characters, Villain. Character Authenticities, Unpleasant. Characters (Women). Church, Meeting House, Religion, Preacher. Coaches, Buggies, Carriages, Wagons. Court, Jail, Hanging, Lawyer. Dancing. Dance Halls & Houses of Ill Fame. Dates. Doctor. Dress, Attire (Men, Men & Boys, Western Women, Women & Girls). Dress & Hair (Women, Women & Girls). Dress & Attire & Hair & Jewelry (Women). Drought. Emigrants & Their Wagon Trains etc. Flora & Fauna. Food, Cook, Chuck Wagon etc. Forts. Furnishings. Childhood (Girl, Boy, Family). Girl, Boy & Family Authenticities on Ranch. Guns & Gunmen. Gunfights Incident. 353 pages.

Notebook 14, H-R, dark blue cloth-covered. [Old Time Western] Horses. Horseman Character. Horse (Wild) Color. Horse Racing. Horse Breaking, bucking. Horse Riding Life & Incident & Riding Equipment. Horse Riding Color, Both Sexes. Humour, Western Incident. Hunting, Game & Warden. Indians. Indian Talk, Songs, Signs. Indians with Whites. Indian Fights, Trouble. Love, Courting, Marriage. Mining (Lead Mine Color). Mine Color (Hardy) Mexican. Mining, Southwestern Treasure. Misc Doings - Events & Acts Oldtime. Misc. Incident. Misc. Objects - Old Days. Misc. Color, Old Days. Misc. Authenticities. Misc. Western Color. Occupation Period Misc., Spanish. Mountains, Hills (New Mexican, Cedar Country). Music, Dances. Obstruction to Journey. Obstruction, Misc. Obstruction, Suspense. Oldfashioned Authenticities. Outlaws. Pets Other than Horses. Pioneer Color, Incident. Plains, Range Color. Plains, Mesa, Desert. Plains & Mesa Stretches. Railroad. Ranch Life, Color (Old Days; Men, Women etc.; Work; Misc. Authenticities) Ranch, Plains Life. Ranch-Mountain Oldtime Life. Range Color (Texas). Range Incident & Color. River, Stream, Boat. Rodeo Misc. 357 pages.

Notebook 11, S-Y, dark blue cloth-covered. [Old Time Western] Saloon Color - Hotels. Schools - College. Sheep, Wool. Sheriff, Peace Officer. Sky, New Mexican. Sky, Weather. Snow Blizzard, Cold. Social Life, Affairs, Visitors. Songs, Verse etc. Stage Line, Coach etc. Store, Trader, Freighters. Store, Post, Trader, Businessman. Story Scenes. Subjects of Talk in Old Days. Talk, Hardy Talk and that of men like him. Talk, Words, Phrases. Talk, Philosophy in Words, Conversation. Talk, Women's Subject. Conversation. Texas Color. Town Color. Town & Street Color & Life. Trade, Commerce, Business. Trade Commission, Business, Trader. Trails. Trails, Topography [hand-drawn maps]. Trail Herds. Trail Occupants. Wagon Train, Freighting, Freighters. Yarning - Windy Cox etc. 278 pages.

Thesaurus I, black leather cover. Index includes: Emotion, Emotional Behavior, Emotional Beauty, Emotional Enthusiasm, Beauty, Delicateness, Derogatory, Face & Body, Impersonation, Movement, Power, Richness, Significant Words, Sounds, Touch, Violent Lavish Words. Also included are pages of Western Adjectives, Verbs, Place Names, Proper Names, Spanish Names, Brand Names, Words of Wildness. 230 pages + 24 loose pages, incl. words for Sayward [trilogy] and Jim Brewton [*Sea of Grass*]

Thesaurus II, black cardboard cover. Index includes: Adventure, Age, Air, Beauty, Color, Coverings, Couplings, Delicate, Depth, Desert & Foothills, Emotion, Evolution, Expression, Face & Body, Fighting, Fireside, Freshness, Gloom, Hard Strong Character, Harmony, Harshness, Height, Horror, Impersonations, Instruments, Intensity, Large, Liveliness, Look, Love, Misc. phrases, Misc Words, Minor Note, Movement, Modern Note, Modern Behavior, Names, Nature, Peace, Person, Places, Plain, Plants, Power, Primitive, Rain, Religion, Rocks, Richness, Shape lines, Significant Words, Sky, Smell, Snow, Sounds, Strength, Taste, Touch, Unwholesomeness, Villain, War, Water (fresh), Water (salt), Weather, Western, Wholesome-warmth, Wildness, Youth. 265 pages + 34 loose pages.

Thesaurus III, marked 8, gray cloth-bound cardboard cover. Index includes: Children, Words, Talk; Clever, Superior People; Color, Light; Dress, Materials, Jewelry, Hair; Drink; Exclamations for Style; Expressions; Fine, Big, Many; Bad, not fine; Food drink; Foreign & Domestic Places, People; House & Household; Human Behavior, Quality, Disposition; Human Cognomens; Human Feelings; Human Parts, Descriptions; Human To Do phrases etc. Also included are pages of Conversation Phrases; Misc. Words & Phrases Construction; Symbolic Phrases; Older & Current Talk Phrases, Expressions; Old time & Pa. Dutch Phrases, Sayings; Sayings Religious; Talk - Phrases Old Style; Talk - Speech, Oratory Old Style; Talk - humorous, old time; Rounds, Sayings; lists of first and last names; pages of Character Talk Flavor [mostly of character who appears as one of *The Grandfathers*]. 284 pages + 19 loose pages.

B. Works by Conrad Richter

Novels (by date of first publication)

The Sea of Grass. New York: Knopf, 1937. 149 pages.
The Trees. New York: Knopf, 1940. 302 pages.
Tacey Cromwell. New York: Knopf, 1942. 208 pages.
The Free Man. New York: Knopf, 1943. 147 pages.
The Fields. New York: Knopf, 1946. 288 pages.
Always Young and Fair. New York: Knopf, 1947. 177 pages.
The Town. New York: Knopf, 1950. 433 pages.
The Light in the Forest. New York: Knopf, 1953. 179 pages.
The Lady. New York: Knopf, 1957. 191 pages.
The Waters of Kronos. New York: Knopf, 1960. 176 pages.
A Simple Honorable Man. New York: Knopf, 1962. 310 pages.
The Grandfathers. New York: Knopf, 1964. 181 pages.
A Country of Strangers. New York: Knopf, 1966. 169 pages.
The Awakening Land. New York: Knopf, 1966. 630 pages. (First publication of the trilogy—*The Trees, The Fields*, and *The Town*—in one volume)
Over the Blue Mountain. New York: Knopf, 1967. 81 pages.
The Aristocrat. New York: Knopf, 1968. 169 pages.

Collections of Short Stories

Brothers of No Kin and Other Stories. New York: Hinds, Hayden and Eldridge, 1924. 340 pages.
Early Americana and Other Stories. New York: Knopf, 1936. 322 pages.
The Rawhide Knot and Other Stories. New York: Knopf, 1978. 215 pages. Foreword by Harvena Richter.

Non-fiction

Human Vibration: the Underlying Mechanics of Life and Mind. Harrisburg: Handy Book Corporation, 1925. 340 pages.

Principles in Bio-Physics. Harrisburg: Good Books Company, 1927. 86 pages.

The Mountain on the Desert. New York: Knopf, 1955. 234 pages.

Articles and Book Reviews

"America Appreciated, Especially New England" (review of four books), *Harper's*, November 1966, 132, 134.

Book review of two novels by Eugene Manlove Rhodes (*Peñalosa* and *The Trusty Knaves*), *The New Mexico Quarterly*, May 1934, 144–145.

"Individualists Under the Shade Trees," *A Vanishing America: The Life and Times of the Small Town*, ed. Thomas C. Wheeler. New York: Holt, Rinehart and Winston, 1964, 34–42.

"New Mexico Was Our Fate," *New Mexico Magazine*, March 1957, 20–21, 45, 47.

"Pennsylvania," *Holiday*, October 1955, 98–112.

"The Peopled Wilderness," *Country Gentleman* (1920; incomplete)

"The Place I Like Best," *Parade*, July 16, 1950, 4.

"That Early American Quality," *Atlantic*, September 1950, 26–30.

"Three Towns I Love," *Holiday*, December 1953, 54–58, 94, 96, 98, 100, 103–105.

"Under Our Feet: A Few Simple Personal Notes," *The Bryologist*, January 1929, 4–6.

"Valley From the Past," *Country Beautiful*, April 1963, 8–13.

Short Stories and Serialized Fiction: First Serial Publication

"How Tuck Went Home," *Cavalier*, September 6, 1913.

"Brothers of No Kin," *The Forum*, April 1914.

"The Old Debt," *Women's Stories*, November 1914.

"The Wall of the House of Ryland," *Illustrated Sunday Magazine*, November 21, 1915.

"The Laughter of Leen," *Outlook*, February 23, 1916.

"The Head of His House," in *The Grim Thirteen*, ed. F. S. Green. New York: Dodd, Mead, 1917.
"The Girl That 'Got' Colly," *Ladies Home Journal*, May 1917.
"The Sure Thing," *Saturday Evening Post*, November 17, 1917.
"Nothing Else Matters," *Every Week*, January 12, 1918.
"The Pippin of Pike County," *Every Week*, March 16, 1918.
"The Go-Getter," *Country Gentleman*, April 6, 1918.
"Swanson's 'Home Sweet Home,'" *Everybody's Magazine*, August 1919.
"Cabbages and Shoes," *Everybody's Magazine*, March 1920.
"The Making of 'Val' Pierce," *American Magazine*, April 1920.
"Smokehouse," *Country Gentleman*, June 5, 1920.
"The Man Who Hid Himself," *American Magazine*, July 1920.
"The Wings of a Swallow," *People's Favorite Magazine*, December 1920.
"'You're Too Contwisted Satisfied, Jim-Ted,'" *American Magazine*, February 1921.
"Tempered Copper," *People's Favorite Magazine*, February 1921.
"The Cheerful Liar," *Munsey's Magazine*, January 1922.
"The Boss of the Works," *Success*, May 1922.
"Over the Hill to the Rich House," *Outlook*, September 6, 1922.
"Rich Relations," *American Magazine*, March 1924.
"Teddy Saves the Day," *American Magazine*, April 1924.
"Father Had No Tact," *Elks Magazine*, March 1925.
"Derickson's Gagoo," *American Magazine*, May 1925.
"The Man Who Loved a Hound," *Elks Magazine*, December 1925.
"The Man Who Retired," *American Magazine*, April 1926.
"The Exaggerator," *American Magazine*, June 1926.
"Mother Cuts Loose," (under pseudonym of Robert Clearing) *Woman's Home Companion*, March 1927.
"Before It's Too Late," *Elks Magazine*, May 1928.
"A Member of the Family," *Farm Journal*, October 1928.
"Rose of Decker Valley," *Farm Journal*, January 1930.
"The Hard-Rock Man," *Blue Book*, April 1931.
"The Hard-Rock Man II: The Taming of the High Point Mine," *Blue Book*, May 1931.
"The Hard-Rock Man III: On Top of the World," *Blue Book*, June 1931.
"The Stampede," *Country Home*, July 1931.

"The High Places," *Liberty*, January 2, 1932.
"The Substitute Daddy," *Home Magazine*, January 1932.
"Try to Stop Me," *Blue Book*, February 1932.
"The White Flower," *Liberty*, March 26, 1932.
"The King Was in the Kitchen," *Woman's Home Companion*, May 1932.
"Her People of the Patch," *Liberty*, May 21, 1932.
"Two of a Kind," *Country Home*, June 1932.
"Mason Climbs the Mountain," *Short Stories for Men*, June 10, 1932.
"The Blood of a Horseman," *Liberty*, June 16, 1932.
"The Sheriff Gets His Man," *Short Stories for Men*, September 10, 1932.
"Cotter's Saturday Night," *Short Stories for Men*, May 10, 1933.
"The Fighting Contract," *Blue Book*, June 1933.
"The Night Riders," *Blue Book*, August 1933.
"Hutcheson's Head," *Liberty*, September 30, 1933.
"A Horse of Another Color," *Blue Book*, October 1933.
"Hoofbeat, Heartbeat," *Liberty*, November 18, 1933.
"The Singing Sheriff," *Argosy*, January 27, 1934.
"The Hard Hombre," *Blue Book*, February 1934.
"Early Marriage," *Saturday Evening Post*, April 7, 1934.
"The Bells of Ichicalli," *Blue Book*, June 1934.
"Long Engagement," *Saturday Evening Post*, June 16, 1934.
"New Home," *Ladies Home Journal*, October 1934.
"The Hands of Minstrel Jim," *Blue Book*, November 1934.
"The New Neighbors," *Success*, November 1934.
"Frontier Woman," *Ladies Home Journal*, December 1934.
"Valhalla," *Blue Book*, December 1934.
"The Square Piano," *Ladies Home Journal*, March 1935.
"Buckskin Vacation," *Ladies Home Journal*, May 1935.
"Smoke Over the Prairie," *Saturday Evening Post*, June 1, 1935.
"As It Was in the Beginning," *Saturday Evening Post*, September 14, 1935.
"Early Americana," *Saturday Evening Post*, January 25, 1936.
"The Sea of Grass," *Saturday Evening Post*. Part I, October 31, 1936; Part II, November 7, 1936; Part III, November 14, 1936.
"The Rawhide Knot," *Saturday Evening Post*, January 1, 1938.
"Life Was Simple Then," *Saturday Evening Post*, March 2, 1940.

"The Free Man," *Saturday Evening Post*. Part I, May 15, 1943; Part II, May 22, 1943; Part III, May 29, 1943; Part IV, June 5, 1943.

"The Good Neighbors," *Saturday Evening Post*, October 30, 1943.

"The Flood," *Saturday Evening Post*, January 6, 1945.

"The Face at the Winder" (from *The Fields*), *Atlantic*, May 1945.

"The Nettle Patch" (from *The Fields*), *Atlantic*, January 1946.

"Always Young and Fair," *Saturday Evening Post*, October 12, 1946.

"The Last Man Alive," *Saturday Evening Post*, August 14, 1948.

"Dr. Hanray's Second Chance," *Saturday Evening Post*, June 10, 1950.

"The Marriage That Couldn't Succeed," *Saturday Evening Post*, June 21, 1952.

"The Light in the Forest," *Saturday Evening Post*. Part I, March 28, 1953; Part II, April 4, 1953; Part III, April 11, 1953; Part IV, April 18, 1953.

"Sinister Journey," *Saturday Evening Post*, September 26, 1953.

"The Lady," *Saturday Evening Post*. Part I, March 30, 1957; Part II, April 6, 1957; Part III, April 13, 1957; Part IV, April 20, 1957.

"The Iron Lady," *Saturday Evening Post*, July 15, 1957.

Additional Short Fiction (data incomplete)*

1914, "A tangle of Lace," *Women's Stories*.

1929, "Reprieve," a Munsey publication (*Cavalier*?).

1929, "Sitting on Sally," *Farm Journal*.

1930, "Bull Pup Brown," *High Spot Magazine*.

1931, "The Mender of the Broken B," *Triple-X Westerns*.

1931, "Monster of the Dark Places," *Ghost Stories*.

1931, "The Toad Man Specter," *Ghost Stories*.

1931, "Lazy Dee," *Complete Stories*.

1931, "Saddle Partners," *Short Stories*.

1932, "Under a Western Star," *Short Stories*.

1932, "The Dark Places," *Short Stories*.

1932, "Bloodshot," *Western Trails*.

1932, "Funny Face," *Home Magazine*.

1932, "Jawbone Kelly," *Short Stories*.

*Dates indicate year story sold or sent to literary agent.

1932, "Lazy Dee Learns How," *Complete Stories.*
1932, "Lazy Dee Lies Down," *Complete Stories.*
1932, "Lazy Dee Rides Along," *Complete Stories.*
1932, "Two Word Talley," *Short Stories.*
1932, "Dumb Bell's Security," *Complete Stories.*
1932, "Cartridges Free," *Western Trails.*
1933, "Tongue-tied Pete," *Complete Stories.*
1934, "Stuff of a Ranger," *Complete Stories.*

C. Books, Articles, and Dissertations about Conrad Richter and his Writing.

Barnard, Kenneth J. "Presentation of the West in Conrad Richter's Trilogy." *Northwest Ohio Quarterly* 29.4 (1957): 224–34.

Barnes, Robert J. *Conrad Richter.* Austin, Texas: Steck-Vaugh, 1968.

Carpenter, Frederic I. "Conrad Richter's Pioneers: Reality and Myth." *College English* 12.2 (1950): 77–83.

Ecenbarger, William. "Richter, O'Hara, Updyke: Enshrining Our Favorite Literary Sons." *Apprise: South Central Pennsylvania's Regional Magazine* 6.9 (March 1987).

Edwards, Clifford D. *Conrad Richter's Ohio Trilogy: Its Ideas, Themes, and Relationship to Literary Tradition.* The Hague: Mouton, 1970.

Flanagan, John T. "Conrad Richter: Romancer of the Southwest." *Southwest Review* 43 (1958): 189–96.

———. "Folklore in the Novels of Conrad Richter." *Midwest Folklore* 2 (1952): 5–14.

Friesen, Paul. "The Use of Oral Tradition in the Novels of Conrad Richter." Diss. Texas Tech U. 1979.

Gaston, Edwin W., Jr. *Conrad Richter.* New Haven: Twayne, 1965.

Kohler, Dayton. "Conrad Richter: Early Americana." *College English* 8.5 (1947): 221–27.

Lahood, Marvin J. "Conrad Richter and Willa Cather: Some Similarities." *Xavier University Studies* 9.1 (1970): 33–46.

———. *Conrad Richter's America.* The Hague: Mouton, 1975.

———. "Conrad Richter's Pennsylvania Trilogy." *Susquehanna University Studies* 8.2 (1968): 5–13.

———. "*The Light in the Forest*: History or Fiction." *English Journal* 55.3 (1966): 298–304.

McCullough, David. "Cross the Blue Mountain." *Country Journal*, February 1977: 63–67.

Meldrum, Barbara. "Conrad Richter's Southwestern Ladies" in *Women, Women Writers, and the West*. Troy, N.Y.: Whitson, 1978.

Milton, John R. "The Novel in the American West." *South Dakota Review* 2.1 (1964): 56–76.

Pearce, T. M. "Conrad Richter." *New Mexico Quarterly* 20 (1950): 371–73.

Schmaier, Maurice D. "Conrad Richter's *The Light in the Forest*: An Ethnohistorical Approach to Fiction." *Ethnohistory* 7.4 (1960): 327–98.

Sutherland, Bruce. "Conrad Richter's Americana." *New Mexico Quarterly* 15 (1945): 413–22.

Wilson, Dawn M. "The Influence of the West on Conrad Richter's Fiction." *The Old Northwest* 1 (1975): 375–89.

———. "Conrad Richter: the Novelist as Philosopher." Diss. Kent State University, 1971.

Young, David Lee. "The Art of Conrad Richter." Diss. Ohio State University, 1964.

Note regarding translations:

Conrad Richter's novels and short fiction have been translated into more than thirty languages including German, French, Italian, Spanish, Portuguese, Dutch, Danish, Norwegian, Finnish, Polish, Rumanian, Yugoslavian, Czechoslovakian, Flemish, Russian, Greek, Arabic, Persian, Chinese, Japanese, Vietnamese, Burmese, Urdu, Marathi, Bengali, Telegu, Halayalam, Oriya, Tamil, Punjabi, Gujarati, and Hindi.

Index